Japanese Politics

JAPANESE SOCIETY SERIES

General Editor: Yoshio Sugimoto

Japanese Politics

An Introduction

Takashi Inoguchi

Trans Pacific Press

Melbourne

This English edition first published in 2005 by
Trans Pacific Press, PO Box 120, Rosanna, Melbourne, Victoria 3084, Australia
Telephone: +61 3 9459 3021 Fax: +61 3 9457 5923
Email: info@transpacificpress.com
Web: http://www.transpacificpress.com

Copyright © Trans Pacific Press 2005

Designed and set by digital environs Melbourne. enquiries@digitalenvirons.com

Printed by BPA Print Group, Burwood, Victoria, Australia

Distributors

Japan
Kyoto University Press
Kyodai Kaikan
15-9 Yoshida Kawara-cho
Sakyo-ku, Kyoto 606-8305
Telephone: (075) 761-6182
Fax: (075) 761-6190
Email: sales@kyoto-up.gr.jp
Web: http://www.kyoto-up.gr.jp

Asia and the Pacific
Kinokuniya Company Ltd.
Head office:
38-1 Sakuragaoka 5-chome, Setagaya-ku,
Tokyo 156-8691, Japan
Phone: +81 (0)3 3439 0161
Fax: +81 (0)3 3439 0839
Email: bkimp@kinokuniya.co.jp
Web: www.kinokuniya.co.jp
Asia-Pacific office:
Kinokuniya Book Stores of Singapore Pte., Ltd.
391B Orchard Road #13-06/07/08
Ngee Ann City Tower B
Singapore 238874
Tel: +65 6276 5558
Fax: +65 6276 5570
Email: SSO@kinokuniya.co.jp

UK and Europe
Asian Studies Book Services
Franseweg 55B, 3921 DE Elst, Utrecht,
The Netherlands
Telephone: +31 318 470 030
Fax: +31 318 470 073
Email: info@asianstudiesbooks.com
Web: http://www.asianstudiesbooks.com

USA and Canada
International Specialized Book
Services (ISBS)
920 NE 58th Avenue, Suite 300
Portland, Oregon 97213-3786
USA
Telephone: (800) 944-6190
Fax: (503) 280-8832
Email: orders@isbs.com
Web: http://www.isbs.com

ISSN   1-443-9670 (Japanese Society Series)

ISBN   1-8768-4321-7   (Hardback)
ISBN   1-8768-4322-5   (Paperback)

Contents

Tables

Preface

There is no better time for rethinking Japanese politics than now. When the Japanese economy was on the rise, as it was in the 1980s, it was often suggested that the Japanese way of doing things was culturally unique and inherently superior. The apparent success of the Japanese approach to issues such as capitalist development, organizational management, decision-making, and education was frequently heralded both inside and outside of Japan. However, having endured the collapse of the bubble economy, and the long economic and demographic stagnation of the 1990s, Japanese are now more sanguine about the prospects for their country in the new millennium. Hence there is no better time for this book to come out. I offer a somber analysis and assessment of Japanese politics during two critical recent periods, 1983–1993 and 1994–2004.

A substantial portion of the book is devoted to a critical analysis of Japanese politics prior to 1993, when the long-governing Liberal Democratic Party relinquished power. The final two chapters examine the last decade of Japanese politics. They identify the incremental and yet steady change which has occurred in Japanese domestic politics and foreign policy. Here, I use the terms "normal party politics" to characterize the emerging contours of Japanese domestic politics, and "normal power" to describe Japan's emerging international profile. By normal party politics I refer to the gradual transcendence of a situation where one party dominates a highly-bureaucratized political system. I argue that the one party system is in the process of being replaced by a more pluralistic, less bureaucratic, and more participatory politics, in the electoral, legislative and policy-formulation domains. With regard to foreign, security and economic policy, Japan has in the past placed all of its eggs in one basket. In doing so it was constrained by the strictures and structures of postwar international politics, and to some extent excluded from "normal" membership of international society. Japan is now replacing its old policies and adopting a more pro-active, yet no less pacific outlook, as it seeks to avoid being "shut out of the sun." These domestic and international transitions are related and have only just begun. They will take another fifteen years, if Kissinger is indeed correct about the number of years which it takes the Japanese to effect important political transitions.

This book's genesis has only been possible as a result of the enormous help I have received from many friends. The portion of the text which addresses the pre-1993 period was initially researched and drafted in 1991–1993. That portion was initially published in 1994 as *Nihon: Keizai taikoku no seiji unei (Governing an Economic Power)* by the University of Tokyo Press, as one of six books in a series on East Asian States and Societies, of which I was Editor. I owe an enormous debt to Hidetoshi Takenaka, also Editor, and my five comrades-in-arms in this series. Tamio Hattori, now at the University of Tokyo, addressed South Korea, and Masayuki Suzuki of Seigakuin University North Korea; Satoru Amako, now at Waseda University, wrote on China, Masaya Shiraishi, also now at Waseda University, researched Vietnam, and Masahiro Wakabayashi, of the University of Tokyo, dealt with Taiwan. Each contributor completed their manuscript as originally scheduled, thereby pushing me to finish my book as the sixth in the series. Terutomo Ozawa of Colorado State University wrote a splendid review essay on this series in the *Journal of Asian Studies* (Vol.53 No.1 1994), which boosted our morale considerably.

I have addressed the decade since 1994 in a number of articles and book chapters emerging from and stimulated by my many and varied roles since the mid-1990s. These include periods as Assistant Secretary-General of the United Nations at the United Nations University Headquarters in Tokyo, as President of the Japan Association of International Relations, as a member of the Legislative Council, and finally as a member of the Science Council of Japan.

I am grateful to the many, many colleagues and friends, both at home and abroad, who induced me to keep researching and writing during the last decade. I was happy to discover that I published more prolifically during this period, the so-called lost decade of stagnation, between 1994 and 2004, than in preceding decades. I am most grateful to those who stimulated and enabled me to consider Japanese domestic politics and foreign policy from a number of diverse and illuminating perspectives. Here I refer to Norio Okazawa of Waseda University, Massachi Osawa of Kyoto University, Steven Reed of Chuo University, and Yoshinobu Yamamoto of the University of Tokyo, who together edited the world's largest *Encyclopedia of Political Science*, published by Kobundo Publishers in 2000. Robert Putnam of Harvard University and Eiko Ikegami of New School University broadened my horizons and challenged me to consider the early modern period of Japanese politics, to complement the more common focus on Japanese politics since 1945 or since 1868. Michio Muramatsu of Gakushuin University, Hideo Otake of Kyoto University, and Ikuo Kabashima of the University of Tokyo together launched *Leviathan: the Japanese Journal of Political Science* with Bokutakusha during the decade ending in 1997, and in doing so waved the flag for Japanese political studies. Samuel Huntington of Harvard University, G. John Ikenberry of Princeton University, and Chung-In Moon of Yonsei University, all kept me busy thinking and writing about Japanese foreign policy. Jean Blondel of the European University Institute, Richard Sinnott of University College Dublin, Ian Marsh of the Australian National University, and Ikuo Kabashima of the University of Tokyo instilled in me an interest in comparative politics as we jointly conducted a large scale cross-national survey on Asia and Europe.

I would also like to thank all of those who have served on the Editorial and Advisory Boards of the two journals of which I have been the Editor, the *Japanese Journal of Political Science* (published by Cambridge University Press since 2000) and *International Relations of the Asia-Pacific* (published by Oxford University Press since 2001). All of the manuscript submitters and reviewers for these two journals deserve my heartfelt thanks for enabling me to read, assess and process many intellectually interesting and rewarding manuscripts.

With regard to the book manuscript itself, I own an enormous debt to Wenran Jiang of the University of Alberta and Tanya Casperson of the Global Governance journal, who together did a marvelous job of translating my 1994 book into English when they spent a year in Tokyo. Paul Bacon of Waseda University masterfully edited and copyedited the manuscript to enhance the clarity and coherence of the book. Ken Firmalino of the Chuo University worked magic in the last phase of submission of the book manuscript to the publisher. Kimiko Goko of the Chuo University sustained the project with her efficiency, overseeing the effective prosecution of thousands of tasks in my academic office. At Trans Pacific Press, Yoshio Sugimoto has been most helpful in getting this book out into the sun. He is the midwife of the book.

Last but not least, the last decade was the decade during which my family members blossomed. My two daughters entered junior high school, and my wife, Kuniko, returned to Sophia University from a two-year ambassadorship to the Conference on Disarmament in Geneva with success and grace. I only hope that I can be of more help to them.

Takashi Inoguchi

1 Japanese politics in the eye of history

This book offers a comprehensive survey of Japan's postwar politics, economics and international relations, with particular emphasis on developments in the last two decades. Although the focus is contemporary, I demonstrate that important elements of Japan's political culture were in place in the early modern Tokugawa period. Whilst subsequent watershed events in Japanese history, such as the Meiji Restoration, the Occupation and the postwar developmentalist state have added distinctive elements to Japan's political culture, all have built on these early modern foundations. This study demonstrates the inter-relatedness of Japan's politics, economics and international relations, and analyses in some detail how these were configured in the postwar context. Initially, Japan was able to draw on centuries of political culture to promulgate a highly successful bureaucratically-driven developmentalist political economy, with the tacit Cold War support of the US.

However, developments in the past two decades have led to a reconfiguration of social forces and the gradual disappearance of the conditions which framed Japan's initial postwar success. During the early Cold War the US was happy for the LDP to dominate Japanese domestic politics as long as Japan could be relied on to remain a stable ally. It was prepared to acquiesce in Japan's embrace of the Yoshida doctrine for this very reason. Eventually, however, as this study demonstrates, the bubble economy burst, an event which can, to a substantial degree, be traced to decisions Japan made in order to buttress the American international economic order. This economic failure, combined with a rash of financial scandals in the early 1990s, served to dramatically undermine the support base of the LDP, leading it to lose power in 1993 for the first time since the 1950s. The 1990s are often portrayed as a decade of stagnation in the politics, economics and international relations of Japan, but this is emphatically not the case. The closer analysis contained in this study reveals that the tectonic plates of Japanese politics have in fact been shifting during this period, and that substantial changes are afoot.

With the end of the Cold War Japan found itself under pressure to liberalize its trade and to make more of a contribution to its own defense, and there have been tensions in the alliance with the US. Although the LDP has tenaciously clung to power during most of the last decade, through a number of electoral coalitions, there has been a clear disillusionment with Japanese party politics. However, after 9/11 the international security environment has changed, with the result that there has been pressure on Japan to become more actively engaged in international politics. Japanese nationalism has also been on the increase in the 1990s, and these two events, taken together, have contributed to calls for reform of the Japanese Constitution. I examine these developments in some detail and conclude that it is likely that Japan will resume its normal statehood in the coming years. What I mean by this is that Japan will re-assert its right to use force in the settlement of international disputes, as other states do. This would, of course, be a seismic development in the international relations of postwar Japan. I also argue that we are witnessing the gradual emergence of a genuine two party system in Japanese domestic politics. I base these two claims on a detailed analysis of the recent Lower House elections, and a detailed analysis of recent events in Japanese foreign policy.

Japan's postwar politics were premised on one-party dominance, economic developmentalism, the military protection of the United States, and the renunciation of the use of force. Each of these premises is undergoing fundamental review and adjustment as a new period of international relations begins to take shape. This book aims to survey and explain the bases of Japan's early postwar success, but, more importantly, to offer a detailed analysis of the way in which the foundations of this earlier period of success have been eroded in the past decade. Japan's politics, economics and international relations are undergoing a significant transformation.

Absolutism founders

Early modern Japan from the late sixteenth century to the mid-nineteenth century was not, by contrast to Europe, a society governed by absolutism (Anderson, 1974; Brown, 1993) Early attempts by Oda Nobunaga and Toyotomi Hideyoshi to establish such absolutist societies foundered midway through the late sixteenth century. Nobunaga rapidly quelled the opposing forces of medieval patriarchal clans and the fiefdoms of religious and commercial organizations. Yet he was prevented from unifying the country when a lieutenant, who felt he would be sacrificed in Nobunaga's march towards unification, assassinated him. His ambitious drive towards the creation of a powerful state based on absolutist rule was thus dramatically thwarted.

Nobunaga's successor, Toyotomi Hideyoshi, was able to unite the country, but not without much compromise. The clearest evidence of compromise with medieval instincts and interests was the nature of the nationwide cadastral surveys that Hideyoshi ordered all the local lords to carry out. Since land would be the key unit of taxation, this was to have laid the basis for a strong, centrally unified government. Recent scholarship on this period indicates that Hideyoshi's regime had a perhaps superior claim to, but lower capacity for, actual governance than Nobunaga's. The land surveys tended to be of a rather superficial nature, and were conducted mainly in areas where the military rule of local clans varied according to developments at the national level, especially in circumstances where there was a frequent turnover of warrior-bureaucrats, who were appointed as local administrators.

Hideyoshi's scheme to conquer Korea and eventually China and India in the late sixteenth century was reckless and ostentatious; he simply wanted to demonstrate his power. But he recognized the strength of medieval instincts and interests and knew that imposing absolutist power on local fiefs and populations would accomplish nothing but the disaffection of local chieftains, which would threaten unity and ignite rebellion among the peasants, thus undermining the facade of stability. Tokugawa Ieyasu, who was not his most powerful military rival, maintained a low profile before finally usurping Hideyoshi's power. He was shrewd and patient in constructing a Pax Tokugawa that lasted until the mid-nineteenth century. But when the West forced Japan open by threat, the way the country had been run until then had to be changed.

The local picture was even less absolutist. Under the rule of the Tokugawa, local lords were forced to move to different domains from time to time. This meant two things. First, they had to make difficult decisions about whom among their retainers they should take with them to their new domains. Some of their retainers were not markedly distinguished from the locally-based peasant/warriors who performed administrative tasks at the grassroots level. The select few warriors who accompanied their lords from one domain to another were thus strangers where they were stationed. Second, the lords had to work through a relatively small number of warrior officials to deal with local peasant officials. Sengoku, for instance, was a shogun bureaucrat of intermediate rank allotted a fief of 2,700 *koku* (an amount of rice expected to support 3,600 persons a year) in Shinano, Kōzuke, and Musashi provinces. He had 32 bureaucrats to run his Edo office and only four to administer official business for the fairly large population of his scattered domains. Two thousand of his *koku* were concentrated in Shinano, but he had only three officials there throughout the seventeenth and eighteenth centuries. Peasant officials therefore had to be co-opted to support the ruling structure. Local notables were the pivotal social force in this governance structure, linking minor officials with the peasants at the grassroots level. The tax ratio of the rice harvest decreased rather than increased in a surprisingly large number of domains, because the lords tended to be more accommodating during the early part of the Tokugawa period.

Because provincial lords chose their close retainers with care, these select warriors developed a pride in themselves as members of an official elite. As they were frequently relocated to new domains and their concentration in the castle towns separated them from direct land ownership, they were essentially stripped of military capacity and power. A comparison of the Japanese and Korean bureaucracies at this time is revealing (Satō, 1978). In Yi dynasty Korea, land ownership was much more closely related to administrative position than in Tokugawa Japan. The Korean elite was much more concerned with family lineage while the Japanese elite was concerned above all with appointment and promotion. Politics in Seoul were much more fierce and competitive than politics in Edo; the former was strongly shaped by politics of land ownership and family rivalry. In Japan primogeniture was the rule, whereas in Korea as well as in China, the inheritance was usually divided equally among sons. Equality in inheritance meant much greater competition among those expected to inherit land, wealth, or position than in the case where inheritance was fixed in principle and known in advance. The basis of the Japanese bureaucracy was meritocratic rather than partisan. Under the Tokugawa regime, the status of the warrior bureaucrats was placed above the other three classes of society; farmers, artisans, and merchants, in that order. The pretension and premise of this hierarchy was that only those possessed of the warrior ethic were capable of restraining the selfish pursuit of profit typical of merchants, as well as the tendency toward tax evasion endemic among farmers.

The warriors gradually came to make up the bureaucracy of the individual domains, taking care of such matters as organizational management, taxation, flood control, crime prevention, and education. They were perhaps the most highly educated members of officialdom, even in the context of the high levels of literacy extant in Japanese society in the seventeenth to nineteenth centuries. Members of the Tokugawa bureaucracy were highly educated, and since they were a select few, social ties among them were quite close. Because of their sense of pride in and responsibility for their mission, they often played a prescribed role in accordance with the spirit of the family codes of each warrior house. The lord as an individual, of course, might not be so virtuous (Kasaya, 1989). If, for instance, the domain's finances deteriorated because of extravagance on the part of the lord, he was often withdrawn from the front line of political life. Since the lords of the domains were often alien to the places to which they were assigned, they tended to be sensitive to local sentiments and preferences. The facade of good governance had to be maintained; it would not do to provoke or invite intervention from the central government. Should rumors or reports of defection or rebellion in a domain begin to circulate, the central authorities had good cause to intervene, a situation that normally had negative consequences for the lords themselves and for most of their followers. Because they recognized that their power rested on acceptance at the grassroots level, they were assiduous in their management of important local issues and events, such as irrigation, flood control, the rice harvest, tax collection, and annual festivals.

The general portrait of the Tokugawa bureaucracy that emerges from this admittedly cursory examination reveals it to have been:

1. self disciplined;
2. an aggregation of inclusive social instincts and interests;
3. cautious but skillful at adapting to constant change, based on the sound and responsive management of specific local conditions.

These features became further entrenched as the modernization drive proceeded during the Meiji era (1868–1912) because the perceived threat from outside, both military and economic, was very serious, and because of high aspirations and ambitions on the part of the Japanese elite. As a comparatively small and as yet reasonably underdeveloped Far Eastern country, the potential constraints on Japan's attempt to consolidate power were formidable.

Rich country, strong military

The threats from the West were manifold. The military threat became real as Japan witnessed the fates of India, Vietnam, and China at the hands of the advancing colonialist powers. After the conclusion of the commercial treaties — the so-called unequal treaties — the economic threat seemed just as imminent. Under the commercial treaties signed with the Western powers in the mid-nineteenth century, Japan was not allowed to set its own tariffs, which were then the major instrument of commercial diplomacy. Determined to address this dual threat, Japan resolved to become a 'rich country with a strong military.' Japan was nevertheless quick to recognize that the threat of the West, both military and economic, was also ideological and organizational in nature. By this, I refer to the capacity of a state to mobilize its resources for national purposes. Commodore Matthew C. Perry noted the speed with which the Japanese were able to look beyond the direct and immediate threat of his gunboat diplomacy to the substantial long-term nature of the military threat he presented (Perry, 1856). To build a rich country and a strong military, Japan had to construct and consolidate the apparatus of a political system that could foster and mobilize national solidarity. They did not have to start from scratch. They had the early modern beginnings of ideological and organizational development, which Herman Ooms eloquently describes as originating in Neo-Confucian, Buddhist, Shinto, and other doctrines readily available at the turn of the sixteenth century in Japan (Ooms, 1985). The modern Japanese bureaucracy came to reflect and embody these early modern ideological and organizational resources.

Two factors prompted the Meiji oligarchy to build a modern bureaucracy. The first was the need for self-legitimization. The Meiji Restoration was engineered by bands of lower-ranking warriors from a handful of domains on the southwestern fringes of the archipelago. It was essentially a military coup d'état followed by a series of political maneuvers and military campaigns. The slogan of this coup was that all people were equal subjects of the emperor. In other words, the new Meiji oligarchy had to present themselves as not fundamentally different from other Japanese. In order to legitimize their rule, they had to uphold the principle that they were promoting the imperial interest, or even more aptly, impartial interests as distinguished from what they referred to as narrow Tokugawa interests. In other words, they had to substantiate the claim that they were working for the public good above and beyond partisan interests. Hence the modern Japanese bureaucracy was created and portrayed as being neutral with regard to sectoral and partisan interests.

The second factor was the need to implement the slogan and execute real policies. The narrow geographical and class basis of the Meiji oligarchy had to be expanded. The Japanese quickly realized that a modern bureaucracy was one of the key institutions of a modern state. The early modern bureaucracy had been much smaller in size and more rudimentary in nature. It had to be developed into an organization based on attributes such as merit-based recruitment and promotion, and a segmented jurisdictional structure better adapted to the more complex tasks that confronted bureaucrats at this time. When the four clearly separated classes were abolished, nonpartisanship paved the way for wider participation in politics. To support merit-based recruitment and promotion, the modern Japanese bureaucracy was developed in such a way as to inculcate national consciousness. Higher education had to be developed in order to widen the base of the bureaucratic elite. With regard to the segmented jurisdictional structure, fairly ad hoc modifications were made to the original and longstanding Sino-Japanese, theocratic-bureaucratic institutions. In cultivating a reputation for nonpartisanship, the Meiji oligarchs were skillful in portraying the bureaucracy as a key institution which embodied the interests of the whole nation.

The tasks confronting the fledgling Japanese bureaucracy until the First World War were not very demanding and could aptly be referred to as those of administering a 'night watchman state', in terms of the ratio of public expenditure to gross national product. In other words, the tasks were far smaller than one would imagine from the much-quoted slogan 'rich nation, strong military.' After all, 'small government' has been the Japanese norm from the early modern period until recently (with the important exception of the 1930s and 1940s).

The new bureaucracy performed the tasks assigned to it steadfastly, not the least because of its ideology. The moral principles which motivate the modern Japanese bureaucrat are reflected in the list of precepts devised by Ōmori Shōichi, a bureaucrat in the prewar Home Affairs ministry (later the Ministry of Internal Affairs) for his son, who was about to enter the bureaucracy himself. The list was regarded as such a definitive account of the spirit of imperial bureaucrats that the ministry circulated it in booklet form every year since 1934.

1. Be pure-minded and immune to criticism.
2. Conduct your affairs without private sentiment and act with impartiality.
3. Exercise common sense and act with restraint.
4. Listen to others; do not be overly self-assertive.

5. Work meticulously and do not turn away from hard labor or toil.
6. Be discreet in speech and behavior.
7. Keep your word.
8. Live modestly and humbly.
9. Do not be ashamed to ask questions and willingly offer instruction to others.
10. Do not fawn over superiors and be faithful to colleagues.
11. Avoid being over-absorbed in hobbies.
12. Devote yourself to the welfare of the state.
13. Do not speak about official duties to those in private life.
14. Be content with your official duties; do not involve yourself in private business affairs.
15. Revere the gods and buddhas and pay respect to the elderly in a spirit of filial piety.
16. Know history, whether it is of your own institution, community, or state.
17. Be calm in handling all official duties.
18. Study your official duties and acquire higher learning.
19. Remain aloof from partisan strife (Daikakai Naimushōshi Hensen Iinkai, 1971).

Other than the largely universal principles that bureaucrats should abide by the world over, there are at least three points here that are important for understanding the peculiar nature of the Japanese bureaucracy. They are: be pure-minded and immune to criticism; be aloof from partisan strife; and act with impartiality.

The first is linked to the high-minded and humble spirit of the warrior administrators of the early modern period. The second reflects the enlightened absolutism of the Meiji bureaucracy, and the third reflects what I call the 'inclusionary bureaucratic' character of the modern Japanese political system. Although all this advice is intended for high-ranking civil servants in the prewar imperial system, it does reflect the standards of the Japanese bureaucracy in general. In other words, they work for a higher cause, but are not highly paid; they eschew involvement in petty controversies, and they are able to present the best solutions for the public good, so that the public is well taken care of by the government.

The similarities in bureaucratic ideology between the early modern and contemporary periods should be immediately apparent: first in the emphasis on discipline, diligence, and devotion; second, with regard to the propensity for 'inclusionary aggregation' of societal institutions and interests; and third, in the emphasis on cautious but intelligent adaptation to changes based on first-hand experience. As Ooms (1985) concludes, Tokugawa (i.e., early modern) ideology provides the basis for the modern Japanese state. A broad and basic continuity exists between the ideologies which govern the conduct of bureaucratic elites in both periods. As the tasks confronting them changed, as the threat became primarily external rather than internal, these similarities may not be apparent at first glance. The major difference is merely the intensity of the latter's use of ideology to legitimize and execute policy. Intense fear of the West led the Meiji oligarchy to institutionalize the state bureaucracy in an extremely consolidated form.

The new millennium

As I have suggested, Japan's bureaucratic ideology, originally formulated in the early modern period, in the late sixteenth and seventeenth centuries, was renewed in significantly more substantial and consolidated form during the Meiji Restoration. After World War II, it became more strategically focused and was tailored to the needs of deeper resource mobilization, both for economic growth and political participation. Both stories are so familiar that I need not recount them (Masumi, 1971). The Japanese bureaucratic ideology played a great stabilizing role with its intense concern for human sentiment at grass-roots level, and with its propensity for the inclusionary aggregation of interests. These qualities were especially critical when the Japanese state had to undergo revolutionary demographic, technological, industrial, societal, and economic change, all within a fifty-year period, and without exacerbating existing political problems.

Now, at the start of the twenty-first century, Japan is again confronted with new challenges. If the early modern challenge was the threat from within, and the modern challenge the threat from without, then perhaps we can describe the postmodern challenge as encompassing threats from both the inside and outside. This derives from the fact that distinctions based on national boundaries seem to be rapidly eroding; the once fundamental significance of geographical distance and national boundaries is diminishing. In tandem with that phenomenon, the domain of the nation-state and the power of nationally-instituted apparatuses of parliamentary and bureaucratic administration are both being undermined. Before discussing the Japanese adaptation to this challenge, let me briefly explain its nature.

The challenge is directly concerned with what may be referred to as the end of the nation-state (Lukas, 1993). This development is no less important than other 'ends,' most notoriously the end of the Cold War, of geography, and, last but not least, of history.

John Lukas refers to the end of the nation-state as a gradual process by which the nation-state is becoming obsolete. Nation-states developed in the context of the evolution of the Western European sovereign states-system, which was largely based on ethnic difference. The model gradually became universal during the twentieth century, but this process of extension contributed to the origins of the most atrocious wars in human history, which took place in the first half of the twentieth century. Many new sovereign states were created. At the turn of the nineteenth century there were only around 20 such states, mostly in Europe; by the end of the twentieth century, the number was approximately 200. The Cold War simply disguised the process by which nation-states were becoming obsolete. The contradictions in the system had already been apparent for some time, but became even more evident as the century drew to an end.

As nation-states developed from the sixteenth through the nineteenth centuries, technological developments and models of economic governance reflected assumptions that the populations of nation-states would be between 5 and 30 million people. But in the twentieth century mega-states with populations exceeding 30 million or even 100 million have become much more common. The growth in size of nation-states is clearly related to technological developments and breakthroughs which make new social formations possible. Here the contradiction between economics and politics becomes stark. In the economic sphere, advanced levels of technology enable capitalism to transcend national boundaries with greater ease. In politics, this has not normally been the case. In many countries, the nineteenth-century European liberal-democratic model was adopted. The supposition was that by instituting universal suffrage, a nation-state could conduct democratic politics in a meaningful and effective fashion. By meaningful, I mean legitimate, and by effective, I mean effective governance; in a related sense Seymour M. Lipset refers to 'legitimacy' and 'efficacy.' The world economy has become globalized at the end of the twentieth century in a far more profound sense than the sixteenth-century European capitalist economy, as portrayed by Immanuel Wallerstein. Accordingly, the cozy premises of the nineteenth-century European liberal-democratic model, which is based on the sovereign state and on the national economy, can not be convincingly sustained (Jaenicke, 1990).

In order to understand more clearly the end of the nation-state, then, we must examine the three 'ends' that confront global politics at the start of the new millennium. The end of the Cold War laid bare the basic contradictions of the nation-state, by dismantling the security structures that had long obfuscated the fundamental difficulties of the nation-state-based system. The end of geography, that is, the elimination of the tyranny of distance in global economic activity, has revealed the difficulties of running a national economy on the premise that democratically elected politicians will formulate national economic policy. The end of history, understood as the end of competition between the two major organizing intellectual currents of the twentieth century, namely liberal capitalism and totalitarian communism, has revealed the basic dilemmas of the survivor, liberal capitalism, in sustaining itself without the threatening presence of an antithetical ideology. Taken together, these three 'ends' seem to reinforce the idea of the ultimate demise of the nation-state (O'Brien, 1991; Fukuyama, 1991; Inoguchi, 1994, 2001).

By now it should be clear that these new challenges are common to all states, not simply Japan. Our question is whether Japan's adaptive but cautious bureaucratic ideology, which has coped with numerous challenges and changing environments in the past five centuries, is equal to the new challenges embodied in the three ends. In order to answer the question properly, I must first paraphrase it. How will Japanese politics, shaped as it is by the ideology of self-discipline, inclusionary aggregation, and piecemeal adaptation, cope with the changing environment? How will the convergence of international security (a major consequence of the end of the Cold War), the globalization of economic activities (a major consequence of the end of geography), and the weakening of domestic governance (a major consequence of the end of history) affect the extent to which Japanese politics can adapt?

Renewing honorific individualism and extending social capital

The above historical characterization of Japanese politics can be enriched by the introduction of two concepts. One, drawn from historical sociology, is the idea of an organizing principle which motivates social action, while the other, drawn from experimental psychology, is the idea of a closed or open social capital transaction system.

Eiko Ikegami suggests that the organizing principle of social action in Japanese society changed dramatically between the late-medieval and early modern periods, from 'honorific individualism' to 'honorific collectivism.' (Ikegami, 1995). Honorific individualism was exemplified by the warriors of the Warring States period in the sixteenth century: their merits and achievements were assessed solely on the basis of individual military strength. Honor and pride were their primary values. This individualist orientation was the key to Japanese politics in the sixteenth century. As the medieval order began to crumble individual power became the strongest type of force in society. This is the period when peasants took up arms and became warriors. The warlords who were the most skilful in organizing them consolidated their power and became the unifiers of Japan: Oda Nobunaga and Toyotomi Hideyoshi. Yet their attempts to create absolutist regimes both foundered. Then came the early modern synthesis of Tokugawa Ieyasu, the basic principle of which was honorific collectivism, although this continued to be based on the warrior's sense of honor and pride.

However, as Ikegami claims, the organizing principle of social action changed. Warriors were transformed into bureaucrats during the seventeenth century. First they were detached from land ownership. Their income took the form of rice stipends which were calculated in proportion to the productivity of the land which they administered. They were forced to relocate to castle towns. Second, they were effectively disarmed. The swords which they carried became mere symbols of their class. Third, their duties shifted from wartime to peacetime duties, namely crime prevention, taxation, flood control, development of infrastructure, management of the political relationship with the Tokugawa bakufu, and education. They became bureaucrats. Fourth, they came to rely on the upper echelon of peasants and merchants to oversee taxation and maintain law and order. The small size of their corps, along with the fact that they often had the status of outsiders forced them to co-opt local people into their official ranks.

Honorific collectivism developed in this fashion. The officials surrounding the Lord, and not the Lord himself, were regarded as the basic collective unit. The honor and survival of this unit became the organizing principal of social action, and the behavioral modality shifted from individualism to collectivism. This shift took place in some 300 domains in a variety of fashions. Out of the coexistence of these roughly 300 domains came the Japanese way of distinguishing 'socially known' others and 'unknown others'. In the former relationship collective assurance and assistance were the norm, whereas in the latter relation little is forthcoming. Honorific collectivism in the early modern period was expanded and reinforced in the modern period, classified here as extending from the beginning of the Meiji period to the end of the Shōwa period (1868–1989). The nation-building effort, starting with the Meiji Restoration in 1868, made Japanese collectivism one of the most intense and concentrated forms to exist anywhere. Economic development and military self-aggrandizement drove collectivism, to a degree that was at times excessive. Under the slogan of 'rich country, strong army', or of rapid recovery and growth, collectivism found a congenial environment in which to flourish.

The three 'ends' which occurred in the final decades of the twentieth century have made all these social arrangements, which were conceived on the premise of national boundaries in the nineteenth and twentieth centuries, difficult to sustain without instituting significant changes. Deregulation, governance problems, and the hollowing out of industry are all symptoms of this difficulty. As these problems emerge, we can observe a great transition taking place from collectivism back to individualism. Many surveys conducted in the last few years suggest that the Japanese are becoming more individualistically-oriented than in the past. As the practice of lifetime employment slowly recedes, fervent loyalty to the company and unquestioning faith in government will soon be things of the past. Identification with the Japanese state has not dissipated completely but is becoming much more diluted.

A parallel analysis is offered by the experimental psychologist Yamagishi Toshio (1995). He compares American and Japanese subjects in the 'prisoner's dilemma' and other games which feature cooperation and trust as key concepts. He argues that American trust is broader and more open, whereas Japanese trust is narrower and more closed. American trust is based on more generalized reciprocity, whereas Japanese trust is restricted more to family and kin relations or to small, known groups. The key function of Japanese social capital among known social groups is to provide reassurance so that uncertainty and risk is minimized, although that reassurance does not extend much further. The key function of American social capital is to express trust so that cooperative and productive reciprocity can be generated. The former social capital can be referred to as 'non-bridging' whereas the latter can be referred to as 'bridging.' In the Japanese case, the tasks of risk assessment and avoidance of the uncertainty of social interactions are optimized within the group, whereas in the American case that task is inherent in any social interaction. In terms of a sense of obligation, the typical Japanese feels a very strong obligation, but only towards a narrow range of socially known others, whereas the typical American feels a weaker obligation, but towards a wider range of socially anonymous others. The former type of social capital can be referred to as binding, whereas the latter social capital can be referred to as extending.

The challenges which Japan now faces can also be expressed in these terms. Japan may be in transition, from a relatively closed society to a society with relatively open social capital, from reassurance-oriented to trust-generating social capital, and from binding to extending social capital. The transition is broadly in line with the transition from what Eiko Ikegami calls honorific collectivism in the Tokugawa-Shōwa periods to what Emile Durkheim might describe as cooperative individualism in the Heisei (1989–) period and beyond. The transition is also in line with the transition from a mode of production based on the massive mobilization of capital and labor in a concentrated and concerted fashion, to a mode based on innovative technology and the skillful manipulation of capital. The relatively closed and binding system of social capital transaction was successful until recently, but has started to function negatively in the age of globalization. Honorific collectivism and the state-led economic developmental model have become obstacles to further success. Furthermore, the very success which Japan has achieved in the recent past seems to have delayed the transition from a relatively closed social capital transaction system, to the more open system which is necessary for the success of contemporary Japan.

The June 1998 Upper House election and beyond

This trend towards individualism could clearly be seen in events surrounding the Upper House elections of June 12, 1998 (Yamaguchi, 1998). The governing party was not able to secure a majority, whereas the month-old Democratic Party made a remarkable advance, as did both the Buddhist lay organization-based Kōmei Party and the Japanese Communist Party.

The following observations may be made. First, the governing Liberal Democratic Party experienced a major setback in its failure to capture a majority. The setback can in large part be explained as a combination of anger and apprehension as a result of the failure of the government's economic policies. Voters are angry with the governing party because its policy failures seem to have locked the Japanese economy into stagnation. This is particularly disturbing because it affects future economic prospects; citizens are apprehensive not only about the undermining of social welfare programs like pensions, education, and unemployment and health insurance, but the bleak prospects for economic growth as a whole.

Second, despite the general adverse trend noted above, the governing party's reassurance-oriented policy package, tailored to the interests of close friends and clients, has worked for some people. This is particularly true of districts that are characterized as non-metropolitan, non-competitive, and consisting of predominantly lower-density, agricultural, or comparatively sedentary populations. This strategy originates directly from the modern collectivist period. It focuses on massive public works, massive subsidies and tax privileges for agriculture and small business, policy finance based on postal savings, and more or less equal treatment of businesses within particular sectors (e.g., staving off bankruptcy for some banks with bad loans). Thus, many conservative friends and clients of the party, although negatively affected by the overall economic and fiscal adversity refrained from voicing excessive criticism.

Third, the governing party's failure to appeal to the electorate on issues unfavorable to its long-time friends and clients is revealed in the extreme difficulties which it encounters in obtaining seats in metropolitan and semi-metropolitan districts. Many metropolitan voters are angry that their money was siphoned off to non-metropolitan districts, and to the United States in the form of deposited postal savings, pension funds and government bonds which were invested in higher-yielding financial instruments. They are also upset at not being afforded equal treatment simply because they are not friends and clients of the governing party and bureaucratic agencies. Both are oriented towards the priorities and preferences of their friends and clients on the one hand, and those less competitive on the other.

These observations clearly relate to the historical and experimental conceptualizations discussed above, and indicate the limits of modern collectivism based on reassurance-oriented social capital. They also indicate that it is necessary for a postmodern cooperative individualism based on trust-generating social capital to emerge. Although more detailed observation and analysis are necessary before drawing definite conclusions about this momentous transition, it seems clear that real changes are taking place. This strongly suggests that Japanese politics is entering *terra incognita*. The changes afoot may be more significant than anything which Japan has experienced in the course of the last five centuries. The current volume is an account of Japanese politics on the eve of this transition.

2 The historical positioning of the contemporary Japanese political system

Introduction

At what point is it appropriate to begin an examination of contemporary Japanese state and society? Although this book's primary focus is on the period after the first oil crisis, it is necessary to be informed about earlier periods because the development of state and society has a historical and continuous pattern. In placing the contemporary Japanese political system in historical context it is necessary to engage in a critical analysis of earlier Japanese history. The purpose of this chapter is, through the provision of such historical context, to provide a fresh perspective in looking at contemporary state and society in Japan.

The origins of pluralism

In tracing Japanese history from the first oil crisis back, one thinks of the following periods as decisive in shaping contemporary state and society: they are, in modern times, the Allied Occupation, the period of national mobilization, the Sino-Japanese War, the Russo-Japanese War, and the birth of the Meiji state.

Why do we prioritize the above periods? Because, firstly, the Occupation led to fundamental systemic changes in Japanese politics and economics. Among these changes the most significant were the rewriting of the Japanese Constitution as the basis for democratic politics, and the signing of the Japan–U.S. Security Treaty, which underwrote Japan's national security. Most works on current Japanese politics begin with this period (Maruyama, 1964; Tsuji, 1969; Masumi, 1965–1980). If one concurs with the view that there is a discontinuity between the contemporary Japanese political system and that of the prewar period, this division is natural. Even those who stress the continuity between prewar and postwar Japanese political systems mostly restrict themselves to arguing that there was administrative continuity. For those who view the democratization of Japanese society as a highly positive development, Japan's defeat and the ensuing period of occupation are usually the starting point for analyses of contemporary Japanese state and society.

Japan's high economic growth ground to a halt in the mid-1930s, rapidly regained momentum in the 1950s, and continued until the first oil crisis of 1973. The basis for this economic growth was the well-prepared infrastructure of the occupation period (Nakamura, 1971, 1978, 1979, 1981, 1985, 1993). Advocates of the discontinuity perspective point to factors such as the dissolution of the zaibatsu, the legalization of trade unions, the acquisition of new equipment and technologies due to the destruction of the old, and the relative stability of both the international environment and domestic politics. On the other hand, those who advocate the continuity perspective point to the ongoing potential for economic growth.

Secondly, during the period of national mobilization, a surprising amount of legislation was enacted that remains in place today. In particular, power was concentrated in the economic bureaucracies for the purpose of mobilizing economic resources. It is now widely accepted that the war mobilization system was utilized in the postwar recovery and the successful period of high growth (Sakakibara, 1990). It is also commonly acknowledged that the framework for government economic operations and the bureaucratic development of the legal system have their origins in the mobilization era. Therefore, discussion of the relatively high economic growth rate in Japan, Germany and Italy is always associated with the influence of mobilization for war (the effects of the fascist era). This continuity thesis is broadly accepted by economic historians, but few are prepared to acknowledge the possibility of such a continuity in the political domain. This is because the defeat, occupation and democratic baptism that followed marked a sharp break from the earlier system.

Thirdly, during the Russo-Japanese War, Japan's desperate struggle to escape from colonization by pursuing a 'rich country, strong army' strategy paid off, with the Meiji state reaching its zenith. Later, national sentiment as a whole was led in the direction of extravagance and arrogance (Shiba, 1969–1970). But if we do not take constitutional monarchy and parliamentary democracy in this period as the starting point, it is difficult to talk about the characteristics of Japan's contemporary political system (Banno, 1971).

With defeat, occupation, democratization and a new constitution, civil rights and general elections gradually became an embedded feature of Japanese politics, marking a qualitative change. However, when analyzing Japan's current political system, few people go back this far. Nevertheless, the military, as a major pillar of the Meiji state ideology, was central to the political operation that was abandoned after Japan's defeat. This makes the discontinuity between past and present systems more distinct (Kōsaka, 1968).

Fourthly, the Meiji state, in the beginning, was based on the emperor system, the bureaucracy and the military. The emperor system successfully provided an ideological basis for political culture in the new nation state. It combined indigenous religious worship with the idea of a single nation, thus creating the foundation for political unification and political stability, both necessary preconditions of modernization (Amino, 1988). During the Tokugawa period the bureaucracy had been broadly inherited by the samurai class, but in the Meiji period a new bureaucratic class emerged as a result of the introduction of a competitive examination system. Despite strong competition from other political actors, the bureaucracy played an important role, as the servant of the Emperor, in the legislation, decision-making and implementation of public policy (Hata, 1981; Koh, 1989). The bureaucracy's role was further augmented in these areas by the necessity of war mobilization in the 1930s and the weakening of other political groups after Japan's defeat in 1945 (Sakaiya, 1991). Those who stress the continuity of the bureaucratic system could fruitfully re-examine this period for further evidence which supports their arguments.

In contrast, the nature of the military changed as a result of the Meiji Restoration, a military coup d'etat that was confined to a very limited geographical area. Universal conscription was adopted as a means of unifying the whole country. The military foundations of the political system were strengthened. Japan's military consolidation made it possible for the Meiji state to confront Western powers and neighboring countries (Inoue, 1985). Thus a new generation of citizens was inculcated with the ideology of the emperor system. In this sense, the military, together with compulsory education and radio broadcasting, provided strong impetus to the process of national unification (Anderson, 1983).

What do we learn if we extend the boundaries of our historical perspective? Generally speaking, the further back in time we go from the present, the more difficult it is to identify the influence of political growth on contemporary national structures. But some argue that, in order to understand the contemporary Japanese political system, it is necessary to study the periods predating the Meiji era: the period of the Tokugawa shōgunate, the Muromachi Warring States period, and the Nara-Heian era.

The Tokugawa period followed the transitional years of the Muromachi Warring era when a society centered on feudal manors collapsed. Although the Tokugawa shōgunate established a central administrative body, autonomous communities remained the basic unit of society, and, generally speaking, the power of the Muromachi Warring States was transferred to the constituent elements of the Tokugawa Bakufu (Ooms, 1985). The Tokugawa regime also created a social and political framework that restricted armed groups, social classes and professions to certain geographical areas, whilst placing more limits on the use of force to settle social disputes. This aspect is significant when discussing the contemporary Japanese political system. The Tokugawa period laid the foundations for a grassroots network that provided mutual monitoring and cooperation in maintaining order and resolving conflicts of interest. This is a key factor in understanding how Japan could later maintain relatively stable social relations when confronted by the destabilizing forces of modernization.

It is generally perceived that Japan's polity is dominated by the state and not by society. However, the nature of this domination differs from that in other East Asian countries, especially China and South Korea, in that the distance between state and society, or between the ruling elite and the ruled, is comparatively small in Japan due to the existence of a fairly large middle class. In addition administrative bodies, due to the ambiguity of their duties, have well-developed rights of discretion and are pragmatic. The foundations of an opportunistic and pragmatic political administration were laid in the Tokugawa era. These same qualities can also be found in the contemporary Japanese political system.

During the Muromachi Warring States period, Chinese-style imperial decrees, the emperor system, agrarianism and central authority were all temporarily destroyed. Instead, there was a high degree of social mobility, prosperity in non-agricultural sectors and decentralization, all of which developed indigenously in Japan from the Jōmon period. In the Yayoi era, the ruling elite had flowed into Japan from China, advanced technologies were spread, and the ancient Japanese state was born. This encompassed the emperor system, agrarianism and a central administration, the key features of Japanese politics. The Muromachi period saw these long-standing arrangements subverted by sheer force. This period was characterized by more dispersed military force, greater prosperity in large-scale trade, a more internationalized society, and a high degree of social mobility, symbolized by the phenomenon of the inferior overtaking his/her superior (Amino, 1984).

The Nara-Heian period saw the adoption and institutionalization of the Chinese imperial decree system, leading to the establishment and consolidation of the emperor system in Japan, thus providing the basis for a single nation-state (Tsuji, 1993; Amino, 1986). This single nation-state was restored and enhanced in the Meiji period. The imperial decree system tied ruled subjects to land and agriculture, resulting in a neglect of other activities such as commerce, fishing and hunting. The tendency to neglect commerce made it possible for the 'island-nation' theory to develop in the Meiji period. It can therefore be seen that if periods prior to the Meiji period are incorporated in our historical narrative, it is possible to acquire a deeper understanding of Japan's contemporary political system.

This study keeps in mind the above historical events but its primary focus remains on state and society in Japan after the first oil crisis. If this analytical perspective is adopted, it is inadequate to study Japan in isolation. Instead, it is necessary to consider the ways in which the Japanese state and society have been shaped by developments in international politics and economics in the second half of the twentieth century. Therefore, this book on state and society in contemporary Japan must begin with a survey of the international environment within which the contemporary Japanese state and society have developed.

Japan was defeated in World War II, and occupied by Allied forces from 1945 to 1952 (Iokibe, 1985; Igarashi, 1986; Finn, 1992; Buckley, 1982, 1992). By 1952, the United States and the then Soviet Union were engaged in mutually hostile relations and the Cold War had begun to take shape. Domestic confrontations in East Asian countries were also shaped to a significant extent by developments in the Cold War (Cumings, 1981, 1990; Tang, 1963; Kolko, 1985). In China, in the regions formerly occupied by Japan, competition between the Nationalists and Communists, both of which had matured as political forces during the war with Japan, developed into an open civil war. In the end, the Communists took control of the mainland and the Nationalists fled to Taiwan, where they were able to assert political control. In Korea, the U.S. and the former USSR each occupied half of the peninsula and soon installed respective puppet governments. In Vietnam, after the Japanese withdrawal, Communist forces came into conflict with conservative forces. When France, the old suzerain, gave its support to the latter, a civil war which was to have significant international implications, and which was eventually to draw in the US itself, erupted. In Japan, as occupation forces carried out political and economic reforms, the struggle between the left and the right intensified. At one point, as Japan suffered economic chaos before setting out on the path to reconstruction, its national income level was one of the lowest in the world. The Philippines had the highest level of national income in Asia at this time.

By the early 1970s the Pax Americana, forged by overwhelming U.S. military force during World War II, experienced a major watershed (Gaddis, 1982, 1987). The Vietnam War was expected to end quickly but had become a protracted, militarily difficult and politically embarrassing conflict. In response to strong anti-war sentiment at home, the U.S. sought a so-called 'peace with honour.' Although the United States was supposedly at the peak of its power, chinks in its armour were unexpectedly revealed (Williams, 1980). The U.S. dollar, as the acknowledged international currency, could at this time be freely converted into gold. However, as the American trade deficit continued to accumulate, the U.S. government abandoned this commitment, which lead to the immediate collapse of the postwar international monetary system, also known as the Bretton Woods system. The new monetary system which emerged to replace the Bretton Woods system essentially allowed the market to determine the exchange rate (Cooper, 1968). The OPEC countries raised prices in an attempt to prevent a decrease in the value of oil, but this decision triggered the first oil crisis. As a result, one of the preconditions of postwar economic prosperity, the cheap supply of primary products, and energy in particular, no longer existed. Oil prices rose, which in the short term led to a rapid increase in the income of oil producing countries, but from a long-term perspective marked a decline in their competitiveness (Bergsten, 1975). The oil crisis also led to expansion by and competition between the Soviet Union and the United States with regard to oil producing states.

In the 1970s and the 1980s, both the former USSR and the United States were highly conscious of their decline in competitiveness as the former Soviet Union moved from perestroika to disintegration, and the U.S. moved from the Reagan revolution to the Gulf War. These changes reverberated strongly in East Asia but they also encouraged

East Asian development. While the defeat of the U.S. in Vietnam highlighted to East Asia the need to adapt to a changing security environment, the move towards a floating exchange rate impressed upon East Asian countries the importance of adapting to international market forces. Skyrocketing world oil prices pushed the energy resource-poor countries of East Asia to implement more thorough energy saving measures, which were to result in a major leap forward in the competitiveness of East Asian manufactured goods (Maddison, 1989).

By the early 1990s the world was again in the midst of a great transformation, with the end of the Cold War, the reunification of Germany, the disintegration of the Soviet Union, and temporary setbacks for the process of European integration (Van den Bergh, 1992; Weber, 1991). In the mid-1970s oil prices were high, and the former Soviet Union, which had the upper hand at this point, as the U.S. suffered from a post-Vietnam hangover, effectively challenged the U.S. to a new arms race. Yet within a few years the Soviet Union's overall economic stagnation became apparent as its intervention in Afghanistan, which had begun in 1979, proved too costly. Neither could the Soviet Union match the American raising of the stakes in the arms race. The U.S. implementation of the Strategic Defense Initiative (SDI) was a key development which prompted the Soviet Union to seek a new detente. Both countries reduced their deployments of conventional forces and the size of their strategic nuclear arsenals, since both already had the potential to destroy the other many times over. These developments occurred as the economies of both countries were showing signs of fatigue in the mid-1980s (Nye, 1984; Kaldor, 1990).

Weary of being manipulated by the superpowers, détente was precisely what Europe had hoped for. The rapprochement between the U.S. and the Soviet Union provided the context for a worldwide detente centred on Europe. One of the more climactic events of this process was the reunification of East and West Germany. Although Germany went through a prolonged period of economic turmoil as a result of this reunification, the sheer size of its population and its economic competitiveness meant that its dominant position in the European Community was never seriously threatened. The Soviet Union, on the other hand, not only had detente to contend with, but also had to carry out far-reaching economic and political reform. As the Soviets experimented during their transition to a market economy, economic chaos ensued and political democratization led to a weakened central authority, ultimately culminating in the Soviet Union's disintegration (Shindō, 1992).

Needless to say the world has changed significantly since 1952. If the two decades after the Occupation years were the era of Japan's high economic growth, then the two decades after 1972 could be described as an era when Japan made a qualitative leap forward. Japan's high growth and qualitative change were a major factor in the transformation of world politics, but from Japan's vantage point, the changes in the world seemed to have come unnoticed. The qualitative change meant an altered domestic structure but it also reflected evolving features of international society. Therefore, in the discussion below I divide my analysis of this qualitative change and of changes in the world into two sections: the world economy and international relations.

From the Japanese point of view, the most critical development in the world economy after the oil crises was the rise of the Asia-Pacific region, with this rise centered on Japan. The emergence of Japan as a significant international player forced the resource-rich regions of Europe, the countries of the former Soviet Union, and the United States to re-evaluate their policies. These countries initially responded by seeking to maintain the status quo, but later both superpowers attempted to change the status quo, as will be discussed below. Furthermore, the implications of the ascent of the Asia-Pacific region were not just confined to the Asia-Pacific region, as this ascent stimulated Latin America, India, China, Russia, and other developing and transitional countries to reach the preparation stage for solid economic development. This situation is very similar to that in the late nineteenth century when European countries could only manage a declining 1–2 percent growth rate amidst a worldwide slump, whilst then-developing countries such as Argentina, Canada, the United States and Australia were able to maintain a 5–10 per cent economic development rate until the outbreak of World War I (Emmott, 1992).

Again from Japan's perspective, the most critical development in international relations after the oil crises was the end of the Cold War. This had a profound effect on Japan. Ten years after the second oil crisis, the two superpowers took visible steps toward ending the Cold War. Yet, even before the second oil crisis, the two countries had taken initial steps by participating in the Helsinki process, talks that were designed to further reduce tensions in Europe. The decisive factor was that as the two superpowers were encountering diplomatic setbacks in their interventions in Afghanistan and Iran respectively, the second oil crisis occurred. By its end, both the U.S. and the USSR had come to realize the severity of their problems both at home and abroad. Later on, the Reagan revolution and Gorbachev's perestroika brought new problems, thus further weakening the positions of the two superpowers (Davis, 1982). The purpose of the remainder of this chapter is to describe and analyze Japanese state and society after the first oil crisis. Before this, it is necessary to consider the position of the Japanese economy within the world economy, and the position of the Japanese state in international politics.

Japan in the world economy

It is important to our analysis of contemporary Japanese state and society that we understand Japan's position in the world economy. There has been substantial progress towards a world economy in the past four centuries and this process accelerated in the latter half of the twentieth century (Wallerstein, 1974). The momentum for these changes has been provided by technological innovation. In communications and transportation advanced technology allows economic transactions to be made immediately. With advanced technology, manufacturing and service industries are able to operate globally in optimal forms. Such is the state of the modern world. In order to discuss state and society in the late twentieth century, the state must be defined as an actor that functions in the world economy, but this economy is also embedded in and permeated by elements of society. Briefly, national states and societies are constituent elements of a much broader world economic structure. Because the nation-state has been the basic unit of world politics during the past four hundred years, attempts to understand international economics in terms of the interactions of national economies have predominated (Kennedy, 1988).

However, with the consolidation of the world market, it has become difficult to analyze the national economy in comparative isolation based on the small state hypothesis. According to the small state hypothesis a country's own behavior does not affect others, but other countries' actions and their collective influence, understood collectively as the international economic environment, do in turn have a bearing on the economy of an individual country. To understand the behavior of the Japanese state and society, it is necessary to look at how the Japanese economy has adapted to a world economy which has developed at a rapid rate in the past fifty years (Maddison, 1991). This century has witnessed an explosion in population growth, revolutionary advances in technology and large scale industrialization. Consequently, it is only natural to consider the possibility that the world economy will become more integrated.

Rapid population growth began in the twentieth century but has its roots in a much earlier period (Cipolla, 1972–1976). Progress in agricultural techniques and improvements in health care and sanitation were preconditions for this population growth. In agriculture, the spread of irrigation technology dramatically reduced the effects of flooding and droughts, thus facilitating sustained increases in grain production. In the case of rice cultivation, shortfalls frequently occurred in the past in cold regions, but once varieties of rice which were more resilient to the cold had been identified and cultivated, the damage inflicted by cold temperatures was minimized. The increased use of pesticides against insects and diseases had a similar effect. Species selection and refinement, allied to the commercialization of seed production, led agriculture to develop over time into a large-scale industry.

There was also progress in health care and sanitation due to factors such as the spread of water-supply lines, better sewage management, developments in the field of medicine, and higher levels of nutrition. The infant mortality rate, in particular, has fallen significantly in many countries. Even in low income countries, wherever there is a good standard of education about techniques of pre-natal care, and a minimum level of health care, there are drastic decreases in infant deaths, and consequent increases in population. The lower the income level of a country, the more likely it is to have a higher infant mortality rate. This, in turn, has led to a systematically high birth rate as the basic unit of society, the family, attempts to secure an adequate number of family members who can eventually join the labour force and contribute to the family's survival. It is particularly important to note that although in the twentieth century many countries have reduced their infant mortality rate, changes in other conditions have not taken place, causing an explosion in population growth (Miyamoto and Hayami, 1988).

Among the technological advances made, the most critical have been those in the fields of communication and transportation, and in the creation of productive and destructive technologies. Communications technology connects different parts of the world instantly, creating a smaller planet. Utilizing electronic communications, financial transactions can be accomplished in the blink of an eye. In the field of transportation, railways developed first, followed by rapid improvements in the speed of overland transportation. Later, with improvements in naval technology, sea-based transportation became more important than land-based transportation. This was followed by the development of large transport airplanes (both passenger and cargo), as air transportation overtook sea transportation as the dominant means of moving people and goods around the world. Today, while seaports are still necessary for such cargos as oil and grain, more than half of Japan's foreign trade goes through airports. In the area of productive technology, there is great demand for iron and steel in the railway and shipbuilding industries, as well as for petroleum for automobile and air transportation. Moreover, the rapid development of mechanical and precision machinery has further increased productivity.

With regard to destructive technologies, the 20th century witnessed the development of automatic rifles, armored vehicles, bombers and atomic weapons. In the battle of Lushun during the Russo-Japanese War, the Russian army was at a clear advantage largely because it possessed automatic rifles. In the German-Polish War that triggered World War II, German armored vehicles were able to comprehensively defeat the Polish cavalry in a very short period of time. This was a traditional cavalry force, not a contemporary cavalry unit; modern cavalry units are now equipped with advanced weapons and helicopters. The Polish cavalry was fighting, one might suggest in the manner of Don Quixote, against thousands of heavily armored German vehicles. This military conflict saw the highest death toll recorded in one day of fighting since the Napoleonic Wars (Singer and Small, 1972). During World War I, bombers also wrought destruction and were, erroneously as it turned out, labeled as the ultimate in weaponry by Giulio Duhet, the early twentieth century strategic theorist. Since then, of course, we have witnessed the full destructive capacity of the atomic bomb in Hiroshima and Nagasaki, and the enormity of these weapons has, for the first time, made humankind reluctant to initiate armed conflict (Brodie, 1959).

In the twentieth century, large-scale industrialization could be quickly achieved by utilizing iron, steel and aluminum as raw materials, and coal and petroleum as energy. Without iron it is not possible to have steel and petroleum industries, and the exploration and exploitation of iron has expanded swiftly. The major producers of iron are states such as the United States, Russia, India, Brazil, and Australia. As regards oil, the major producers are states such as the United States, Russia,

Saudi Arabia, Kuwait, Iraq, Indonesia, Venezuela, Bahrain, China, etc. Unlike iron, petroleum is produced in only a limited number of regions. The possession of oil is very closely related to military power, thus it is also related to the occurrence of wars in the twentieth century.

In the twentieth century the speed of industrialization quickened. In comparison with the economic growth rate of the second half of the twentieth century, nineteenth century industrialization was very slow. This was the case for the most advanced country at that time, Great Britain, as well as for comparative latecomers such as the U.S. and Germany. A fundamental feature of this technological leap was the cheap supply of energy (and primary products). Large-scale industrialization primarily entailed the production of mass consumption goods such as automobiles on the one hand, and capital goods such as machine tools on the other. One indication of the rate of industrialization is that the GNP of more than half of the world's 190-plus countries is less than the total sales of large multinational corporations. As these large enterprises make judgements based on economic calculations, the world economy becomes globalized and interdependence deepens. These large enterprises not only transcend national borders to constitute a world economy, they also shape the states and societies in which they operate. This is quite similar to the absolutist era of the early modern period in Europe, when the Prussian army founded the Prussian state. Large enterprises in the twentieth century have comparable influence to the Prussian army in the seventeenth century. This is an inescapable characteristic of highly industrialized society.

Japan's case is even more extreme. Large corporations not only produce a significant proportion of GNP, but also acquire most of the foreign reserves which are used to import energy and food. Furthermore, the huge profits derived from the domestic market have enabled Japanese enterprises to engage in technological innovation and enter overseas markets. In Japan, manufacturing industries produce most of the GNP. The export of automobiles, machine tools and electronics could by itself provide all of the foreign currency which Japan requires, and still leave Japan with one of the world's largest trade surpluses.

In addition, one third of the government's revenue comes from the corporate tax levied on several thousand enterprises (another one third or more comes from personal income tax). One view is that in comparison with recurring profit, corporate tax is too low. But the Japanese government's philosophy on corporate and personal income tax is that neither should be too high. Lower taxes can stimulate people's work incentives, which in turn will ultimately generate more government revenue. In other words, the government does not want to create a high tax system that will ultimately dampen entrepreunerial spirit. At the same time, certain regulations, cartels, systems of consultation and customs have become central to the security, safety, stability and operation of Japanese society. Although these regulations contribute significantly to a higher cost of living, the Japanese people have tolerated them in the past (Ohmae, 1989). For instance, elevators could be bought from abroad at a cheaper price but if they do not meet Japanese safety standards, then the purchase cannot be made. Another example is that foreign corporations are prevented from entering Japan's construction industry since they may disturb the existing industrial order in this sector.

Japan experienced a number of significant changes in the twentieth century. Explosive population growth, technological progress and large-scale industrialization have taken place, and all have exerted a considerable influence on the Japanese state and society which continues to this day. In the Tokugawa period, the Japanese population grew substantially (Hanley and Yamamura, 1977). Before then, rice production in low-level areas was difficult because of flooding and disease. Technological progress remedied this problem, making it possible for agriculture to be more productive, thus leading to a population increase. In this instance, increased productivity was based on improvements in traditional technology rather than the kind of drastic leap in productive capability that occurred in the twentieth century. The critical element in all of this was what Miyamoto Matao and Hayami Tōru have labeled an 'industrious revolution,' a set of diligent habits that gradually permeated Japanese society (Miyamoto and Hayami, 1988).

However, just as agricultural yields had to be monitored and cropped, population growth also had to be controlled to a certain degree through comparable methods. Cold weather played a vital role in controlling population in the Northeast region, and this could explain why Tokugawa Japan built a self-sufficient agricultural system. After the mid-nineteenth century, Japan began experimenting with mass industrialization, which was soon followed by a rapid leap in productive capability which in turn led to a faster growing population. As Japan entered the twentieth century, this population growth trend was reinforced and accelerated by a steady drop in the infant mortality rate. It is worth noting that population issues were an important factor in the various disturbances which impacted on the international political economy in the turbulent first half of the twentieth century. A vicious circle of distrust spawned increasingly restrictive policies in the areas of immigration, trade, and international currency management. Eventually, this distrust and the ensuing competition led to military conflict.

In the second half of the twentieth century, the reverse was true. In the era of Pax Americana, it was widely believed that the economy was in a healthy cycle. The prolonged period of peace led to political stability, which in turn helped to stimulate economic growth. Japan's population grew quickly in the high growth period of the third quarter of the twentieth century. This in turn supplied the necessary workforce required to sustain high growth, paving the way for Japan to become a major world economic power. Japan's population has reached a plateau at around 127 million people, making it more populous than any of the major Western European countries.

At the start of this century, technological progress in Japan was slow but when the conditions for economic take-off were met, advances were achieved with incredible speed. This can be illustrated by reference to the spread of firearms technology which the Portuguese brought to Japan when their fleets arrived in 1543 (Inoguchi, 1992a). Three days after the fleet's arrival, Lord Tokitaka of Tanegashima Island met with the Portuguese, and within a couple of days of his first meeting the Japanese had already learned how to shoot. Lord Tokitaka then ordered an ironsmith to make more than 600 guns. Although there were problems with the trigger device, these firearms were used to conquer the adjacent island of Yakushima. The Japanese also reached an agreement with the Portuguese that on their next visit they would bring an ironsmith to help the Japanese to perfect their firearm manufacturing techniques. By 1556, in the Warring States Period, firearms were widely and readily available in Japan. According to an account by Mendes Pinto, there were 300,000 firearms in Japan, with 25,000 already being exported to the Ryūkyu Kingdom. When Oda Nobunaga defeated Takeda in the battle of Nagashino in 1575, he formulated a new strategy whereby soldiers armed with rifles made repeated attacks. This method of fighting, called the 'musketry volley' tactic, did not appear in Europe until fifty-six years later, in 1631, when it was employed by Gustavus Adolfus of Sweden.

At the end of the Bakufu period, there was an urgent demand for ship-repairing facilities at Deshima in Nagasaki. This gave increasing momentum to the idea that Japan should not only have facilities to do repair work, but should also build its own shipyards and iron and steel mills. Just as with Tanegashima's acquisition of firearm-making techniques, it was argued that Japan should develop the capacity to make things on its own (Nakanishi, 1982–1983). The logic was that until Japan took the next step and upgraded its existing ship-repairing capabilities, or, indeed, built its own ships, it would continue to be dependent on foreigners. Furthermore, Japan could not make its own ships until it produced its own iron and steel. The Tokugawa Bakufu built shipyards for these reasons. The Meiji government was similarly concerned to promote the indigenization of these processes because of their significance for national security. Ultimately, however, the government feared that expenditure would be too high and that such enterprises would be unsuccessful, going as they did against the logic of the market, and sold its state ventures to the private sector. This led to the establishment and development of Mitsubishi's Nagasaki Shipyard. Interest in foreign things, and especially in foreign science and technology, was a feature of Japan not only during the open door policy of the Warring Period, but also of the Tokugawa era, when Japan officially pursued a closed door policy. These precedents all contributed to the steady development that Japan experienced after it officially opened its doors to the world (Toby, 1984).

With the moderate increase in population which occurred in the Tokugawa period, the government attempted to minimize foreign trade and technology transfer from abroad. The Japanese economy as a whole at that time was essentially self-sufficient, and from a long-term perspective this system would shape the way that Japanese thought about economic development. The principles of self-help and self-reliance were emphasized even during the acquisition of technology from abroad. A technologically backward country must be enthusiastic about importing foreign technologies, but once introduced, these technologies should become indigenized and be further improved to achieve competitiveness. This belief became an important pyschological driving force in Japan, providing the foundation for the so-called Japanese developmental model.

The opening of the country and the implementation of modernization policies planted the seeds of technological progress in many fields. At that time, the Japanese economy faced difficulties in two areas. First, by the end of the Tokugawa period, resources (silver, etc.) had been exhausted. They had been discovered and mined from the Warring States Period to the mid-Tokugawa era. Energy resources were also limited and primary products, such as food, that had once been exported, had become scarce due to population growth. Second, Japan was forced to relinquish its sovereignty over tariffs when signing trade treaties with foreign powers, thereby losing control of a tool which could have helped Japan to protect its industries effectively. Although state-run enterprises did have some success in promoting industrialization in the early stages, the government also realized early on that a system that went against market principles would not be competitive in the medium to long run. In short, Japan had to try and survive for more than half a century within a global free trade regime that had been imposed on it. The lack of foreign reserves was a constant problem for Japan during these years, creating many bottlenecks in the early stages of industrialization.

Japan's industrialization took off during the First World War, and continued at a steady pace until the national mobilization period of the 1930s. Until this time Japan was able to attain a solid level of technological development. But after the mid-1930s, the dissemination of technology was severely restricted by the international economic blockade. This situation persisted for years even after the Second World War. Technology transfer was strictly limited in military-related sectors such as aeronautics, rockets and submarines. This provided a window of opportunity for civilian production technologies to become mainstream and grow in the postwar period. Since limitations had been placed on Japan's sovereignty in the area of security, it concentrated its energy on manufacturing and trade. Although the product lines shifted to foodstuffs, textiles, shipbuilding, machinery, and then later automobiles and electronics, Japan's large volume of production and exports still earned the foreign currency required to import food, energy and raw materials, thereby establishing a fixed pattern of economic behavior. The bottom line had remained constant: technology transfer and technological innovation guided by the principle of self-help and self-reliance (Tsurumi and Kawata, 1989).

Japan's industrialization in the twentieth century was initially stimulated by the demand for weapons during the First World War. But this was more than a temporary increase in demand. It created the conditions for the beginning of a structural adjustment. First, Japan regained tariff autonomy. Second, based on the initial achievements of industrialization, more than fifty years after opening up to the world Japan now possessed the necessary political stability and sufficient social and productive infrastructure for economic development. Third, the first half of the twentieth century was an unstable period in international affairs, with all states striving for hegemonic status.

This instability in turn renewed impetus for greater industrialization. The most critical constraint was the fragility of the economy, which was compounded by a general lack of awareness of the need for a comprehensive economic policy. This could explain why there were dramatic peaks and troughs in the world economy in the first half of the twentieth century. Japan was then a newly industrializing country. At this time market access at the global level did not exist; instead the prevalent trends of the period were towards protectionism and regionalism. By the 1930s, war mobilization, protectionism and economic blockades had all intensified. For an economy such as Japan's, which was dependent on energy and raw materials from abroad, and particularly from the United States, this was devastating. When the military-governed economy also proved unsuccessful, Japan turned to the idea of a Greater East Asian Co-prosperity Sphere, and set out on the road to self-destruction.

After World War II, Japan's economic recovery proceeded apace due to the removal of conservative capitalist forces, the destruction of old production facilities, the setting of new national goals, and the birth of a global free trade regime under the Pax Americana, the emerging U.S.-dominated world order. The dissolution of the *zaibatsu* and the implementation of anti-monopoly legislation completely decimated the old capitalist class. In their place, enterprises with a low percentage of their own capital, balanced stock holdings and wage-earning managers emerged. This led to the birth of new operating strategies: cooperation among firms, consultation with supervising government offices, thorough monitoring of market trends, and a complete commitment to adapting to market changes (Johnson, 1981).

The destruction of old production equipment meant that everything started from scratch, giving great freedom to new industrial enterprises, and making it easier to construct new industrial facilities and production systems. The vast investment in equipment which was necessary for this new beginning provided a strong boost to the economy. Moreover, because of restrictions on the role of the Japanese government in the security arena, both state and society were able to set the same new economic development goals and then focus all of their energy on attaining them (Amaya, 1984). The global free trade system was made possible by the acceleration of world economic growth, driven by the overwhelming economic power of the U.S. and the spread of the free trade ideal. From a long-term perspective, the postwar Japanese economy developed, for the most part, within this beneficial environment and under these favorable conditions, although that is not to say that it did not encounter numerous difficulties along the way.

Japan in international relations

What is Japan's position in the international system? The relationship between state and society will not be clear until this question is answered because both are constituted within the structures of modern international relations (Gilpin, 1981). Here the term 'modern' refers to the structure of the international system in the four centuries since the conclusion of the Peace of Westphalia, which marked the end of the Thirty Years War in Europe. In this Westphalian system, the complex interactions between nations and states have been the basic feature of world politics.

Needless to say, the twentieth century belongs to this modern world. However, if we agree with John Lukacs' assertion that the modern world is a world of states interacting with each other, then it is impossible to understand domestic politics and society without positioning them in the context of international relations in the past four hundred years. The structure of the international system has placed constraints on the types of state form which could emerge. Understanding these constraints helps us to understand how societies developed within states which were structured by the international system. Between 1648 (when the norms of the Westphalian system were codified) and 1945 (the end of World War II) states engaged in fierce military competition. Nationalism was a central element of the international relations of this period, from at least the time of the French Revolution in 1789. Ideas of national self-determination became significant, and nation-states fought increasingly intense wars, competing for Empire and for predominance in the European states-system, a process which was to culminate in the First and Second World Wars.

If we look briefly at the major events in modern Japanese history, the opening of Japan, the Meiji Restoration, Japan's defeat in World War II and the ensuing occupation, we can immediately recognize that all were related to international relations. Both Japanese state and society have of course been deeply affected by these events. Not only have there been fundamental transformations in state and society viewed independently, but the relationship between state and society has also undergone significant changes as a result of leadership changes and the changes in policy that this has entailed.

The most salient feature of twentieth century international relations, and its most dramatic change, is the unprecedented number of casualties generated by the two world wars. War casualties from the twentieth century alone exceed the total number of casualties for all pre-twentieth century wars combined (Inoguchi Kuniko, 1989). This fact demonstrates the strong impact which international relations have on the domestic constitution of states and societies. Even if we limit our focus to international society after 1870, war has had momentous implications (Russett and Stein, 1980). An estimated 2.5–3 million Japanese died during the Second World War. By contrast, in the second half of the twentieth century, few countries use their armed forces to settle international disputes. Japan's constitution and the postwar Japan–U.S. Security Treaty limit its foreign policy options, as Japan has pledged not to use military force in settling international disputes. Japan could indeed be regarded as semi-sovereign with regard to its security policy, partly by its own design, and partly at the instigation of the US.

The second salient feature of twentieth century international relations is the establishment of American hegemony in the latter half of the century, after the major shifts in position among leading world powers in the first half. This was a century when two periods – the preparation for, and the establishment of American hegemony – were closely linked. From a Japanese perspective, Japan was a rival of the U.S. in the first half of the century, and a dependent cooperator in the second half, especially in the third quarter (Iriye, 1965). As is generally known, Japan's competition with the U.S. began at the time of the Russo-Japanese War. The US believed that if Japan achieved a decisive victory over Russia the balance of power in the Far East would be lost, and American interests would be harmed as a result. For this reason President Roosevelt mediated the signing of the Portsmouth Treaty. Later, the Japanese were angered by state legislation in California which discriminated against Japanese immigrants. Even so, Japan cooperated with other major powers in reaching an agreement on the reduction of naval capabilities after the First World War. However, Japan was eventually pushed to adopt an independent foreign policy as a result of the worldwide economic downturn, political instability on the Asian continent, and more importantly the uncertainty of domestic politics. The struggle for hegemony over China, Southeast Asia and the Western Pacific eventually brought Japan into suicidal military conflict with the United States (Borg and Okamoto, 1973).

In the second half of the twentieth century, it was possible, with the acknowledgement of absolute U.S. hegemony, for Japan to recover its position in the world. First of all, Japan's military expenditure was at a minimum. During the prewar period, for several consecutive years military spending had accounted for as much as one third of total government expenditure. In the early postwar period military spending dropped to just over one per cent of GNP, and decreased steadily thereafter. It was only in the 1980s that military expenditure again exceeded the one per cent ceiling. The main task assigned to Japan's Self Defense Forces (SDF) was to assist the U.S. military personnel stationed in Japan, the Far East and the Western Pacific region. In its supplementary role, anything other than indirect assistance by the SDF in instances of regional war, nuclear defense and nuclear war was beyond consideration. Although at this time Japan was not able to defend herself independently of the U.S. there was little that could be done to alter this arrangement. The SDF's role in maintaining domestic order was quite significant in the period when it was established, but as Japan's political situation stabilized the need for such a service decreased (Inoguchi, 1993a).

Japan's political fortunes have fluctuated in the twentieth century but its GNP has grown almost continuously from 1870 until the present time, with the exception of the 1945–51 period. If we simplistically equate GNP to international influence, Japan's importance in international relations has been increasing consistently throughout the twentieth century. Japan's extraordinary progress since the Meiji Restoration can be attributed to its aspiration to hold a respectable place in international society (Inoguchi, 1992b). This goal led to military conflicts in the first half of this century which were not necessarily intended, while in the second half of the century the same goal led to national economic policies that made it possible to maintain peace (a policy of one-country pacifism).

Why is it that the objective of occupying a respectable place in international society became such an important guiding principle? This aspiration can ultimately be attributed to the overwhelming impact of the 'black ship' effect. Commodore Perry led the American fleet of black ships which forced the Tokugawa Bakufu to open its doors. Perry, as well as other foreign representatives who came after him, also imposed extraterritoriality conditions and limitations on Japan's tariff autonomy. These impositions reinforced Japan's conviction that in the future it would be necessary to become economically and militarily powerful in order to guarantee national autonomy. In today's world of free trade zones, universal diplomatic immunity and customs concessions these conditions do not seem unusual. But in an era when European and American colonialism was at its height, the Japanese government would have been seen as an agent or indeed, a subject of Western power if it had accepted these practices. At this time, as a substantial scholarly literature attests, Japan came to understand international politics in terms of colonialism, imperialism, anarchy, self-help and the survival of the fittest (Duus, Myers and Peattie, 1989; Myers and Peattie, 1986).

In the postwar era, a U.S.-maintained peace was realized but a different kind of rivalry persisted in the realm of economics, particularly in the areas of manufacturing and trade. Postwar economic competition in world markets is different in nature from the rivalries of the prewar period. Competition in the marketplace is full-scale, including market monitoring and production and sales. From the early postwar years when goods were scarce, Japan has developed competitive industries with considerable export potential. Such industries include foodstuffs, textiles, ship-building, machinery, automobiles, electronics and new materials. Industrial growth was accompanied by the raising of technological standards, growth in capital investment, high productivity in manufacturing facilities, and strong networks for sales and services. In the latter half of this century, Japan has achieved its goal of occupying a respectable place in the world. Today this is how Japan is viewed and also how Japan views itself.

Certainly, ambition alone can not increase a countries wealth and significance in international relations. Yet the primary reason for Japan's growing importance in international society has been its economic activities and successes, firmly based on the principles of self-reliance and hard work, as described in the previous section. In addition, the self-sufficient economic system that was already in place in the Tokugawa period made it possible for Japan's economic take-off after the country's opening and the Meiji Restoration (Flynn, 1991). Japan's literacy rate was the highest in the world in the eighteenth century, and this was another valuable element of social capital which assisted Japan's take-off (Dore, 1973). By the twentieth century, Japan's population was sufficiently large to provide the workforce required for the coming explosion of industrial progress. In 1850 Japan's population of 32 million was second in size only to that of France, which had a population of 35 million. At this time Germany had not yet been unified, and both Britain and the U.S. had populations of less than 30 million

(Nishikawa, 1985). Japan's population provided a large and dependable domestic market when the nation's international competitiveness was weak, and a sizeable pool of potential recruits when soldiers were needed for war. The relative size of Japan's population at this time was a significant national resource.

Japan thus emerged as a non-western state which aspired to a respectable position in international society. It had come to believe that it was necessary to develop a strong economy and a powerful army to negotiate an international anarchy where only the fittest survive and prosper. After achieving these twin objectives, Japan began to contemplate the possibility of competing with the western powers. This sense of competitiveness was heightened by a perception that Japan was being discriminated against on racial grounds. Ultimately Japan resorted to war as a perceived solution to its problems.

In the second half of this century, Japan relinquished its quest for self-reliance in the domain of national security, instead limiting its objectives to the securing of a respectable position in the world economy. It is often argued that a state which does not have autonomy in making its own national security decisions is only semi-sovereign. This view predominated in the nineteenth century, when Japan first acknowledged its own relative lack of power, and remained popular throughout the latter half of the twentieth century, in an era when Japan's foreign policy choices have been circumscribed by its relationship with the United States. States whose distinctive features are their ability and willingness to trade are often characterized as merchant states, somehow implying that they belong to a lower rank. De Gaulle's disparaging reference to Japanese Prime Minister Hayato Ikeda as a 'semi-conductor salesman' is a clear example of this line of thought. Such a characterization is especially galling for Japanese, given the low status that merchants have traditionally been accorded within Japanese society.

In the last few decades of the twentieth century, however, the importance of an economic and technological base for national security became more widely recognized. It is often suggested that U.S. hegemony is in relative decline, and American policy-makers have attempted to adjust policy to reflect this possibility (Zysman, 1983; Zysman and Tyson, 1983; Tyson, 1992). Throughout the nineteenth century, and indeed until comparatively recently, war and trade were clearly distinguishable. War belonged to the realm of 'high' politics and was dealt with by senior diplomats, while trade was accorded a lower priority and dealt with by consuls.

By the end of the twentieth century, however, it had become apparent that national security is highly dependent on production and technological capabilities. The approach to technological innovation differs between the United States, Japan and European countries. In the U.S., money is invested in military technology as a matter of priority, and the benefits of this research are then spun off into the private sector. The Internet is a good example of this process. In Europe and Japan it is the other way around: the development of civilian technology is prioritized and benefits are then transferred into the military domain. In an ironic twist, those responsible for the production of American weaponry have been adapting more and more civilian technologies from Japan and Europe. Japan is ahead of its American competition in the areas of electronic production and innovation. Moreover, with the declining competitiveness of the American manufacturing industry, many enterprises have been forced out of business, in turn causing concern that this will adversely affect American national security. American hegemony is premised on superior military technology, and yet many vital parts can not be produced domestically. American primacy is therefore in part underwritten by the excellence and innovation of the Japanese electronics sector. There are different views within the U.S. regarding the extent to which this should be tolerated. Some believe that Japan has exploited its superior technology to achieve concessions in its multi-faceted relationship with the U.S.

To conclude, it is clear that economic and technological prowess are important elements of a successful national security strategy. To the extent that this is true, it is necessary to re-appraise the conception of Japan as a semi-sovereign state. At the end of World War Two Japan was forced to acknowledge the role that America's production and technological capabilities played in its own comprehensive defeat. Half a century later, many respected American commentators suggested that Japan had been the real winner of the Cold War. This line of reasoning acknowledges that economic and technological success provide the foundations of national security.

3 The nature of the contemporary Japanese state

Introduction

Most countries with significant traditions of political science have generated a variety of theories about the nature of state-society relations. Japan is no exception to this rule, and, accordingly, there are numerous theories about the role of the Japanese state. In this chapter, I survey the most influential of these theories, and offer my own interpretative synthesis. I focus on the role which the Japanese state plays in guiding economic development, maintaining social order, guaranteeing political stability and fostering national culture. This discussion will pave the way for a more detailed analysis of the political mechanisms which support Japan's role as an economic superpower, in Chapters Four through Seven.

The Japanese state: Guiding economic development

The most significant role of the Japanese state has been considered to be that of guiding economic development. The best-known work written from this perspective is Chalmers Johnson's *MITI and the Japanese Economic Miracle* (Johnson, 1981). In this work Johnson characterizes the United States as a regulatory state and Japan as a developmental state. According to this characterization, the central task of the US government is that of removing obstacles which hinder the effective functioning of the market, punishing those actors who violate established rules, and guaranteeing an environment within which entrepreneurs are able to operate freely. By contrast, the focus of the Japanese government is on economic development: it plays an active role in the consolidation of social infrastructure, it grants subsidies to cultivate infant industries, and it provides incentives for technological innovation. The Japanese state participates directly in the market place, utilizing a variety of policy measures to promote economic growth. This developmentalist approach yielded some astonishing achievements, to the extent that it was suggested at one point that the US and other major regulatory states were engaged in 'unfair competition' with the formidable Japanese developmental state.

A major problem with such a characterization is a lack of historical perspective. To illustrate this claim, let us look briefly at the Japan-U.S. trade relationship in the latter half of the nineteenth century. At that time, the fledgling Republican government in the United States consistently pursued a high tariff policy. After the Civil War, the US economy enjoyed a rapid takeoff. As a newly industrializing state it implemented comprehensive protectionist policies (Kolko, 1965), which were appropriate during the fourth quarter of that century; the world economy, centred on Europe, was then experiencing major recession. The American experience can be contrasted with that of Japan in the same period. In the commercial treaties which were signed after the arrival of Commodore Perry's black ships in 1853, Japan's sovereignty over territorialities and tariffs was forcefully limited. In losing its tariff autonomy, Japan lost a vital means of promoting economic development. As a result, Japan had to practice free trade from the mid-nineteenth century until the beginning of the twentieth century, when Tokyo regained control over customs operations (Ishii, 1966). Germany, similar to Japan in that it was a newly industrializing country, had achieved political unification but was divided on the economic issue of whether to pursue protectionist or free trade policies. Prussia, with agriculture as its main industry and grain as its strongest export, advocated free trade. The Rhine, which was prosperous in manufacturing, insisted on protectionism. Through a compromise resulting in the so-called 'iron and rye' coalition, Germany as a whole eventually adopted a basic policy of protectionism in order to strengthen its national power (Gerschenkron, 1989, 1962).

It is often overlooked that Japan began its pursuit of economic development in the context of a global free trade system in the latter part of the nineteenth century, and that at this time Japan's room for maneuver was limited by foreign pressure and regulations. Japan produced silk instead of iron and rice rather than rye. Although silk was not a high value-added export product, it provided a means by which Japan could take its first tentative steps on the road to industrialization. The Japanese state's developmental nature has its origins in the need for Japan to industrialize in an international free trade environment. The period from the 1930s to the 1960s was a golden age in terms of rapid economic growth for newly industrialized countries. It was also an era in which the state was both able and expected to play an active role in the international system as a result of the recessions and wars which took place. Japan was a developing country during the period when the Japanese state began to intervene actively in the market. It must also be emphasized that Johnson's book focused on this period.

But now it is time to place the developmental role of the Japanese state in a much broader historical context (Umemura, 1988–1990). It should be stressed that, as a regulatory state, the US was also attempting to facilitate economic development. To shape American society as a market society, the central function of the American government was to let entrepreneurs assume most of the risk, create a minimal legislative framework to encourage unfettered and transparent economic activity, and prosecute miscreants when these rules were breached. Understood in this way the American Civil War was fought to determine the nature of federal government: it was a conflict between forces that wanted to copy the medieval Tudor state in Britain (Huntington, 1981), and forces that were attempting to establish a modern state (Skowronek, 1982; Orren, 1991).

After the Civil War, the US gradually transformed into a modern state but its essential nature as a market society did not change. The implementation of New Deal policies in the 1930s can be interpreted as the consolidation of a modern welfare state (Berkowitz and McQuaid, 1980). Developments in US foreign policy in response to the international political events of the 1940s and the 1950s can be interpreted as the consolidation of the military and diplomatic aspects of US superpower (Kolko and Kolko, 1969, Yergin, 1977). Notwithstanding these impressive signs of the consolidation of state power, the predominant view within US society remained that the essence of economic development lay with unfettered entrepreneurial capitalist activity. This view predominated until the fourth quarter of the twentieth century. Then, in response to a perception of diminishing American economic competitiveness and overall hegemonic decline, the methods of and rationale for the developmental approach began to infiltrate the American way of thinking. Policy issues related to this perception of diminished competitiveness, such as the establishment of national standards for compulsory education, were tabled for discussion in the early 1990s for the first time (Rosen, 1993).

Different characteristics of state formation can be illustrated by a comparison between the United States and Australia, also originally a white settler country. Australia is a regulatory state, but the state also plays an active role in industrial development, such as the exploration of mining industries (Tsokas, 1986, Capling and Gilligan, 1993). Although Australia could be characterized as a regulatory developmental state, the US as a regulatory state, and Japan as a developmental state, we should also consider the historical circumstances in which each state evolved, with 70 to 80 per cent of the measures being taken for economic development in each country appropriate to its respective state form.

Now let us turn to an historical examination of the role which the Japanese state played in economic development. In the Tokugawa era, the establishment of a social classification system contributed to the pacification of civilian life for most of the population. Although the samurai lived in residential districts, their primary tasks were notionally military, personnel and financial affairs. However, the prolonged period of Tokugawa peace saw finance become their chief preoccupation; significant numbers of samurai became economic bureaucrats in their districts of residency. There were interesting interactions between the market and the state in the Tokugawa era. Firstly, the financial affairs of each han were strictly monitored by the Tokugawa Bakufu, with all han having to pay fealty to the shogunate in the form of tax and tribute, thus making it imperative for each han to pay close attention to its economic management. It could be said that the han practiced tight fiscal policies, and that individual han established self-sufficient economic systems. To depict each region as self-sufficient is a slight exaggeration, since essential goods that could not be produced in the han were purchased on the market. The more goods that were locally produced and which therefore did not require cash transactions, the better for the han in question. During these years, nationwide commercial routes were developed, with salt, rice and seaweed becoming major commodities in the national economy. This nationwide market economy, while outside of han control, gradually enhanced han understanding of market forces and promoted the idea of han coexistence with the market. Under these conditions, the individual han began to collect annual revenues from farmers, monitor markets and supervise exchange in order to maintain a fiscal balance. Thus the market was not laissez-faire, rather it was monitored and supervised.

Beyond the borders of individual han, the desire for a self-sustaining and self-sufficient way of life was strong throughout Japan. The Tokugawa Bakufu kept foreign commodities and technologies to itself through its monopoly of international trade. This restriction on the volume of foreign trade shaped Japan's countrywide drive for self-sufficiency. By way of contrast, at a time when European countries were establishing overseas colonies in their search for goods and markets, Tokugawa Japan was endeavouring to create a self-contained economic unit. Hence, the concept of self-sufficiency has been prevalent ever since the Tokugawa period. It should be noted that this policy of seclusion did not impact negatively on Japan's accumulation of scientific and technological expertise from abroad, which was actually quite advanced even before the fall of the shogunate and the opening of the country. Although a developmental industrialization program was not comprehensively implemented in Japan until after the Second World War, the notion of a self-supporting economy existed as early as the Tokugawa era.

During the Meiji period things changed dramatically: Japan was forced to practice free trade in the world economy. As a developing country, Japan had few exportable commodities, with the exception of primary products such as silk, cotton and tea, the proceeds from which were then used to import energy and machinery. This market order was certainly imposed by Western powers, but Japan, without the means to determine its own international trade policy at the time, could do little other than depend on the successful and efficient mobilization of internal forces. As a country with few natural resources, this strategy for attaining foreign currency made it feasible for Japan to achieve economic success. Even today, after Japan has transformed itself into an economic superpower, such ideas continue to preoccupy those charged with guiding Japanese economic development. It is no exaggeration to argue that the belief in mobilizing internal forces for economic development was a key strategy that was consistently pursued in both the Tokugawa and Meiji periods.

The idea of large-scale domestic industrialization was formulated in the Meiji period. It was believed that in order to promote modernization, it was necessary for Japan to be able to produce goods domestically whenever possible. Many foreigners were hired on high salaries by government institutions, for the purpose of advancing this drive for industrialization. However, all of these positions were short-term, and foreigners' jobs were soon taken over by Japanese; foreigners were used as a means to the end of transferring technical know-how to Japan. State enterprise is another method by which a newly developing country can attempt to modernize in a free trade environment. Although industrialization began via private enterprises, severe competition made it difficult for them to survive and succeed. State ventures, on the other hand, with their cost-accounting considerations, were soon transferred to private ownership. The parallel development of both types of enterprise was a learning process for Japan in adapting to the world market. Therefore, Japan's demonstrated ability to adapt to world market conditions was learned in the Tokugawa era, when self-imposed limits were placed on foreign trade, and in the Meiji period when a free trade system was imposed on Japan from abroad.

The process of industrialization intensified as Japan entered the twentieth century, and the government sought a more active role in guiding economic development. It was also in this century that Japan's image as a developing country emerged. For the first fifty years, the government's increased role was to be expected, in the context of such a volatile world economy. Mobilization for war provided a further opportunity for the Japanese state to augment its guiding role in economic development. During the Depression, the Japanese government had implemented a proto-Keynesian public investment policy, but this was closely associated with the preparation and mobilization for war. On this point, the experiences of the US and the other European powers offer a striking contrast. The first half of the twentieth century was an era of zero-sum competition in the international political economy, and Japan was understandably attempting to discern the rules of the game and play by them. There was intense colonial rivalry and competition for scarce resources. The latter was often accompanied by state intervention in the form of economic blockades and protectionism. Depression and the psychological uncertainties it engendered completed this heady cocktail.

It was unfortunate for Japan as a developing country to be industrializing in such an environment, since this prompted the state to take on an extremely large role. Over one half of state expenditure went to the military, or on other expenses that were related to the war effort. Power came to be excessively concentrated in the hands of the Japanese state, with all of the negative consequences which usually accompany such a development. Yet some aspects of the nationwide war mobilization system that was established in the 1930s and 1940s remained in the postwar period. This could be seen in areas such as resource development policies, technological policies, regional policies, food policies, social welfare policies, health policies and education policies. In each of these issue areas the origins of postwar policy can be traced to the period of war mobilization. What is more, policy formation in each of these areas continues to be informed by patterns which were established in this earlier period (Sheldon, 1981, Garon, 1987).

After the Second World War, the state's role in guiding economic development did not differ significantly from the prewar era. There was a second national mobilization, but this time the objective was economic prosperity and not war. What were bureaucratic institutions like in the postwar period of high economic growth? First of all, while the Japanese military, the Privy Council, political parties, and even Naimushō (the Ministry of Home Affairs) all had to endure painful purges under the occupation forces, the Ministry of Finance emerged relatively intact to assume a more powerful position. It became both the supervisor and monitor of Japan's financial system. The Ministry of Finance collected taxes, wrote budgets, and utilized public funds such as postal savings and government pensions to finance economic and social policy. With its control over fiscal policy, the Finance Ministry cultivated its role as the most important office among all government ministries and agencies. The role of the Ministry of International Trade and Industry (MITI) was to foster industrial development and supervise the industrial structure. MITI retained a high degree of authority over the innovation and transfer of technologies, and also possessed overwhelming influence in the area of energy supply. In a society where economic success is so important for national well being, it was natural for the position of MITI, the ministry in charge of industry, technology and energy, to become so important. Other government offices which dealt with economic issues, such as the Ministry of Agriculture, Forestry and Fisheries, the Ministry of Transport, the Ministry of Construction and the Ministry of Posts and Telecommunications were responsible for the physical aspects of public property, such as land, roads, housing, communications, airports. Extensive state regulation and protection ensured that all of these Ministries gained in importance with economic development. The Economic Planning Board (the predecessor of the Economic Planning Agency) effectively played the role of joint high command in the immediate postwar economic recovery, and in the period of high economic growth.

However, in the past quarter century, the positions of the government economic bureaucracies such as the Ministry of Finance, MITI, and the Economic Planning Agency have weakened as a result of the rapid expansion of the private sector, the relative decline of the public sector, and surprising progress in economic liberalization as a result of increased international interdependence. There were demands for the creation of a separate Ministry of Budget and Ministry with Monetary Authority, which began when the LDP was in power. MITI lost control over several of the policy tools with which it had successfully promoted industrial development (such as credit supply, energy distribution, assistance with technological innovation, etc.). Finally, the status of the Economic Planning Agency's plans were gradually downgraded, from mandatory planning, to indicative planning, to the decorative planning of today.

How did the government guide economic development so successfully? Through the consistent pursuit of which principles did Japan achieve its high economic growth in the twentieth century? At the risk of being over-simplistic, there are three main explanations (Inoguchi, 1990b). The first is the harnessing of the strengths of Japanese society to provide a firm basis for economic development. The most salient qualities here are determination and self-reliance. Special emphasis is placed on the ability to adjust and respond to market changes at a structural level. The ability to respond efficiently can only be realized through the appropriate mobilization of internal resources, since reliance on external resources cannot continue for extended periods. Japan's strengths, or distinctive social resources include high general levels of education, a highly trained labor force, a strong sense of nationalism, a strong sense of loyalty and devotion to one's organization, and the relatively well-established social values of egalitarianism and collectivism.

The second is the acknowledgment that market forces are much more significant than state economic directives. State directives may have sufficient power to counter market forces in the short term, but they will not endure. Market forces reflect fluctuations in supply and demand at a global level, and it is impossible even for a superpower to directly confront the market for a prolonged period. Therefore, a critical task in economic development is to actively detect market trends. In order to transform a situation from one of comparative disadvantage to comparative advantage, a country must have considerable administrative capability, in order to assess all relevant market information, determine its significance for specific industrial sectors, and implement consistent and flexible policies that can absorb the impact of sudden change.

Finally, the Japanese government realized that it was necessary to provide the private sector with both information and incentives. The government supplied information to private enterprises and guided them to appropriate decisions through persuasive argument. The government had to be able to reassure private enterprises that long-term benefits would follow from the pursuit of recommended strategies.

Although the government guides the private sector through permits, licences and subsidies, it must at the same time make appropriate assessments of market trends or offer incentives. If government policies are designed for the short-term, they might be able to offset market forces, and alter the short-term trajectory of world markets. But such policies, even if some of them cover a diverse range of possibilities, can only have a limited and temporary restrictive function. Thus, the government's role, in principle, is to provide the private sector with information, guidance and advice. If we consider the relationship between the economy and the state in Japan since the Tokugawa period, then these principles are obvious. And yet not all corporate managers and bureaucrats agree on them. However, if we want to understand the role which the state plays in guiding economic development, many useful observations can be derived from a consideration of these three principles.

The Japanese state: Maintaining social order

Japan is said to be a highly controlled state, with very comprehensive police monitoring and a low crime rate (Morris-Suzuki, 1988). Anti-crime networks are pervasive, enabling the police to collect detailed information on criminal activities or about any given neighborhood. In addition, the nationwide postal network also functions as a social monitoring device in confirming neighborhood information. It was reported that as a result of the establishment of special postal networks by a young Tanaka Kakuei, then Minister of Post and Telecommunications, it was possible to forecast election results the day before voting took place with a surprising degree of accuracy (Tanaka, 1972).

Private enterprise exists under the administrative umbrella of the Japanese state. As a result, private enterprise adopts a co-operative attitude, superficially at least, in order to promote harmonious relations. The fact that private enterprise is effectively obliged to do this constitutes a kind of control. However, it is also the case that private enterprise has considerable room for maneuver. The activities of private enterprises can also be implicitly or explicitly defended by government institutions. This type of intricate relationship, displaying elements of both control and latitude, is common. For example, when the securities scandal was exposed in 1992 (large investors who lost money trading in securities were compensated by the securities firms in question), the reaction from the Ministry of Finance and the security firms was ambiguous as to whether this action had been approved by the Finance Ministry or not. At such times, private enterprises and the bureaucracy display a symbiotic relationship of intriguing interplay (Alletzhauser, 1990).

For this same reason, the government likes to supervise non-governmental organizations (NGOs). For instance, NGOs like Amnesty International Japan must be placed under the supervision of one or more government ministries/agencies in order to organize large-scale activities in Japanese society. This makes a degree of government control inevitable. Moreover, in 1991 the Ministry of Post and Telecommunications set up an international volunteer postal savings account, offering relatively high interest rates, with a portion of the interest being donated to international volunteer organizations working in developing countries. But organizations which receive this donation can not escape the feeling that they are influenced by the ministry, and that in the future it might be difficult to avoid *amakudari* in some cases.

Since a system of constant mutual consultation and mutual adjustment has become a part of the Japanese way of doing business, it is difficult to take independent action. The business world prefers to make incremental progress through partnership, or at the minimum expects coordinated action. This is why, in their activities, private sector enterprises often seem to be adhering to the dictates of the relevant state office.

The mass media in Japan, especially newspapers, are viewed as monolithic in what they produce, and journalists are seen as lacking in critical analytical skills. One important reason for this is the institution of the *kisha* (journalist) club, where the timing and content of news releases are decided by the government. These are largely taken at face value by the media and faithfully reproduced in the newspapers (Yamamoto, 1995). For the individual reporter, admission to a *kisha* club is dependent on his/her journalistic style and previous deeds. This gives the institution of the *kisha* club formidable powers of exclusion; those reporters who violate certain rules are excluded from a club, often making it impossible for them to arrange the interviews which are necessary to carry out their work.

As long as Japanese newspapers write coherent, accurate and detailed reports based on information provided by government offices, they do very well. In contrast, the American newspapers that are regarded as first rate are excellent in reporting stories that are interesting, but fall short when it comes to supplying continuous and detailed information. Japanese newspapers have many reporters stationed abroad, but they face the challenge of not having a journalist club-type institution where they can acquire information. They are unable to depend on the government offices of their host countries to make announcements. This challenge is invariably compounded by a lack of critical analytical skills, and as a result Japanese journalists have yet to produce stories of consistently high quality.

However, as Michel Foucault points out, it is inevitable that highly industrialized societies will find themselves under some form of supervision or surveillance, because they are also highly developed information societies. In such societies, it can often be difficult to ascertain who controls whom. Rather, everyone is a component of a highly complicated machine in operation. At the same time, each part of the system has its own form of order. This kind of social evolution is made possible by technological progress, which makes it easier to store a wealth of information in readily accessible ways. The more advanced and complex a society becomes, the easier it becomes to collect, classify and utilize information in a form that society can accommodate. Hence, higher levels of information make it easier to monitor and detect social trends, and also make it possible for the government to intervene when it sees fit (Foucault, 1995).

In ancient Japan, rulers used to assess whether the country was well managed by observing the smoke coming from people's cooking fires. Similarly, in the sixteenth century William Petty, one of the founders of statistics in Britain, believed that cooking smoke coming from people's homes was an important indicator in studying family and population in his book, *The Political Anatomy of Ireland*. In order to study society, it is necessary to collect and evaluate many types of information, and contemporary industrial societies generate infinite amounts of such information. However, the most vital items in the National Census are still about population, family and occupation. In the national mobilization period of the 1930s, a mother-child notebook system was set up. This proved to be the most effective means of recording childrens' health, and as a result of the adoption of this process the infant mortality rate was substantially lowered. An immediate understanding of the history of illness and vaccination records of children was made possible by reference to the mother-child notebook.

Japanese society has a long tradition of tight organization. This further reinforces the features of a controlling state as analyzed by Foucault (Murakami, 1979). The Japanese government has traditionally considered its role in the maintenance of social order to be fundamental. Let us briefly review how the Tokugawa Bakufu and the Meiji government, as the predecessors of the current government, carried out their tasks as self-appointed supervisors of social order. The rule of the Tokugawa shōgunate did not depend on military hegemony or economic power. Its maintenance of social order was based on an effective class system (Nihon no kinsei, 1991). When this class system was not sufficiently embedded, in the Muromachi Warring States period, it was common for the lower classes to resist the attempts of their superiors to impose order on them. This situation was transformed with the rapid process of national unification and the disarmament of society (samurai being the sole exemption). Beginning with the elimination of armed shrines by Oda Nobunaga. Toyotomi Hideyoshi launched a nationwide campaign to confiscate swords. Then, to facilitate Tokugawa domination, samurai resided in cities, and the nationwide disarmament was completed with surprising speed. Under Tokugawa rule, not only samurai bureaucrats in residential districts, but all lower ranking officials such as village heads performed a vital function in maintaining social order. These local officials were located at the interface between state and society. They strove vigilantly to unify social actors above and below them, to prevent a division or split between state and society.

Exemplifying this diligence, in 1813, Umeki Tadaaki, the village head of Iyonokuni wrote to his successor Heijirō in *A Village Headman's Notes*, setting out what he felt were the most important attributes of a village headman (Suzuki, 1991). Essentially, the village head was in a position of 'being close to both those above and below.' Hence, he should be able to 'accomplish his duty both by detecting the intentions of his superior and by sensing the feelings of his inferior,' to recognize and interpret the behavior of rulers as well as villagers, and to 'carry out the duties assigned from above and please the hearts of those below.' A village head must possess the wisdom to implement appropriate policies, display benevolence toward villagers, and have the courage to make quick judgments and prompt decisions. Umeki also sincerely advised that it was entirely counter-productive to be disliked by the villagers, and that benevolence was the only path to wealth and prosperity.

In this way, officers at the lowest level operated at the key interface of society, maintaining social order through their daily contact with ordinary people, while displaying a clear sense of purpose and direction. There can only be a stable society when this interface between state and society is conscientiously managed. When there is a split between state and society there will also be turbulence and unrest, and when these occur it is possible that the momentum to effect a reorganization of social order will be generated. This system was first established in the Tokugawa era. There must be some correlation between the prolonged period of peace which Tokugawa Japan experienced and the effective functioning of such a controlled system of social order. It is evident that the leaders of this period already had a strong understanding of the appropriate dynamics of interaction between state and society. For instance, according to Hayashi Razan, 'The world under the heaven does not belong to one person but belongs to the world itself'. Yamaga Gorui further argued that:

> A ruler's supreme power is derived from the masses under heaven, thus a ruler must not behave in a selfish manner ... It is with the people's support that a ruler emerges, and it is the ruler who establishes the state, thus the essence of the state is the people.

Akita Chiranki also suggested that 'The ruler is like a boat and his subordinates like water. Water can carry the boat but it can also sink it' (Sasaya, 1988). As these citations indicate, in the Tokugawa era bureaucrats operated in an environment characterized by limited power. In implementing policy, considerations of wisdom, benevolence and courage were never far from their minds.

Under the Meiji government, bureaucratic institutions had more sensitive matters to consider. The Meiji state was founded as the result of a military coup d'etat, and this rendered the legitimacy of its ruler a very delicate issue. In order to establish its legitimacy, the Meiji state had to demonstrate its efficiency. This provided a great deal of motivation for the Japanese bureaucracy to carefully monitor societal trends (Inoguchi, 1985). Firstly, the emperor, who had been politically mute for centuries in Kyoto, was reintroduced to the public to give the impression that the Meiji state governed at the request of the emperor. The leading conspirators from the Meiji coup were the new power behind the old throne. But these leaders knew that an emperor system alone was not enough to sustain their rule.

Recognizing that an efficient bureaucracy was also indispensable to the management of a modern society, the Meiji government began the incremental construction of bureaucratic institutions from the late nineteenth century onwards. At first bureaucrats were primarily recruited from the old samurai class. Later, with the rise in national education standards and the development of selective examination as the meritocratic basis for recruitment, the number of bureaucrats drawn from the old samurai class halved by the 1920s. The customary priority given to candidates from the strong southwest han was also withdrawn, and capable individuals were recruited from all over the country. According to the ideology of emperor supremacy, all citizens under the emperor were supposed to be equal. It therefore followed that bureaucrats themselves must be treated the same as ordinary citizens. This was the second factor which demonstrated the sensitivity of the modern Japanese bureaucracy to social trends and shifting preferences.

Many of those from the old samurai class who were unable to enter the new Meiji bureaucratic system, and those from the landlord class who bore the heaviest tax burden in the form of land rent, organized anti-government uprisings throughout Japan. After initial armed rebellions and the later emergence of the Freedom and Popular Rights movement, these two groups were eventually absorbed into local assemblies or the Imperial Parliament. Therefore, most Japanese politicians in Japan at that time came from anti-government opposition parties, with their support bases located in regional strongholds. In general, they lacked policy direction, were eager to promote local interests, and lusted for power. Effectively heads of regional kingdoms, they could not disguise their sources of political motivation when it was necessary to address issues relating to development at the national level. With regard to the design and implementation of the technical aspects of national policy, these regionally motivated politicians left things to the bureaucrats in Tokyo.

Thus, the contact point between state and society was maintained in the following manner: bureaucratic offices in Tokyo were charged with monitoring and directing social trends through a technical, professional and administrative division of labour. Local politicians represented and articulated locally distributed interests. As a result of these dual features society was represented, as well as monitored and supervised. Admittedly such mechanisms exist in all societies to a certain extent, but in the modern Japanese context this was a vital change which was designed to fortify and legitimate the Meiji coup. These mechanisms further strengthened the interaction between the bureaucracy, the Diet, political parties and Japanese society (Inoguchi, 1983).

After the Second World War, the government paid even greater attention to its relationship with society at large. The emperor's status was reduced to that of a symbol. The military, the bureaucracy and the prewar political parties that had provided the pillars of the emperor system were all humiliated by the occupation forces. To put things in their proper perspective, the normal procedure for a defeated nation such as Japan would have been for its prewar governing apparatus to be dismantled in its entirety. But the United States allowed substantial parts of the prewar infrastructure to remain in place. This meant that Japan was the only country among the former Axis states not to have its political system undergo a fundamental change. This also led to a weakening of the legitimacy of the Japanese state. The bureaucracy, having been tainted by association with the war, had to undergo a process of transformation, from servant of the Emperor to servant of the public. In this new climate bureaucratic institutions had to justify their existence by demonstrating value. To demonstrate their value, bureaucratic institutions had to be acutely aware of and highly sensitive to societal preferences. Hence, a major task for the government was to identify and respond to social needs. Moreover, the Americans took on most of the emerging responsibilities in the area of national security, a former policy concern of the Japanese government. This made it easier for the bureaucracy to focus exclusively on economic recovery and economic development. The postwar Japanese government therefore sought to enhance the tradition of sensitivity to social needs which it had inherited from both the Tokugawa and Meiji governments. With continuous technological development and advanced industrialization, Japanese bureaucratic institutions have further refined their special talent for monitoring society and maintaining social order.

The Japanese state: Guaranteeing political stability

Japan is often described as a politically conspiratorial country. That is to say, politicians, bureaucrats, corporations and the mass media conspire with each other, or at the very least coordinate their activities by sending out signals to each other, as part of their efforts to maintain political stability while pursuing certain policy agendas. In this respect, the Japanese state is seen as actively pursuing political initiatives. To illustrate this, it is worth noting that the Tokugawa Bakufu, the Meiji state and the postwar government were all fragile in the beginning. Hence, a considerable amount of work had to be done to establish political stability. Although political outcomes are related to economic conditions, to the social environment and to international trends, there are also other considerations, especially during periods of major adjustment. In the following discussion I consider the possibility that the Tokugawa, Meiji and postwar governments share common characteristics in terms of their attempts to guarantee political stability.

The Tokugawa shōgunate came to power by taking advantage of a split within the Toyotomi camp. Its military dominance was not obvious, and in the beginning it did not possess economic clout, nor did it enjoy overwhelming political power. Militarily speaking, the Tokugawa Bakufu was on thin ice in its military actions (*Ōsaka natsu no jin*, *Ōsaka fuyu no jin*) against Toyotomi's threat and in its crackdown on the Christian rebellion on the Shimabara Peninsula. In economic terms the Bakufu was not strong, if one measures the power of individual han in terms of their rice output. Politically, there were signs that the rival han forces under Toyotomi were about to form a coalition, which would have been a nightmare scenario for the shōgunate. Therefore, the Tokugawa government's stability and peace depended on skillful and effective political maneuvering.

The Meiji government was born out of a military coup d'etat. Militarily, the coup forces would not have had an overwhelming advantage over the Bakufu forces had the latter been centralized. What was astonishing was the fact that the coup forces were gradually able to politically outmaneuver their shōgunate counterparts and ensure that a decisive counter-coalition was never able to form. In fact, the anti-Bakufu military force was relatively weak at the time of the coup, and was fortunate in many subsequent military conflicts. But the most significant aspect was that repeated conflict, and even the avoidance of confrontation by the coup forces, gave the public the impression that the days of the Bakufu were numbered. The Meiji Restoration was accomplished before many pro-Tokugawa han in the Northeast took any political or military action.

The postwar government was set up after Japan's defeat in World War II. How could the defeated regime successfully re-group and keep the conservative government continuously in power in the aftermath of comprehensive military defeat and economic ruin? It succeeded by doing the following: it persuaded the public that the bureaucracy was indispensable in administering on behalf of the occupation forces; it convinced the people that it was important for Japan to have a conservative government at the height of the Cold War between the East and the West; and it pushed the occupation forces to carry out a fundamental reform of Japan's political system. Although Japan surrendered unconditionally, it was able to maintain the emperor system, and to keep its bureaucracy almost intact with the same authority to govern. It was also able to prevent the further strengthening of left wing forces, which were expanding their influence in the wake of selective purges by the occupation forces, and economic turmoil. These actions provided a firm foundation on which the conservative government could construct the support needed for its prolonged stay in power.

There are three features which are common to the efforts of the governments in question to maintain political stability. The first is their utilization of the emperor system. The Tokugawa shōgunate made more use of imperial authority than did the Ashikaga Bakufu. The Tokugawa government attempted to buttress its legitimacy by having the emperor on its side. Confirmation of this strategy can be seen from the construction of a shrine for prayer at Nikkō. This was designed to give the impression that the Tokugawa Bakufu was above even the emperor's authority and power. The Meiji government adopted a similar approach to this matter. If it had not restored the emperor to centre stage, the Meiji state might not have succeeded. By promoting the emperor system, and under the slogan of a fresh start, the Meiji elites mobilized a nationwide political transformation (Bitō, 1992). Since the imperial family had resided in Kyoto for centuries with very little military power, this was an exceptionally good opportunity for those who wanted to take advantage of the political authority of the imperial system. The postwar government did the same.

It is often said that the postwar imperial system is symbolic, but as Ishii Ryōshuke points out, the imperial system has always been symbolic except for a brief period in ancient times. Even setting aside the immediate postwar political ramifications of the status of the emperor, the symbolic nature of the emperor system has been the rule and not the exception for most of Japan's history. This symbolic status is reflected in the principle of 'reigning but not governing'. The symbolic value of the imperial system also provides an element of stability in times of political change. The Japanese people did not disown the Showa Emperor, who was a focal point in occupation politics, precisely because they knew that the imperial system was the key to political stability. It is worth noting that the Showa Emperor conducted an intensive inspection of the entire country, with the exception of Okinawa, after the end of the war.

An important ingredient in these three political transformations, then, is that the emperor's role was always very significant. Changes in the political structure are not usually viable unless there are major changes in the military balance. But even if changes only occur in the former, military competition can develop, which can in turn easily lead to political instability. In either scenario, restoring the emperor reduces the likelihood of exclusively military solutions. In the middle of the seventeenth century the Tokugawa Bakufu carried out a large-scale military mobilization to deal with *Ōsaka no jin* and the Shimabara rebellion. Initially there was political uncertainty, but Tokugawa governance later became relatively stable. Similarly, the Meiji government endured the Seinan War and other rebellions in the 1870s, but by the 1880s and 1890s it had successfully absorbed anti-government forces into the political establishment. The postwar government experienced setbacks in their dealings with anti-government and anti-American opposition parties in the late 1940s and early 1950s, but it ultimately managed to relegate opposition forces to peripheral political status.

Secondly, factors external to Japan played a role in all three cases. A major motivation in cracking down on the Shimabara rebellion was the prevention of the penetration of Christian forces and the possible colonization of Japan. In the process, the Tokugawa government confiscated weapons, expelled foreign forces, and centralized foreign trade. The Seinan War was triggered by the advocacy of foreign conquest, a theory that was put into practice when the government sent an army to Taiwan. Conquest there ended the resistance of anti-Bakufu forces, who were then incorporated into the political system. In 1947, the decision by occupation forces to ban a general strike was based on the belief that a political confrontation between the left and the right might lead to political instability in Japan. This would create unnecessary complications for the US in one of its Cold War satellites. The prohibition of the general strike fragmented left-wing forces and transformed them into political organizations that were peripheral and parasitic in nature. These conditions enabled a stable conservative government to be born (Ōtake, 1987).

The third and most salient feature is that all three governments persistently fortified their established systems from within. The Tokugawa shōgunate continued to repress Christians while trying to assimilate those who returned to the system. Those han that were seen as potential threats to the Tokugawa regime were reduced in size, isolated and marginalized (Nihon no kinsei, 1991). The government also achieved its goal of consensus through pressure tactics, such as propagating the belief that it would be difficult for those who did not keep pace with the new rules of the system to survive. In the

Tokugawa period, an isolationist policy of *sakoku* was skillfully developed in order to give the Bakufu a monopoly on foreign trade and information. Traveling abroad was also prohibited. By contrast, during the Muromachi Warring States period, Japanese had been allowed to interact with the outside world, engage in piracy and migrate abroad. The sudden shift to an inward-looking *sakoku* policy was an indication that the system was being strengthened from within. In this way, the Bakufu was able to both control and utilize foreign influence.

In brief, the *sakoku* policy marked a turning point in the development of Japan's political system, and fostered assimilation, inclusiveness and self-sufficiency. This is in sharp contrast with Latin American political structures which were expellant, exclusive and externally-linked. According to Albert Hirschman, if Japan is compared with Latin America at times of systemic crisis and strong popular discontent, Japan conforms to a pattern of voice while Latin America exhibits a pattern of exit (Hirschman, 1970). Loyalty, voice and exit are the choices available to people in times of political uncertainty. Some continue to be loyal even when a political system is breaking down. Others voice their concerns. Still others, those who can no longer tolerate the deterioration of politics, may choose to exit from the system altogether.

The relationship between loyalty, voice and exit is complicated. For instance, when a small number of people swear allegiance to a deteriorating political system, the leadership may be encouraged to acknowledge its mistakes and respond by initiating the necessary structural reforms. Loyalty in this case might have the effect of promoting reform. It is also true that the voicing of concern or protest from a group of people may force the leadership to concede its faults and implement reforms. Voice in this case also achieves the result of reform. In another scenario, when more and more people choose to exit the system, the leadership may feel compelled to resign, leading to systemic change. Exit, in this context, is also conducive to reform.

In the Japanese system, the majority is seen as displaying loyalty. When discontent with the system is high, many people will change to a voice approach, but once the source of their discontent is gone, their loyalty to the system returns. People in the exit category are few in number. This is why Japan is referred to as a non-exit system. In Latin America, those who are highly discontented with the system are either expelled or seek asylum abroad. In 1983, after the overthrow of the military government in Argentina as a result of the Falklands (Malvinas) War, a temporary route was opened at the delta of the

Laplata River, for Argentine political dissidents residing in Uruguay to return home. This vividly illustrates just how many Argentines had sought asylum abroad in this instance.

As mentioned above, the old samurai and landlord class, a substantial number of whom were cast aside by the Meiji government, initiated rebellions and riots but were eventually absorbed into the system. This process was very thorough. Its effectiveness is demonstrated by the many ambitious leaders who subsequently emerged from the pro-Bakufu clans (and their offspring). For example, Enomoto Takeaki was one of the leaders of the Bakufu; both Hara Takashi and Nitobe Inazō were from Iwate prefecture; and Yamamoto Isoroku was from Niigata prefecture. But not all were assimilated. The migration of the so-called continental *rōnin*, the nationalists and Asianists, can be viewed as a form of exit from the system. However, with continuing Japanese penetration into Asia and the expansion of its colonies, those who relocated from Japan to the Asian continent were also re-integrated into the system, eventually functioning as advanced forces of the Japanese empire.

The processes of absorption and adoption were a major factor in the systematic incorporation of opposition forces. When the government was faced with opposition and was forced to consider alternative policies, it at first resisted and then appropriated opposition policies as its own. When the Freedom and Popular Rights movement advocated the establishment of parliaments in the prefectures that had autocratic governments, the Meiji government initially created local assemblies, and then an Imperial Parliament, thereby completely incorporating the opposition into the establishment within a short time. In the 1960s, Japan's anti-pollution movement accused the government of favoring large businesses which were responsible for health and environmental damage. Over the next ten years, the government established the Environment Agency, giving most non-governmental environmental organizations the appearance of being government satellites or government-coordinated groups. Of course, not all were successfully co-opted, but Japan's anti-pollution efforts were among the best in the advanced industrialized countries, which reduced opposition dissent to a more acceptable level. This too was the result of a policy of systemic assimilation.

The announcement of the Large Store Act in 1973 illustrates a similar pattern. The purpose of this legislation was the implementation of the Medium and Small Retail Store Renewal Act, through the introduction of limited competition into the retail industry, and the simultaneous encouragement of efficiency in small and medium-sized retail stores. The government put through the legislation in an attempt to regain support from small and medium-sized businesses after the Communist Party made significant headway in the Lower House elections of 1972. Afterwards, the small retail business sector went into decline, and the funds for improving retail management committed by the Medium and Small Retail Store Renewal Act were also reduced. When the Large Store Act was revised for the second time in 1993, there had been a great deal of deregulation. By then, most people in the retail industry had been absorbed into the system (Kusano, 1992).

This type of mechanism exists in many political systems. In postwar Japan, this systemic incorporation was most conspicuous in the area of social policy. In policy areas such as diplomacy, defense and national identity, systemic assimilation did not proceed as quickly. Issues such as self-defense versus military alliance with the US, and the promotion of patriotism versus its containment, were as divisive as they have ever been in the past fifty years. But after the end of the Cold War, the government and opposition parties have, to some extent, increased their cooperation with regard to foreign policy and defense-related issues. At the same time, however, there has been a worldwide rise in nationalism. There has also been an increase, albeit a small one, in the number of people who support the Japanese government's position in the areas of national identity-related education and ideology.

The more systemic the assimilation in a political system such as Japan, the more restrictive a society becomes. As a result some people complain that they can no longer tolerate the suffocating Japanese environment. Even today there are some people who, as if trying to escape from the restrictive structure of Japanese society, travel and live in America, Europe, Asia and Australia. The people who choose this subtle form of exit from the Japanese system, although few in number, are noticeable. When systemic assimilation becomes too pervasive, it also becomes constraining and repressive in nature.

Japan, as argued above, has a non-exit type of political system. In this situation what kind of political dynamics are being produced by the combination of forced non-exit and repressed voice? Japan at the end of the Tokugawa era and the former East Germany at the end of the Cold War are two such examples. In the final years of the Bakufu, the Japanese were, with some exceptions, forbidden to travel overseas. The debate on whether the Bakufu should open Japan transformed into a confrontation between those who supported the Bakufu and those who wanted to overthrow it. As the fate of the Japanese nation hung in the balance, the Tokugawa government, without consulting public opinion, tried to suppress the forces that wanted to yield to foreign pressure and open Japan. The German Democratic Republic had a similar experience. It practiced non-exit by force and suppressed voice, even though it was evident that the Cold War was coming to an end. As a result, many escaped via neighboring Central and East European countries, while at home the political structure of the German Democratic Republic, premised on the ideas of national solidarity and loyalty to the national homeland, collapsed from within (Hirschman, 1993).

The Japanese state: Fostering national culture

Japan is said to have a ritual based culture (Pye, 1989). Accordingly, Japanese politics can be characterized as one more theater where cultural rituals are enacted. The actors' roles are further obscured by their adoption of cultural roles, making it difficult to discern authority's presence or its precise location, much less identify coherent policy development. Such a view characterizes power in a Western sense, as an identifiable influence on policy outputs. In contrast, power in Asia is located in categories of formality, symbol and ritual, with authority given more emphasis within norms of cultural practice and not necessarily closely related to policy matters. Politics in Asia are embedded in broader cultural movements and dynamics. They can be meaningful without consciously asserting influence, or being strongly linked to rigorous discussion of policy issues. Politicians can seem like characters in a Japanese Noh drama. Their expressions do not appear to change a great deal unless careful attention is paid, in which case subtle changes can sometimes be discerned. Many of the politicians' speeches also do not appear to make much sense. And as with the silence and austerity of a Noh play, there can suddenly come the thunder of drums, prompting events to move at a faster pace. Politics is considered to share some of these features, but it is also a real life drama that is repeated with only the actors changing.

When I refer to Japanese politics as 'cultural politics' I am referring to the full impact of cultural forces. As Watanuki Jōji observes, it is difficult to determine the support base of a political party with any accuracy by using conventional sociological categories such as class, occupation, income, and region (Jōji, 1967; Flanagan, 1992). Common cultural experience, mediated by generations and epochs, is an important factor. Then how has Japan's civic culture formed and how has it promoted or hindered the functioning of Japan's political system? Why is it difficult to understand Japanese politics without positioning them in terms of their relationship to Japan's civic culture? And what has been the state's role as the creator of civic culture? The three functions of Japan's civic culture can be summarized as follows: the first is to coordinate even in competition; the second is to create consensus on issues of potential conflict; and the third is to reform based on loyalty to one's organization. From these features, some static characteristics are emphasized, such as consensus, the vertical society and subject culture (Nakane, 1968; Almond and Verba, 1963). But what is problematic is that these regularities do not adequately explain the dynamics of Japanese society in adapting to change. Although Japan's civic culture can indeed be characterized as concerned with consensus, the vertical structure and subject culture, *this is only the case at the surface level*. We can not understand Japan's civic culture in a comprehensive way unless we look at the motivation for competition, confrontation and change at the basic level of society. Whether in the family, the school or in the workplace, there is an emphasis on coordination, connection and solidarity, but these are all superficial aspects of Japanese culture. There are often opposing movements, clear differences and substantial fragmentation at the basic level of society, even though on the surface society can appear as if it is eternally unchanged. But just like a geyser that intermittently ejects hot water and steam into the air, movement at the basic level of society may at some point lead to alterations on the surface. Many people have offered such a structural explanation, but few have developed its implications in an integrated, coherent manner.

Umehara Takeshi also argues that what Prince Shōtoku in ancient times referred to as 'harmony being the best' is a superficial cultural feature. Ancient times were full of confrontation, competition and contradiction at the grass roots level. Harmony was emphasized precisely because of the nature and extent of confrontation and disharmony. Merry White claims that the twin emphases on the accumulation of standardized knowledge and the pursuit of collective activities in Japanese schools does not mean that there is a lack of competition or a barrier to individuality. Rather, Japanese practices lay the foundations for the development of competition and individuality. In contrast, the compulsory education system in the US did not, until comparatively recently, have a standard curriculum or common textbooks, and depended too much on the individual teacher's ability and enthusiasm. In many cases, it could be said that the US system fell short in fostering the development of student individuality (White, 1987; Rohlen; 1983; Kamata, 1984). Thomas Rohlen observes that Toshiba's corporate song places equal value on both cooperation and strength, and that the source of the company's organizational strength is competitiveness based on internal solidarity. Team-based manufacturing not only involves competition among individual team members but also a sense of competition with other teams. Here the general premise is coordination within the team. As each member of the team strives to finish his/her part of the team's quota in a given time, the team's overall record has the potential to improve, and while this can create an intense amount of stress for the individual, management does not consider this to be a problem unless it causes trouble for the other members of the team (Rohlen, 1974).

As Maruyama Masao argues, a major stream of Tokugawa thought was the coexistence of loyalty and betrayal. When one's loyalty was not only to the master but also to the community of which the master was apart, one's betrayal of the master could be conceived as loyalty to the community when the master did not meet the expectations of the community (Maruyama, 1964). Bitō Masahide further observes that the distinction between the state and society in Japan after the Tokugawa era was not as clear as Hegel would have argued it to be. Rather, there was a strong recognition of community, leading people to expect their leaders to acknowledge their responsibilities when mistakes were made. When these responsibilities came in the form of Japan's defeat in the Second World War, Emperor Hirohito did not acknowledge the part he had played, leading to more and more discussion of his responsibility for the war in the days leading up to his death in 1989.

If we understand Japan's civic culture in this way, then how does the state shape such a civic culture through schools and the mass media? The acquisition of standardized knowledge and the pursuit of collective activities in enterprises and government offices are an expanded and more concentrated version of what Japanese people have learned at school. Both are very strongly emphasized by the Japanese. Whether it is the Japanese army in the prewar period, or Japan's International Cooperation Agency in the postwar era, both have extremely similar knowledge bases and implementation directories. The agricultural field research project in Indonesia is a good example of this. The training involves both the acquisition of basic agricultural knowledge (such as the treatment of seeds, irrigation, weed control, harvest and agricultural financing) and an introduction to the collective activity required for agricultural work (Kurosawa, 1992). Japanese fondness for conducting studies and field research has a long tradition.

Basic training is stressed, followed by orderly competition. As a result, the collective expectation of achievement through competition results in an increase in productivity. Orderly competition is conducive to the creation of a solid work ethic, as the environment encourages colleagues to feed off each other's hard work. It is also impossible for workers to give less than 100 per cent effort in the work place or to sabotage the work of others. This is directly related to the existing competitive spirit among work groups. The heavy workloads of auto-workers, as described in Kamata Satoshi's book *The Desperate Automobile Factory* (Kamata, 1981) are the result of such practices. There is not only competition between and among different firms in the same industry, but there is competition between and among work groups within one company. These methods generate a competition that some would characterize as excessive. They also produce results which are sufficiently prolific that rival national manufacturers are driven to complain that they are unfair.

Factions within the LDP are another good example of this coordination and competition (Inoguchi, 1993c). The LDP as a political party was initially a coalition of right-wing parties organized for the general purpose of preventing left-wing parties from gaining power. This purpose serves as a bond and a source of solidarity among the factions, but a system of mutual competition also exists in each electoral district. In Lower House elections, most districts elected two to five representatives, with a few exceptions. In such circumstances, especially given the ideological preferences of the Japanese electorate (more than half of voters are located on the middle or the right of the political spectrum) and the current state of political parties (non-LDP political parties can also be found on the middle or thr right of the political spectrum), LDP candidates have found themselves competing with each other. LDP factions existed in approximate proportion to the electoral distribution of two, three, four and five member districts. Small factions, unlike large factions which could easily win seats in all types of districts, had little chance of winning seats in one and two member districts and relied mostly on four to five member districts. Election campaigns in districts had little to do with ideological or policy issues, but focused on factors such as personal connections or the securing of benefits for the region in question. This is one reason why politicians in Japan do not like policy-oriented debate. Competition among conservative party candidates is a key feature of Japanese party politics.

Candidates not only compete in electoral districts but also within their factions. It is common practice for faction heads to distribute election funds (political funds) to faction members. Although these amounts are not large, candidates must compete for funds because rival candidates in the same district belong to another faction. Since this is all internal LDP politics, it is possible to form cartels based on geographical agreements, a loosely arranged custom within the LDP. Despite the existence of such competition, LDP members in the Diet usually strictly adhere to the party line when voting, just like other political parties. Even the most serious cases of internal LDP conflict are acceptable as long as politicians toe the party line. In some ways, LDP politics appear to be frozen in time. This image of politics as static and immutable is reinforced in the minds of the Japanese public by the shameless levels of corruption and scandal that have been revealed in the media. Yet LDP politics do possess the ability to change when circumstances demand it. This adaptive capacity is very evident from the LDP's recent changes in policy direction. The most important consideration when formulating policy is to be as inclusive as possible with regard to the general public. When policy change occurs, it is often driven by such a desire to please the masses. To borrow Nakane Chie's vivid description, policy changes are like molasses, that is to say they move slowly when changing direction (Nakane, 1978).

Although there are clear indications that confrontation and competition exist in Japanese society, on the surface only a sharp image of order, regularity, stability and harmony is presented. It may be surprising that such an image originates within Japan's civil culture and that this image was formulated by the modern state. This image of Japanese society is contrary to the drastic changes that the Japanese economy and Japanese society have actually experienced, but is instead derived mostly from Japan's political system. Japan has enjoyed relative stability for a considerable period of time, if the instances where it over-reacted to foreign stimuli and the accompanying domestic changes are set aside. A frozen society with fossilized structures would not be able to cope with sudden change in the way that Japan has on numerous occasions. Order, regularity, stability and harmony can be seen as short term and superficial characteristics of Japanese society, while its medium- to long-term, and more salient characteristics are adaptability, flexibility, change and competition. The modern Japanese economy experienced rapid development, digesting and absorbing major economic and social transformations. If the Japanese political system, which supported these new economic and social structures, had not been able to make policy adjustments, then it could not have endured. We may say that the nature of Japan's civic culture formation has made it easier to have order in competition, to have agreement emerge from confrontation, and to have change centred on loyalty.

Japan's schools are mostly controlled by the Ministry of Education, and there are detailed regulations on curriculum content and teaching qualifications. A standardized and shared curriculum is the basis of a civic culture. Yet it was not until the end of the twentieth century that the United States, in legislation initiated by the former President George Bush, began to make standardized, universal and compulsory education the pillar of its own education policy. In this particular sphere, Washington lags far behind Tokyo (Rosen, 1993). Needless to say, apart from the formation of civic culture, compulsory education is one of the vital ingredients of modernization. Not only does compulsory education provide an opportunity for all citizens to acquire basic reading, writing and arithmetic skills, it is also a means through which the public can be socialized to adhere to social norms and to respect collective ethics. In the Tokugawa period, educational institutions such as private schools put Japan at the forefront of the world in terms of reading, writing and calculating capabilities. Compulsory education, coupled with nationwide standardization, further improved the level of education. It was natural for a nation that was desperately trying to adapt and emulate the West to emphasize respect for social norms and group ethics. Japan's compulsory education was similar to conscription in this regard, in that it was a powerful method of inculcating appropriate social norms and values.

4 Japan's international economic responsibilities

Introduction

By the mid-1990s it was widely acknowledged that Japan, as an economic superpower, should take on greater international responsibilities (Inoguchi, 1992). Although the US remained a superpower, its credibility and competitiveness would be severely undermined without the cooperation of other allied nations. The US has maintained its overwhelming military predominance in the post-Cold War world, and American supremacy was undeniable in terms of both strategic nuclear weapons capability and conventional war-making capability. When it came to economic and technological potential, however, US predominance had weakened in the medium-to long-term. The era of absolute US economic hegemony was over, and the US needed the cooperation of Japan and Germany, both allies and major economic powerhouses, to manage the world economy (Nye, 1990; Sanholdtz, 1992). Japan and Germany were both defeated in the Second World War, but have long since been rejuvenated as substantial economic powers in their own right. The idea that they should assume an international responsibility commensurate with this economic power gained increasing momentum in the early post-Cold War world. It was already apparent in the 1992 Declaration of the Group of Seven Summit that Japan and Germany were strongly expected to assume more responsibility in managing the world economy (Asahi shinbun, 1992). It was understood that progress would be slow in the area of security, due to various significant domestic and international constraints. But in the field of economics, the US and other leading states indicated much higher expectations of both Japan and Germany. In this chapter I examine the economic background to this emerging assumption of Japan's international responsibility.

In reviewing Japanese economic development after the oil crises, especially the second oil crisis, I will demonstrate how the notion of an 'international economic responsibility' greatly affected Japanese economic management. I will examine the conceptual and political tensions between a responsibility to the management of the international economy, and the management of one's own domestic economy (Sachs, 1993). These tensions provided a major test for Japan, which had been historically accustomed to managing its economic affairs from a narrower and more self-interested developmentalist perspective. It was necessary for Japan to expend a great deal of energy, and exercise acute judgement, to address the complicated issues involved in the management of the world economy. Second, as international economic integration intensified, Japan strove to reform aspects of its economic structure to meet emerging international standards. These reforms entailed increased policy adjustment, policy harmonization and policy coordination.

Japan, in its capacity as one of the countries increasingly regarded as responsible for the fate of the world economy, was also expected to ease the economic troubles of the United States. Japan coordinated its activities with international financial institutions to support a low dollar, a high yen and a high German mark, as part of an effort to mitigate mounting US fiscal and trade deficits. This often had negative ramifications for Japan's own economy. As a consequence of fulfilling its responsibilities to international economic management, Japan was often unable to implement policies that were optimal in terms of its own domestic economic management. Japan was also obliged to adjust its domestic economic structure to meet emerging world standards. The world had high expectations of Japan's capacity to enforce international regulations and customs as it took on its responsibilities for economic management. The inevitable result was that some sectors of Japan's domestic economy and society suffered. Before I justify these claims in more detail I will survey the characteristics of Japanese economic management (Umemura, 1988–1990).

Characteristics of Japanese economic management

It is undeniable that businesses are the driving force in Japanese society, because Japan has a capitalist system. More than half of Japan's GNP is created by larger companies, and most of the foreign currency acquired by Japan comes into the coffers though the business dealings of the twenty largest corporations. Japanese society is business-centered, and many laws and practices have evolved to facilitate the functioning of business in society. The strategy for economic development in postwar Japan shifted the focus from light industry to heavy industry, on to high-tech industry, and finally to high value-added industries. Japan's strategy was based on three fundamental objectives: securing food supply, restructuring the financial system, and ensuring energy supply.

The first task facing Japan in the aftermath of the war was to secure its food supply. The government had specifically rewarded rice production through the Staple Food Control Act as a means of ensuring its food supply during the war mobilization period. Although rice production in Japan required subsidization as early as the Russo-Japanese War, concern about the competitiveness of rice production weakened later on, due to rice imports from Japan's colonies. In the postwar period the competitiveness of rice production declined continuously, to the extent that it is now impossible to grow rice without substantial government subsidy. Japan's preparedness to subsidize rice production is premised upon its cultural significance and the fact that rice is the only basic staple which is produced domestically (Hayami, 1990).

Starting in the prewar period, the government's paramount concern was the restructuring of Japan's financial system. This had been developed under strict public regulation in response to the bankruptcies and related financial turbulence of the 1920s. Furthermore, as their activities were tailored to the goal of wartime mobilization in the 1930s, Japan's financial institutions were placed under tight public monitoring and sponsorship. Japan recognized that as a society with few natural resources, and little energy or food, it was necessary to make flexible use of financial systems to manage stable economic development and reinforce economic competitiveness. Therefore, Japanese financial institutions have, in both the prewar and postwar periods, continuously restricted free competition.

The government assigned most of the energy industries to the public sector, making them priority industries. Thus, the companies associated with the energy industry, like Japan's financial institutions, are recognized as key enterprises and have remained the most profitable throughout the prewar and postwar periods (Yamazaki, 1991). Businesses in both the financial and energy sectors have close ties to the government, and continue to be stable ventures protected by state regulations. We can easily understand this by looking at the Ministry of Finance's attitude towards the liberalization of financial markets at the Japan–US Structural Impediments Initiative Talks, or MITI's attitude towards the transportation of plutonium. The government is more interested in intervening in these two areas than in other sectors of the economy (Iida, 1992). The high profile of certain industries is also reflected in the selection of leaders for Japan's major economic organizations, such as Keidanren, Nikkeiren (Japan Federation of Employers Associations), the Chamber of Commerce and Industry, and the Japan Committee for Economic Development. These organizations mostly draw on banks, the electrical industry, or the iron and steel industry when they select their leaders. It is evident that these economic organizations represent industry when it comes to overall questions of economic strategy and management, and that they also represent the interests of capital, in the broader sense of that term.

By contrast, the number of agricultural and small- and medium-sized businesses have been decreasing as their competitive edge has diminished. Yet, because they are weak, they have continued to receive public funding for social and political reasons. From the societal perspective, except for public ventures run by local governments, agriculture and small- and medium-sized businesses are major local players. Politically speaking, as major supporters of the LDP, the party which has been in power for most of the postwar years, agriculture and small- and medium-sized businesses have received protection through government fiscal policy (Inoguchi, 1983; Calder, 1989).

Conditions for manufacturing industries differ from conditions for those industries which are subsidized by the public. Although a substantial number of manufacturers received subsidies, the basic policy approach, based on the principle of comparative advantage, is that manufacturers expand their own production, calculate their own profits, and acquire their own foreign currency. Comparative advantage entails competition and change. In adapting to and managing these changes, the primary emphasis of Japanese manufacturing has shifted from sector to sector. The original focus was on food and textile products, followed by light industrial products. The focus of competition then moved to heavy and chemical industrial products (such as iron and steel, ship-building and petro-chemical products), and then to machinery, and then to high-tech industrial products such as electronic and new material products. Successful manufacturers in these sectors have successively provided the main source of foreign currency.

The government tends to be more receptive to the needs of those manufacturers which are successful and which provide foreign currency (Phillips, 1991). For example, oil and gasoline prices and road taxes have not increased dramatically. This is due to implicit requests from the motor industry. Auto emission standards for family cars are also not as strict as those applied to industrial vehicles. The government has generally treated the motor industry very well. Later in the postwar period, due to increased international environmental consciousness, the government finally established regulations regarding the emission of nitrogen oxide. However, the calculation involved here was that a greater burden should not be placed on the motor industry, as this would weaken the competitiveness of an industry whose success has a significant bearing on the nation's economic fate. In similarly calculating fashion, when the government introduced a 3% consumption tax in 1989, which was a dramatic event in itself, it also reduced automobile sales tax from 18–23 per cent to 6 per cent. (To help understand the magnitude of this move, automobile sales tax in Singapore, which is small and does not have its own motor industry, is over 100 per cent.) This decision was one of the significant factors causing a dramatic increase in car sales during the peak of the bubble economy from 1990–91. By the end of 1992 there were as many as sixty million automobiles crowded on the narrow roads of Japan. Later, as we know, there was a steady drop in domestic sales, and as a preemptive measure to avoid a sharp decrease in overseas sales, Japan's car manufacturers implemented self-imposed export quotas. This was a major turning point for the Japanese motor industry (*The Economist*, 1992).

The Japanese government believes that the positive effects produced by competitive industries and businesses will trickle down to those industries which are relatively uncompetitive. Thus delays in responding to the needs of weak industries are tolerated. The logic of providing public regulations and public aid to certain industrial sectors is as follows. Certain sectors, such as finance, energy, communications and transportation, are under government regulation. The rationale behind this is to ensure a stable supply of vital goods to the market. Japan has the lowest tax rate among advanced industrialized countries, but Japan is also a permanently high cost society because, apart from taxation, consumers have to bear the costs resulting from public regulation and the related informal cartel system (Ohmae, 1990). Automobile safety inspection is a good example: although the purpose is to maximize safety through fixed term inspections for automobiles, the costs are exorbitant, with the profits going into the coffers of the Ministry of Transportation and associated firms.

As far as financial services are concerned, the government strongly believes that rather than allowing private citizens to provide financial services and take risks, the state should provide an umbrella of monitoring and protection, and avoid dealing with services which might threaten Japan's financial stability. The government also tends to avoid foreign financial services, regardless of how high the interest rates are. Therefore, pricing policies have always been the number one concern in polls which solicit information on the public's expectations of the government. People expect price stability, and Japan has an economy with stable retail prices and a relatively low inflation rate, which is an uncommon combination. However, in the publicly funded and less competitive sectors, the government places an emphasis on social and political considerations. The government subsidizes agriculture and small- to medium-sized businesses, not only because they are less competitive, but also because they are major stabilizing forces in Japanese society. But these subsidies do place an extra burden on consumers.

The government treated manufacturing industry as the champion of competitiveness, and constantly regulated finance, energy, and other economic infrastructure related sectors, despite the high cost. At the same time, it provided subsidies to less competitive sectors. In the 1987 Lower House election, the LDP's campaign slogan, 'safety, security and stability', had its basis in this policy orientation and the slogan strongly appealed to the majority of Japanese voters (Inoguchi, 1987a).

However, by the 1990s there was strong public support for the notion that Japan was rich while the Japanese were poor. The government responded by proclaiming the goal of making Japan a 'superpower of high living standards'. Disaffection was especially strong among high income earners and urban dwellers. Combined with a series of scandals in the Liberal Democratic Party, this stimulated a mushrooming of political dissent and calls for the reform of Japan's excessively centralized, production-centred and bureaucracy-oriented society. But Japan was and is not in a position to implement Northern European social policy for the time being. Most people who support an improvement in living standards are strongly opposed to tax increases. One reason for this derives from the traditional Japanese psyche. Another stems from public distrust of government. To stress again, many of those who advocate higher living standards are strongly against increased taxes. Japan is not expected to adopt a North European type of social policy, introducing high taxation and high levels of welfare expenditure. There are a number of arguments for rejecting such policies. The traditional Japanese sense of self-help and self-reliance is very much alive. Another reason is that people are suspicious of government based on the experience of war, inflation-related high taxes and the purchase of government bonds. These experiences play on the minds of the public, creating moderate levels of distrust for government.

There are many arguments about what role the Japanese government should adopt in an economy with such developmentalist features. Modern economic development has basically been centered around markets. The market is the outcome of utility calculations by a countless number of actors. Thus, even though government institutions consciously attempt to influence actors by providing guidance, it is doubtful whether they can successfully and decisively shape market outcomes in the long run. But market theory alone cannot completely explain the relationship between government and economic development or economic management. One theory claims that the Japanese government promoted economic development by intervening in the market from the period of war mobilization to the era of high economic growth. This theory is mostly advanced by foreign scholars who have been impressed by Japan's economic achievements (Johnson, 1981).

Economic management after the first oil crisis

In observing the way the Japanese state directed economic development from the first oil crisis to the mid-1980s, three major trends are visible. First, disturbances in the energy and foreign exchange markets increased the government's commitment and readiness to deal with market uncertainty. Second, Tokyo continued to adopt a macroeconomic management approach, with price stability as its central objective. Third, the government adopted temporary measures to provide relief, always in the context of the goal of self-reliance, for sectors and regions that had trouble adapting to some of the structural adjustments which were necessary.

On the first issue, the government responded to market disturbance by intervening in the foreign exchange market. This was in reaction to the abandonment of the US dollar standard, which had been a symbol of the Pax Americana, by the American government. The Bretton Woods international monetary system that had been based on the US dollar standard ceased to exist, and states and markets negotiated the transition from a fixed exchange system to a floating system. The Japanese government had been a beneficiary of the dollar standard, and did not wish to see the system collapse. In the beginning, Japan tried to aggressively defend the old standard, leading to the loss of a large amount of US dollars in a short period of time (Angel, 1991). Opposing arguments on whether the dollar purchase strategy was necessary or effective are heated. Some viewed the strategy as completely ineffectual and foolish. Others argued that it was inevitable that Japan, as a beneficiary and a supporter of Pax Americana, would continue to support the US until the end. Inevitable or not, a plausible explanation for the Japanese government's behavior could well be that it regarded Pax Americana as a given condition. It can also be said that such an attitude is typical of Japanese behavior in the face of a larger changing environment: Japan never surrenders until the last moment, when it realizes that it is futile to do anything else (Blaker, 1977). As the floating exchange rate system developed, the government highlighted preparation measures so that the domestic economy would not be damaged by temporary disturbances, and also utilized the power of the Japanese yen to ride out turbulence in the international currency markets (Inoguchi, 1983).

The Japanese government's response to the first oil crisis was similar to its reaction to the collapse of the Bretton Woods system. Faced with a crisis, the government formulated various policies for ensuring a continuous and stable oil supply. The government pursued three paths simultaneously. One was to strengthen friendly relations with oil producing countries, revising existing policies towards Arab countries where necessary, and securing oil supply routes. The next was to emphasize the development and import of oil resources from countries such as Indonesia, China, and Mexico, in order to avoid excessive dependence on oil from the Near and Middle East. Japan's efforts to stabilize its oil supply also included the possibility of approaching the former Soviet Union, a policy which might, however, have created problems with the United States. Third, the Japanese government allocated resources to the development of alternative energy sources, including the development of nuclear power. In these ways the Japanese government was able to enhance its readiness to cope with market turbulence. The crises in the currency and oil regimes removed two of the major pillars of the Pax Americana. From the Japanese government's responses to these two events we can discern a pattern of reaction: the government is at first confused, and then recovers to implement consistent and effective remedial policies.

Turning to the second trend in economic management, Japan's macroeconomic commitment to price stability was consistent from the first oil crisis to the end of the second oil crisis. The government pursued an appropriate money supply policy, effectively containing the rapid rise of inflation following the first oil crisis. Furthermore, the persistent efforts of Japan's financial authorities to achieve price stability did influence the market. This lead to a situation that differed from that in the US, in that inflation did not occur in Japan when the second oil crisis hit. Although the government had to issue deficit bonds to prosecute its fiscal policy, a high savings rate enabled Japan to absorb the government bonds without triggering inflation. A tenacious belief in the virtue of price stability was prevalent among the financial authorities after the first oil crisis, and it demonstrated the government's determination to provide the guidance it felt was necessary to attain stable economic development. However, weighed down by recession and the slow growth of the entire economy after the first oil crisis, fiscal deficits accumulated. Since Japan's tax system is largely structured around direct taxation, state revenue declined significantly during the recession, leaving the government with no other choice but to issue deficit bonds (Noguchi, 1992). Financial policy became a primary tool in controlling the money supply, preventing inflation and stimulating business activity. There are constant demands, both domestically and internationally for economic powers, as part of their international responsibility, to utilize financial policy to end recession and stimulate the economy. These demands chime with the theory that it is necessary for certain states to act as engines of the world economy (Ueda, 1992).

In the 1960s, real GNP was the economic variable that fluctuated the most, while in the 1970s it was commodity prices, and in the 1980s it was interest rates. In other words, the 1960s featured changing material goods, with the 1970s and 1980s being witness to price changes and changing money markets respectively. We might also depict the 1960s as the age of industrial policy, the 1970s as the age of financial policy, and the 1980s as the age of monetary policy. The 1960s could also be characterized as the era of the nouveau riche, the 1970s as the era of recession, and the 1980s as the era of the bubble economy.

Lastly, the surge in energy prices and the turbulence in foreign exchange rates altered the structure of competitive advantage in the marketplace, causing business failures and unemployment. The Japanese government provided certain rescue measures, but these were primarily to encourage re-orientation to market forces and changes. It also offered technical skills retraining rather than permanent assistance. In many instances, the rescue efforts took the form of temporary legislation. In short, assistance was offered through emergency and temporary measures, based on the principle of self-reliance.

Although the large increase in energy prices after the first oil crisis was felt throughout the entire manufacturing industry, the net effect was the promotion of energy conservation and labor-saving measures, leading to a new overall orientation, which helped many corporations overcome the difficulties brought about by high energy prices. In spite of initial fears, the adjustments and changes in policy were consistently effective. By the time that the last tremors of the first oil crisis had faded away, Japan had become one of the most resilient economies in the world in terms of adapting to crisis. Japan succeeded not only in solving the problems of its energy supply but also in stabilizing prices. Its competitiveness had also been steadily enhanced in many fields.

Economic management after the second oil crisis

The Japanese government had a further challenge to confront after the second oil crisis. President Reagan advocated a set of economic policies which sent the US economy into shock, as a result of which the Japanese economy was in turn severely affected. Reaganomics consisted of massive tax cuts, reductions in government expenditure, deregulation and a tightening of the money supply (Uekusa, 1992). This economic ideology attempted to address the problems of the Carter administration and the second oil crisis through a market forces-oriented strategy. However, with the exception of tax cuts and the tightening of the money supply, the objectives were not fulfilled. There was a rapid increase in defense expenditure to meet the needs of the Second Cold War; the US government was unable to reduce its expenditure; and many deregulation measures withered on the vine. This economic policy led to a dramatic growth in the financial deficit. It also caused the current balance deficit to worsen as economic activity and the expansion of domestic demand brought about by tax reductions increased. Because the US government simultaneously attempted to stimulate the economy and limit the supply of money, real interest rates increased substantially. The high interest rate attracted capital from all over the world, thereby boosting the value of the US dollar.

Against this background the US became a debtor nation in 1984, and protectionism was rampant. In September 1985, Japan, the US and other major European countries concluded the Plaza Accord. According to this agreement, the floating exchange rate system was revised, and became a managed floating system. In addition, each country agreed to currency adjustments that were designed to mitigate the effects of the high value of the US dollar. Japan agreed to an appreciation in the value of the yen, and the exchange rate fell dramatically, from 260 yen to the dollar in February 1985 to 121 yen in January 1988. Consequently, Japan's exports decreased, the economy was sent into recession with the appreciation of the yen, and the domestic inflation rate dropped as the price of imported goods fell. In response, the Japanese government implemented a lower interest rate policy to relieve the pressure on the overvalued yen. The official discount rate was lowered from 5 per cent to 2.5 per cent, and the interest rate on ten year maturity government bonds was also cut from 7.2 per cent to 3.7 per cent. This decrease in long-term interest rates caused the value of stock prices and real estate to rise significantly. Due to these changes, about 90 per cent of the loan balance increases of financial institutions were related to asset transactions. Creating credit in this way paved the way for the emergence of the bubble economy. For example, the ratio of investment in plants and equipment to the amount of corporate bonds issued in the 1986–91 period was 2.1 per cent (Seika industry), 5.2 per cent (Itoman), and 8.6 per cent (Marubeni). This new credit market was created outside of the traditional primary trading sectors of these firms, and, one might argue, outside their areas of expertise (Nihon keizai shinbunsha, 1993).

When the US stock market crashed in October 1987, the American government relaxed monetary controls and requested that other nations did the same. Although Japan had at that time already started to recover from its recession, it acquiesced in this. When the US reverted to its policy of tightening the money supply in March 1988, Japan continued with its relaxed control of the money supply until May 1989. The logic behind Japan's approach was that if countries that are in the black on their current accounts limit the supply of money, then countries which are in the red will face hardship. If Japan had done anything else but maintain its relaxed control of money supply, this would have been an abrogation of its international economic responsibility. In May 1989, however, the official discount rate finally went up. Market conditions which required a tightening of the money supply had emerged. These were an overheated economy, intense pressure caused by inflation, a protected Japanese yen, and dramatic increases in the supply of money. The Japanese stock market eventually crashed in 1990.

The 1980s was an age of interest rates and monetarist policy. First of all, faced with the growth of twin deficits and strong protectionist forces, the US government, lacking the ability or will to select appropriate policy measures, asked for cooperation from its allies. It requested creditor nations to carry out a low interest rate policy. Although Japan accepted the request from the US, it was unable to implement appropriate fiscal policy due to the accumulation of deficits from the first oil crisis, leaving its monetary policy to function alone. Because the government over-estimated the deflationary effect of a high Japanese yen, and made the political decision to coordinate with the United States, its monetary policy further stimulated the formation of the bubble economy.

Trends in market liberalization

Market liberalization, another major pillar of Reaganomics, was also gradually promoted in Japan during the 1980s. In particular, privatization and deregulation gained momentum under the Nakasone administration. Although there were fears about the accumulation of deficit bonds from the first oil crisis onwards, the government's desire to increase taxes was stymied by public opinion. In 1979, for example, the Liberal Democratic Party lost a lot of seats because Prime Minister Ōhira raised the possibility of a tax increase. Afterwards, the government recognized that without serious attempts at administrative and fiscal reform, it would be difficult to reduce the deficit and calm public opinion. Based on these considerations, the government attempted to implement sweeping reforms of the administrative and financial systems in the 1980s.

One of the major items on the reform agenda was the privatization of public enterprise. Two of the strongest advocates of this approach were Prime Minister Nakasone Ysauhiro, and Dokō Toshio, the chairman of the Provisional Council on Administrative Affairs (*rinji gyōsei shingi kai*). Influential figures in the world of finance suspected that although corporations conserved resources and made strenuous efforts to respond effectively to the oil crises, the government, on the contrary, appeared to waste money and leave corporations to clean up the mess. The business world stressed the need for a reduction in government spending. It was also convenient for Prime Minister Nakasone, a Presidential Prime Minister, to push for reform of the administrative and financial systems in order to weaken the power of the bureaucracy and reinforce the power of politicians.

The idea that there should be substantial administrative and fiscal reform, promoted by the financial sector, met with stubborn internal resistance from the bureaucracy. The latter skillfully managed to shift the goal of the reforms from the cutting of fiscal deficits to privatization, deregulation, and creating an environment in which the private sector could more actively pursue its industrial activities. But as is often the case with bureaucratic practice, new public regulations were established to deal with the new market conditions even though privatization and deregulation measures were being implemented. The Japan National Railway and The Japan Telegraph and Telephone Company are prime examples. Although the transportation and postal services were privatized, this did not necessarily translate into many similar-sized corporations being able to freely compete in the same field. A more critical point is that there were and are networks of communication between the public and private sector through which the government could effectively retain management of the privatized, pseudo-public sector, whilst reducing the financial burden of direct subsidy. These networks include communication with people through such means as *amakudari*. (This means 'descent from heaven', and refers to the process by which retired bureaucrats acquire jobs in those areas of the private sector which remain under bureaucratic purview). Other forms of communication and control are administrative guidance in the form of informal requests, and councils where the government listens to opinions from representatives of industry and professional groups. These groups often share objectives with the government.

Relaxed public regulation, together with a shrinking public sector, encouraged the private sector to be more active. Especially, deregulation in construction, transportation, real estate and finance laid the groundwork for large-scale industrial activity. This became one of the most important pillars of the Heisei boom. At the same time, deregulation made the following activities very common. Land takeovers were often facilitated by threatening landowners with the involvement of gangsters. It was also common for land to be reclassified. For example, when land for agricultural use was reclassified for commercial use, the type and the amount of tax also changed, and the price of the land increased sharply. Corporations, politicians and bureaucrats received a share of the dividend from this process under the guise of administration. Businesses also found new ways to create capital. It was easier to create capital by holding real estate as collateral, and large amounts of money were lent to corporations or gangsters who pretended to be corporations. These institutional changes subsequently led to the Recruit scandal (1988) and the Sagawa Kyūbin scandal (1992).

Needless to say, reducing the fiscal deficit was also a priority, with stringent budget cuts implemented across the board. But the government did not achieve short-term success in its attempts to promote new initiatives or reduce fiscal deficits. Market liberalization not only affected administrative and fiscal reforms but also influenced the trade relationship between Japan and the United States. Trade friction between Japan and the US had existed since the 1960s, but with market liberalization it expanded into the areas of textiles, iron and steel, televisions, machine tools, automobiles, VCRs, semiconductors, agricultural produce, tariffs, alcoholic beverages, construction and finances. It was also apparent from some of these conflicts, in agriculture, construction, tariffs, taxes and finances, that Japan's domestic economic structure was increasingly the cause of much of this friction. While this demonstrates a deepening of international economic interdependence, it is in the same instance a reflection of domestic politics in the US. The Republican Administration believed that without the promotion of strong market liberalization measures, the US trade deficit with Japan would not be reduced. Accordingly, it put a check on protectionist legislation proposed by the Democratic Party, which at that time held a majority in the US Congress (Destler, 1992; Tyson, 1992). Given these circumstances, the liberalization of financial markets had a great impact on the formation of Japan's bubble economy. The permission to issue commercial papers and freely determine deposit interest rates directly affected the Japanese economy.

Here, I would like to briefly touch upon the international trend towards market liberalization. The source of market liberalization is technological progress. Advanced communication and transportation technologies have made it easier to conduct global transactions. The US and the UK, both of which have market-oriented economic operations, were increasingly interested in acquiring profit on a global scale. The movement towards market liberalization in North America and Western Europe, both of which are large markets for Japan, was one of the major factors behind Japan's own market liberalization. Moreover, as an economic superpower with significant global reach, Japan not only benefits from the market liberalization of other countries, but its own market liberalization drive serves to generate reciprocity in areas of trade, investment and finance. As a result of this, foreign governments have high expectations for Japan, and from a long-term point of view, market liberalization will also serve Japan's own national interests.

In addition to these technological and economic factors, a political factor was also pivotal. The US government was especially enthusiastic about liberalizing foreign markets. Recognizing its relative decline in competitiveness, the US never wanted to fully acknowledge the protectionist push from those domestic sectors that were losing their competitive edge. If the government accepted this, then there was a danger that the US as a whole might lose even more of its competitive edge, as confidence in its economic power would have been eroded still further. Therefore, the American government had to be more adamant about its requests that other countries liberalized their markets, in order to soften the protectionist push at home. Washington was convinced that the main reason for the decrease in its competitiveness was closed foreign markets. The excuse given by the U.S. government in containing and delaying protectionist legislation at home was that it had demanded the liberalization of foreign markets, thus eliminating the need for any protectionist domestic legislation. The government was engaged in substantial economic conflict on the domestic front, and partly as a result, its request for the opening of foreign markets was also very straightforward and ideologically aggressive.

The demand for market liberalization entailed gradual changes in the bureaucratic regulation which was characteristic of the Japanese economic system. This included the informal and collusive self-regulatory relationship between industry and the government agencies that oversaw them (Aoki, 1988). Japanese bureaucratic organizations initially viewed the demands for change as interference in domestic affairs. However, as global economic interdependence deepened, they came to realize that there is a necessity for standards by which to regulate economic activity and also the standardization of products and technologies. However, even though the medium- to long-term advantage of market liberalization is recognized, in the short run it is difficult to overcome opposition from those who have vested interests, including government offices, the business community and *zoku giin*. This is especially true for those government ministries and agencies which have the power to grant licenses and permits, or which regard themselves as guardians of the national interest. These government bodies are actively opposed to market liberalization as promoted by the US government. Aside from the competitive manufacturing industries, sectors which factor in the national interest as part of their operational considerations do not regard free competition as a priority consideration. Together with the financial and communications sectors, these sectors are all strongly resistant to market liberalization and standardization.

If we observe individual government institutions, the Ministry of International Trade and Industry (MITI), which had manufacturing industry under its purview, took a positive attitude toward market liberalization. Most of Japan's manufacturing industries are very competitive, and the tariff on these products is either zero or near zero. MITI was also fully aware of the tendency of Japanese corporations to form cartels (in other words, symbiotic relationships), and of the protectionist sentiment that such behavior engenders. In contrast, because the Ministry of Agriculture, Forestry and Fisheries supervised industries that were not competitive, it naturally favored protectionism. For example, the price of rice produced in Japan is five to six times higher than that produced in Thailand. Another government body that pursued protectionist policies was the Ministry of Health and Welfare, although here the motivating factor was not always related to trade issues. Sanitary standards sometimes become non-tariff barriers. For instance, it was the regulations regarding the prevention of plant diseases, not the 20 per cent tariff, that were the stumbling block for the import of apples from the US and New Zealand. Apple imports were only allowed where harmful insects were terminated on the spot.

The Ministry of Finance is responsible for both currency and finance and at this time gave the impression that it preferred protectionism or mercantilism to liberalism. Some people, such as Bill Emmott of *The Economist* in Britain, referred to such attitudes as financial socialism (Emmott, 1991). But market liberalization has had a great impact on financial and fiscal policies. The Ministry of Finance was extremely wary because issues such as currency and finance, both vital elements of national sovereignty, were up for discussion at the Japan–US Structural Impediment Initiatives talks (Sakakibara, 1990). In spite of these misgivings, the Ministry of Finance, albeit in an informal way, did suggest some rather liberal ideas, such as removing all tariffs imposed on the manufacturing industry. The Ministry of Finance is proud of the role it has played in maintaining long-term financial and economic stability, through a system that has ensured a stable supply of capital at low cost, and also shielded banks from bankruptcy. Ultimately, the Ministry of Finance was not in a hurry to take decisive action on market liberalization, and questioned whether liberalization of the entire market was necessary or desirable.

One of the reasons Japan was reticent about US demands for market liberalization, which was reflected in the Japan–US Structural Impediment Initiatives talks, was that the call for change directly affected the core of Japan's socio-economic system. As an example, the US, in seeking to reform Japan's financial system, sought a reduction of working hours for Japanese workers because it constituted unfair competition. It also demanded an increase in public expenditure at a certain level and within a given period, to improve insufficient social infrastructures such as housing and roads in urban cities. Requests for such thoroughgoing reform could be construed as interference in domestic affairs (Inoguchi, 1989a). Yet, given the intensification of economic integration and global interdependence on the one hand, and the repeated calls for reciprocity and the standardization of social systems on the other, such requests from the US do not appear to be out of the ordinary. We should also remember that while the United States continues to treat Japan as a dependent state, it still expects Japan to take its share of economic responsibility as an allied nation. This tension provoked strong disagreement within Japanese society and generated substantial anti-US sentiment, as was manifest in the book *The Japan That Can Say No* (Ishihara and Morita, 1989).

International responsibility as an economic superpower

The 'strong America' policy includes market liberalization, but it also involves other issues. The Japanese government finds many of these issues disturbing (Nye, 1990, 1992–1993). The main goals of American policy were, as discussed earlier, market liberalization, a revival of competitiveness in terms of technology and industry, requests for expansionary policies by allied nations through macroeconomic policy, cuts in its own security expenditure, and a greater sharing of responsibilities among allied countries. Here, I will examine the latter two issues.

US military forces were deployed all over the world during the Cold War, and the US has expressed strong dissatisfaction over the costs it has incurred in maintaining military forces to defend its allies. Ever since the US significantly increased its military expenditure in pursuit of its hardline policy against the former Soviet Union in the 1980s, its demands on allies has grown. These demands became even greater after the end of the Cold War. It is an undeniable reality that the American public wanted to benefit from the peace dividend, and as a result the government has had to drastically reduce its defense spending. Under these conditions, the US government proposed that its allies make more equitable international contributions. In concrete terms, for Japan burden-sharing meant shouldering an increased amount of the cost of maintaining the US military presence in Japan, increasing the exchange of military technologies, and sharing the costs of involvement in international conflicts more equitably.

The US government was especially keen for Japan to share the cost of the Gulf War. In fact, as it transpired, Japan's financial contribution was so substantial that Tokyo had to put on hold parts of the general account budget during the war. This was one of the factors which contributed to the creation of a bubble economy (by this time the economy had already shown signs of overheating). The Japanese Diet also passed the Peace Keeping Operations Law, making it possible for Japan to contribute financial aid and manpower to the United Nations Transitional Authority in Cambodia (UNTAC) (Inoguchi, 1992d). In the same period, there were also loud appeals for advanced industrial countries, including Japan, to provide joint financial assistance to the former USSR. In the Munich Summit declaration of 1992, G-7 countries agreed to supply a relatively large amount of financial aid, in stages, to the former Soviet Union. The World Earth Summit in Rio de Janeiro was another occasion on which Japan was called upon to make financial contributions.

Hence, it was not just the US but the world community centered around the US that had demands on and expectations of Japan. Some believe that the hitherto interventionist and developmental role of the Japanese government was compromised by such requests. This is a significant potential development when one considers the autonomous role that the Japanese government has played in the domestic governance and emergence of modern Japan. An increase in government revenue is the only viable way to cope with unexpected expenditure, but it is difficult for the Japanese government to raise taxes because of the credo of 'small government, low taxes.' Japan had little choice but to maintain a low tax rate even if this perpetuated the cartel system that made living costs so high. Alternatively, instead of raising taxes the government could have chosen the option of promoting market liberalization, breaking up the cartels, and reforming the high price system. However, it is doubtful whether most Japanese, who, remember, have enjoyed 'security, safety and stability' would have accepted such a decision. Given that Japan is simultaneously an aging society and an economic powerhouse, it is necessary to restructure its financial capabilities in a corresponding manner. In this sense, it is impossible for the Japanese government to swim against the tide of economic integration and market liberalization brought about by technological progress, without a decline in the quality of people's living standards in the medium- to long-term.

Aside from security concerns, aid to Russia, and environmental matters, other issues raised in the Western summit declaration, in the form of macroeconomic policy coordination, presented difficulties for the Japanese government in the prosecution of its developmentalist role. This was because on occasions when Japan saw the need for a tightening of the money supply and high interest rates, other countries firmly believed that Japan should stimulate its economy, expand consumption, and increase imports. The most damaging example of this tension was the stimulatory and expansionist policies which were pursued in 1985–87. Even though the US economy had started to show signs of recovery, the Japanese economy was still in a prolonged period of low economic growth. This led the government, supported by the Ministry of Finance, to maintain its policy of tight control of the money supply. During this period, priority was given to price stability, followed by a reduction in government expenditure. However, pressure from the US government was severe, and finally the Prime Minister, the Minister of Finance and the Minister of Foreign Affairs, all of whom preferred to cooperate with the US, agreed on a policy direction which was more palatable to their American counterparts. As part of this process the Maekawa Report, drafted by an advisory body of the Prime Minister, suggested that liberalization should be promoted, and domestic consumption should be expanded. Public opinion also shifted in favor of market liberalization. Administrative and financial reforms were again embraced even though the private sector had made great efforts to eliminate waste (saving energy, improving labor productivity, etc.) after the first oil crisis. However, these efforts were not matched by the government. In particular, the Nakasone administration forcefully pushed for these reforms. However, while administrative and financial reforms were partially implemented, economic policies that had entirely opposite objectives were also implemented in response to other aspects of the report.

This macroeconomic policy adjustment began as a complementary measure to support the recovery of the American economy. But once the policy was introduced it overheated the economy, and caused the boom and subsequent bursting of the bubble economy at the end of the 1980s and the early 1990s (Phillips, 1991; Emmott, 1991). The partially liberalized financial markets and the collapse of the bubble economy sent shock waves through Japanese society. Incomplete market liberalization policies were carried out in other fields, and when monetary policy was tightened in 1989, the bubble economy started to burst as the knock-on effect spread from industry to industry. The collapse finally led to the reform of all industries with regard to inventory, capital investment and overtime work. As a result, individual income declined, which had a negative impact on consumption. By the beginning of 1992, total recession had set in across the board.

International economic responsibility after the Cold War and the bursting of the bubble economy

In the 1990s negative views on macroeconomic policy coordination became more predominant. The Maekawa Report (1986), following the assessment of international finance as laid out in the Plaza Accord and signed by the US, Western Europe and Japan, encouraged market liberalization, the expansion of domestic demand and policy cooperation with advanced industrialized countries. The report was considered by some segments of society to be the key factor in the collapse of Japan's bubble economy in the late 1980s and the early 1990s. This viewpoint is sometimes called the counter-Maekawa course. Yet, as long as technological innovations that promote international economic integration continue, this viewpoint lacks credibility, if one adopts a broader and long-term perspective. Only from a partial and short-term perspective are some points valid.

First, whenever a severe recession is experienced, the emphasis on domestic priorities is strengthened. Recognizing that without a stable and prosperous world economy the Japanese economy cannot improve, there was a strong desire to see the GATT's Uruguay Round succeed. However, there was an increasingly pessimistic attitude towards the adoption of a set of unified rules (Nihon keizai shinbun, 1993). Moreover, as the recession worsened after the end of the Cold War and the bursting of the bubble economy, the idea of taking on fewer international responsibilities grew. Japan was pressured into paying a large amount of the unexpected costs of the Gulf War. It is not surprising that the Ministry of Finance, which considers finance to be one of the key elements of national sovereignty, found it difficult to accept this demand. Japan was in the midst of trying to cope with the collapse of its bubble economy, and recession was at an all time low. Despite this there were still extravagant discussions about Japan's international economic responsibilities, covering topics as diverse and costly as the environment, aid to Russia and UN peacekeeping activities. Not unnaturally domestic economic difficulties meant that the Japanese government gave these discussions a cool reception. The comprehensive set of economic policies announced in August 1992, the large scale expenditure on public projects included in the 1993 fiscal budget, and the cut in personal income tax were all policies which were developed with domestic priorities in mind. Support for these policy measures was far more emphatic than previous support for the reduction of the fiscal deficit.

Second, Japan's distrust towards the US grew. According to opinion polls taken in both countries on the subject of Japan-US relations, the benevolent sentiments that Japanese people held towards the US were steadily weakening, although the change was not as dramatic as that which occurred in the attitude of American people towards Japan. This change in attitude could clearly be seen in the fact that a book that speculated about the US's key role in the formation and bursting of Japan's bubble economy became a bestseller in Japan. More generally, the demands which the US was making of its allies at this time were not finding wide support. A commonly held view was that because American prestige was waning, the government in Washington was expecting its allies to take up more of the burden than was fair. This shift became apparent at the Munich Summit in 1992. Although the US requested that both Japan and Germany should lower their interest rates, this was not included in the declaration. Indeed, rather than lowering interest rates, the German government immediately increased them after the summit. Representatives of the European nations thought that the Munich Summit itself had lost a great deal of significance in the relaxed post-Cold War world. The US also exhibited a strong domestic politics-oriented posture. Therefore, there were no country specific clauses in the declaration itself. As a result, only the basic macroeconomic management measures of individual financial authorities (in particular, European nations headed by Germany and Japan) were laundry-listed in the declaration. Needless to say, the Japanese government was expected to accomplish its five-year economic plan, achieve an annual average economic growth rate of 3.5 percent, finalize its revised budget, and generally meet the expectations of the US before the next summit. As the impression that US power was in decline grew, articulate voices within the Japanese government pointed out that Japan had its own distinct qualities and domestic priorities, just as the US does. The US has traditionally viewed Japan as a revisionist state, and this has been the motivation behind many of the demands which the US placed on Japan thoughout this period (Murakami, 1992). Some Japanese wanted to counter this with a more pluralist interpretation of Japan's role, which explains why Japan hesitated, or acted against, the liberalization of its financial markets after the collapse of the bubble economy.

Third, it was widely recognized that it would be ridiculous for Japan to isolate itself in the Asia-Pacific region, and that policy coordination with the US in the second half of the 1980s had not really benefited Japan that much. Prime Minister Kiichi Miyazawa himself established a consultative council on Asia-Pacific issues in the spring of 1992, maneuvering public opinion to reinforce diplomacy toward Asian countries. This could be seen in his approach to Beijing and the commemoration of the twentieth anniversary of Japan's diplomatic rapprochement with China. Also, at the beginning of 1993, Miyazawa visited ASEAN, rather than the United States, even though a new US administration had just taken office.

On the issue of free trade, there has been a gradual acceptance that regional regimes are more effective than universal regimes. The delay in the conclusion of the Uruguay Round of the GATT confirmed the suspicion that it was difficult to reach universal arrangement on free trade. The deadlock between the US and the then European Community on agricultural products was a good example of this. Doubts about the value of universal regimes were demonstrated in the rapid increase in the number of regional agreements which were reached in the 1990s. In Europe the Maastricht Treaty was accepted by all member-states because it provided economic coherence, protected cultural homogeneity and was ultimately a political necessity. Most countries agreed that barriers to the free transaction of goods and services, and the free movement of people should be eliminated, while the liberalization of domestic markets was promoted in stages. The North American Free Trade Agreement (NAFTA) was also formed between the US, Canada and Mexico, and was based on bilateral free trade arrangements. The purpose of this agreement was to create a large common market by removing trade and investment barriers through the liberalization of domestic markets. Since Mexico is one of the member nations, the future of most Latin American nations will be greatly affected by this agreement.

In the Asia-Pacific region, the Asia Pacific Economic Cooperation forum (APEC) was initiated. The most important feature of this forum is that it was neither institutionalized nor exclusive. Its goal was to promote the economic development of Asia-Pacific countries, and to enhance free trade worldwide. At the same time, there is also a shared sentiment akin to that articulated by the East Asia Economic Caucus (EAEC), that US pressure for market liberalization should be resisted. This group includes Asia-Pacific nations but excludes North American and Oceanian states. However, there was also a recognition that without a global free trade system functioning in the Asia-Pacific region, the prosperity of some countries could be threatened. This logic in turn works against the formation of a regional group. Looking at the region as a whole, income levels remain low, and local import capacity is not sufficiently large to absorb the export volume produced by the region. Thus a worldwide market is required. In terms of food and energy supply, Asia-Pacific countries still have to rely on other regions. Considering their demographic structures and population growth potential, Asia-Pacific nations do not have enough energy and food within their own region to sustain themselves.

To summarize, the Japanese government gave universal agreements first priority. Secondly, it enhanced cooperative relations in promoting regional economic development. Finally, the Japanese government tried to enhance human resources to achieve coherence in managing the economy. In other words, the conclusion of the GATT treaty, the active promotion of trade, direct investment, technology transfer and ODA, and the sharing of economic management skills through training and education, are the government's priorities. There is a possibility that the universal free trade regime might disappear, and that the regional trade regimes in Europe and Northern America might become institutionalized. Accordingly, the Japanese government is seeking to realize a non-institutionalized, open structure that corresponds to the APEC spirit, and which can guarantee regional solidarity and coherence. In short, even though there is a growing awareness of Japan's international economic responsibility, more and more people feel that Japan should meet these responsibilities in its own way. Since there is not absolute confidence that the Japanese developmentalist model will be accepted by other countries, the predominant view is that states should implement policies which are appropriate to their own situations, and demonstrate greater tolerance towards others.

5 One party dominance and political hollowing-out

Introduction

The Liberal Democratic Party (LDP) was established when the Liberal Party and the Democratic Party merged in 1955 (The Liberal Democratic Party, 1978). The LDP managed to stay in power continuously for nearly four decades, until 1993. This is probably the longest time that a single political party has retained power in any liberal democracy. Some political parties, such as the Christian Democratic Coalition in Italy, and the Christian Democratic Alliance in Belgium, have been able to stay in power for lengthy periods, not as a single party but as majority parties in a coalition government. Their ability to hold onto political power makes these European parties similar to the LDP in this particular regard. Other parties have dominated the political scene for an extended period as single political parties, such as the Social Democratic Party of Sweden, the Congress Party of India and the Labour Party of Israel. However, all of these parties lost power as a result of economic downturns and political instability in the 1970s (Inoguchi, 1990a). What are the main factors behind the LDP's extended and unbroken domination of Japanese politics between 1955 and 1993?

To answer this question, we must examine both the political and the economic spheres, and further subdivide each sphere into private and public sectors. The political sphere is made up of political parties and an administrative section, and the economic sphere has both a private and a public sector. Political parties include Diet members and the political parties that back them. The administrative section, on the other hand, is led by a Prime Minister who is selected by Diet members, and his appointed cabinet, which oversees the bureaucracy. It also includes other surrounding organizations with supporting functions. The private economic sector consists of ordinary private enterprises and the economic organizations that represent them. The public economic sector includes government enterprises and semi-governmental and semi-private ventures. In this chapter, the main focus is on the political parties which are closely related to the politicians. Why, as a structural feature of Japan's party politics, was one party domination able to continue for so long? To answer this question we must analyze the relationships between the political parties and the administration on the one hand, and the political parties and the economic sphere (both private and public sectors) on the other.

Political parties and the administration

It was only possible to choose politics as a career after the Meiji Restoration, with the introduction of the constitution and parliamentary politics in Japan. In this sense, politics as a vocation is a comparatively recent development. The emergence of a distinction between the administrative role of a politician and the administrative role of a bureaucrat therefore came later in Japan. But how were these administrative functions allocated before the Meiji Restoration in practice? During the long process of de-feudalization up until the Edo period, the samurai warriors who served as civil officers in the cities, and the landlords who took on the duty of village heads in the countryside were the ones who fulfilled these administrative roles. Prior to this arrangement, warriors were separated from the land to which they had been closely attached and moved to urban areas as a group. Effectively disarmed, they served as civilian officers, conducting political and administrative work. In local areas, power-holders such as village heads held concurrent positions as politicians and administrators at the grassroots level. The characteristics of this political-administrative structure were 'strict and serious on the surface but very rough and pragmatic in reality' (Mizutani, 1972). In other words, the birth of Japan's political-administrative system was not based on a grand design for the future. Rather, it was born out of a careful and ongoing monitoring of social reality, and characterized by an ethos whereby practical problems were dealt with through political and administrative means. As one administrator of the old bakufu government once put it: 'To spend a lot of money on building dams is very much western in style, but on the matter of flood control, it is best to trust those who have experience and who often suffer from flooding on their own land' (Mizutani, 1972).

This political arrangement was completely revamped after the Meiji Restoration. At that time, there were about 400,000 unemployed samurai warriors. After the Restoration, most of them were absorbed into the modern mass bureaucracy which was gradually being established. A large number of others who did not join the government were elected either to a local assembly or the Imperial Parliament, thereby becoming politicians. Still others utilized the opportunities afforded by the privatization of official enterprises to pursue their own business ventures, effectively transforming themselves into entrepreneurs and capitalists. The new bureaucracy contained many features that enabled the new administrators to carry on some of the meritorious practices of their Edo predecessors.

In early Meiji Japan many politicians experienced unemployment, either because they had failed in their initial attempts to win government office, or because they had been activists before they were elected as assembly representatives. Sometimes they militated on behalf of regional resistance to central government's coordinated attempts to reduce or withdraw local powers (Masumi, 1965–1980). In the Edo period, these people would have been the leaders who brought matters of local dissatisfaction, inequality and poverty to the attention of senior central administrators. In this sense, as representatives of grassroots interests, today's politicians differ little from those in Edo Japan. However, politicians in the Edo era were also administrators, a qualitative distinction which set them apart from their modern counterparts.

A major change after the Meiji Restoration was the bureaucratization of Japanese society. It was not until the twentieth century that bureaucratic institutions became dominant but the foundations of their predominance were laid in the period between the 1870s and 1890s. In a parallel development, politicians emerged as an active force in social movements, expressing their dissatisfaction and resisting the imperiousness and exploitation of the central government. Politicians were in part stimulated to become social activists by their experience of the Western-style parliamentary system. It is well-established in political histories of this period that, up until the mid-twentieth century, these social activists, who began as freedom fighters and defenders of the popular rights movement, successfully articulated anti-government positions in the Imperial Parliament. Later, however, they became members of an internalized party system in the Taisho Democracy period, after which they finally became a branch of the Taisei Yokusan Kai. Through this process these activists systematically assimilated themselves within existing institutions, thus terminating, by their own actions, their original mission.

As the bureaucracy emerged to institutionalize legislation, monitor society and implement policy in an orderly and relentless fashion, the role of politicians in the legislature was reduced, in comparison with that of the Edo era. With the perfection of the bureaucracy's supervising mechanisms and its increased capabilities in dealing with complex issues, the role of politicians became increasingly marginalized (Kawato, 1992). As a result, politicians came to fulfil a more symbolic but also more emotional function, in representing ordinary people and voicing public opinion (Kyōgoku, 1983). In concrete terms, politicians have become more and more specialized in dealing with issues such as the following: highly politicized problems that the bureaucracy is unable to solve directly, or problems posed by social groups with powerful grassroots support. Examples of the former include the symbolic nature of the Emperor, the intentions of the US government, and the loss of confidence in Japan's business community. Examples of the latter include the challenges posed internally by extreme rightist groups and gangsters, and fierce public protests. There are two sets of issues involved: legitimacy, state leadership and the interests of big capital on the one hand, and the threat of powerful internal groups and rejection by the public on the other.

While politicians are vexed by these difficult and sensitive problems, the scope of their daily work has narrowed with the ever widening and deepening scope of the bureaucracy's activities (Inoguchi, 1992c). A politician's acknowledged sphere of competence and responsibility is now very much limited to his electoral constituency, thus reducing the role he is able to play in formulating public policy, and in contributing political ideas or initiatives that might form the basis for such policy. It is the bureaucracy which is in charge of formulating and implementing public policy, and this limits the work of politicians. There are, however, some opportunities for members of the ruling party to provide input through the Policy Research Committee. Although the bureaucracy has a rigid organizational structure, politicians' policy ideas carry more weight in the policy-making process through coordinated intervention than through confrontational methods. Policy input through this latter approach becomes especially difficult and unproductive in the long run. While 70 to 80 per cent of LDP Diet members are highly prominent within their own electoral districts, they are only minor players in Tokyo, where the Diet only sits for brief periods. This reflects the political reality that politicians are more important within their own constituency than outside it, and secondly, that the short Diet sessions suit the bureaucracy.

Under this arrangement, the bureaucracy expects politicians to play a complementary role to it, while remaining receptive to public opinion. This has contributed to the LDP receiving a majority of votes and staying in power for a long time. The larger the number of citizens represented by the party in power, the easier it is for bureaucratic institutions to coordinate policies. The LDP, as an inclusive party, was able to retain control of the political sphere for a prolonged period. In addition, the LDP has been successful in maintaining and guiding Japan's market economy, and sustaining a friendly relationship with the United States, and this has helped it to remain in power. If we look at twentieth century history, this transformation in the role of politicians is more or less common in advanced industrialized countries. In Japan, this process was accelerated due to particular aspects of its modern and contemporary history.

The political and economic spheres

The separation of the political and economic spheres, and the distinction between the public sector and the private sector are both derived from principles of democratic politics, which in turn have their basis in nineteenth century European capitalism (Van Wolferen, 1989). But when we consider Japanese state-society relations, it is difficult to determine the lines of division as neatly in practice. The political-administrative system in the Edo period was designed both to maintain order and guide economic operations. For instance, politics and economics were entwined in such administrative realms as flood control and corvée, harvest and taxation, crime and the justice system. 'Edo's public administrative system was really a system which required self-responsibility from the peasantry and the urban dwellers. On the surface, this administrative machinery appeared strict and severe but in reality it was very flexible and pragmatic. These features were crucial in sustaining a vibrant society characterized by a high degree of population mobility and intense economic activity whilst simultaneously nurturing a stable and peaceful social order' (Mizutani, 1972) This is similar to my earlier point, but the Edo period is described as 'paradise' (Fukuzawa) precisely because it had a social framework that highlighted state guidance whilst allowing for societal self-adjustment (Mizutani, 1972). It was an administrative system that was not harmful to the internal development of society. This system placed some restrictions on peasants and merchants who engaged in economic activities, but it took into consideration such changes as economic development, demographic movement, technological progress and the environment. Hence, it was a pragmatic political framework that did not interfere with immediate and longer term market forces.

Although the political system of Meiji Japan borrowed many elements from the West, the core of Japan's approach to governance did not undergo a fundamental shift (Bitō, 1992). The Emperor's status continued to be used politically to meet the nation's desire for symbolic unification, while real political and administrative power resided with the bureaucracy. Given that Japan was being bombarded with foreign ideas, particularly in relation to issues of constitutionalism, parliamentarianism and democracy, the approach which was adopted at that time could not have been more efficient in limiting the negative impact that these foreign ideas could have had on the country (Ooms, 1985). The economic system was certainly capitalistic but there was no real industrial base to speak of. As such, the prioritization of political stability, financial regularity and the nurturing of social infrastructure proved farsighted. Years of accumulated administrative experience from the Edo period were very beneficial in this regard. For instance, when the Meiji government, which possessed neither capital nor technology, planned to construct a communications network, it gave prominent local figures official positions, in exchange for their financial support in constructing specific post-offices and electrical poles (Yoshimura, 1993). Another example is the government's use of foreign loans, technologies and managers to support and sponsor public enterprises. Once in operation, these enterprises were sold to the private sector, thereby strongly encouraging private entrepreneurship (Umemura and Nakamura, 1983). By the middle of the nineteenth century, Japan had been forced to open its ports. The unequal treaties caused Japan to lose tariff-setting autonomy, which was a very important aspect of international economic relations at that time. To overcome this disadvantage in pursuing economic development, the government set up official enterprises that were relatively unaffected by the unequal treaties, and privatized them at an early stage, thus ensuring that they were not in conflict with market forces. These methods are still applied today.

This approach was appropriate to the political-economic conditions of the late nineteenth century, when capitalism was still young, the technological levels were low and tariff-setting autonomy had been suspended. It is also important to note the political and economic system which Japan adopted in the stormy years of the mid twentieth century (1925–75). This was a system of economic operations guided by the state (Nakamura 1971, 1973, 1979, 1981 1985; Inada, 1993). At the time, communism, fascism and Keynesianism, with the last not yet having its own name, were at their peak. Japan's economic activities through military mobilization combined elements from each of these 'isms'. In this mixed policy orientation lay the beginnings of what has subsequently come to be known as the model of Japanese economic development.

The most significant political factor, when one considers economic development, is the extent to which state intervention is consciously and successfully harmonized with mid- to long-term market forces. The state can participate in key industrial sectors and intervene to stimulate competition, both of which go against market forces in the short run, as long as it consciously considers mid- to long-term trends in the market. Needless to say, there is a disparity between theory and practice, and in reality Japan experienced many failures. In the prewar era, there were no clear mid- to long-term targets, with the result that the economy was mostly managed in an ad hoc and reactive manner. In contrast, in the postwar period not only was the international environment dramatically improved, but the Japanese government was better at coordinating and harmonizing its market interventions with the mid- to long-term trajectory of market forces. This demonstrated the merits of the Japanese economic development model. For short periods, or in particular cases, the government forcefully intervened in the market, arguing that it was trying to shape short-term market trends in order to reap long-term benefits. It was recognized that some political interventions would incur net losses, but compensation would be provided to cover such eventualities for given periods of time. This approach also facilitated the development of networks of cooperation among various actors in Japanese society. This grand framework, which originally emerged tentatively, has become a standard feature of political/economic operations, making it possible for different actors to regulate and coordinate their activities. Since the constituent elements of the now well-known Japanese triad-politics, business and the bureaucracy – function according to the same social dynamics and rules of interaction, it is easier for them to form social networks. But to successfully put these networks into practice, the dynamics of particular sectors must be respected. This provides a means for achieving relative balance during political interventions in the marketplace (Kōsai, 1992).

Let me make some concrete observations. First of all, politicians assert influence on the government budget process at two levels. At one level input is highly political, and comes from the top echelon of government, such as the US government's attempts to improve overall economic conditions, or a budget amendment to stimulate the economy, when public support for the cabinet is low. In the second case influence takes place at more of a micro-level, for example through the Tax Commission of the LDP's Policy Research Committee, or through LDP Diet members who are active on other committees. A typical example is the so-called 'Telephone Book' of the LDP Tax Commission, which has listings according to LDP priorities – concrete and individual issues related to constituencies and business. Except for top level contributions, it is common that input by politicians is limited to the micro-level. In other words, the original draft of the government budget at both the macro- and the micro- levels is determined by the bureaucracy, and input by politicians is minimal.

The more we observe the micro-level, the clearer it becomes that decisions are based on what politicians deem valuable. This is only natural in democratic politics. The point here is that this type of democratic input creates a self-perpetuating mechanism that does not generate a surplus for economic operations. This mechanism was taken for granted when politicians as tribal Diet members (zoku-giin) had a significant amount of input at the micro-level (Inoguchi and Iwai, 1987).

The mechanism of party politics

From the above analyses, political parties and politicians appear to be relatively weak. Indeed, it is the bureaucracy that does most of the day-to-day political and administrative work, while the political actors specialize in micro-level inputs. In general, when politicians cannot insist on a specific policy direction, the political process is weakened, because the work of politicians becomes superficial. Although there are some exceptions, this is an overall weakness of the Japanese political system, especially since political parties are supposed to represent citizens, and are supposed to reflect the wishes of society.

The private sector operates within its own framework. Two important points must be made about the private sector and the bureaucracy. First, the overwhelming accumulated power of the private sector is not limited to Japan; it is a common international trend. If we compare Japan's GNP and the total output of Japan's largest enterprises at both the beginning and at the end of the twentieth century, or if we compare the scale of accounting between the Japanese government and large private companies, the latter's strength becomes immediately obvious. Many Japanese firms have assets which are greater than the GNPs of many countries (Sakamoto, 1992). These factors are common to all advanced industrialized countries.

Second, the accumulation of power by bureaucratic institutions is also a twentieth century historical trend. The bureaucracy has been steadily growing and increasing its capacity to process and organize information, due to technological progress and the expanding legal structure of the state. Today, the bureaucracy has become a specialized institution which conducts professional and technical work (Weber, 1980). The development of the bureaucracy has been a universal occurrence in industrialized countries. Democratic polities share the following similarities: there is freedom of expression and free competition; political parties compete with each other according to their policy platforms, coming to power via free but secret ballots; and public policies are decided by a majority vote before being implemented. Mass democracy in the above sense is qualitatively different from nineteenth century democracy, where the scope and scale of public participation was extremely limited. Nevertheless, no universal system of thought has offered a sustained challenge to liberal democracy, or threatened to replace it (Lukacs, 1993). Judging from the above two points, Japan's political framework follows worldwide trends towards bureacratization and the consolidation of liberal democracy.

There are three other characteristics which form an integral part of Japan's political system. These are realism, pragmatism and opportunism. The very birth of the LDP itself creates the impression that it is superficial in terms of social representation (Masumi, 1988). When Japan was defeated at the end of World War II, the ruling elite accepted the occupation forces. But the political and economic reforms carried out by the occupation forces were based on the following considerations: a purging of the militarists from the ruling elite in order to make the occupation easier, and the utilization of Japan in pursuit of a new international agenda. From the viewpoint of the United States, Japan had to accept the reality of a close and subordinate relationship, and it also had to accept capitalism. These were non-negotiable conditions. From the viewpoint of Japanese business and the bureaucracy, it was important that the interests of the Japanese people were represented. The only way to meet these various conditions was to unite all of the conservative forces. The occupation forces therefore encouraged the reorganization of the conservative ruling class. However, due to a general loss of confidence, a lack of support from the public, and financial difficulties, the conservative parties were not politically strong in the early years following the end of World War II.

Throughout the period of occupation and the extremely poor economic conditions that followed the war, the conservatives benefited from the largesse of a right wing individual who had control of a special secret fund from the wartime Japanese military. As was subsequently witnessed, conservative social movements countered the demonstrations against the renewal of the Japan–US Security Treaty. There was also a considerable amount of right wing involvement in the Lockheed scandal, as well as in the formation of the Takeshita cabinet. Whenever events that rocked the system took place, right wing groups were involved. The predecessor of the LDP was established under such circumstances, and this has placed restraints on the function of political parties in Japanese politics.

The role of political parties is to attract the support of as many citizens as possible, from as many diverse constituencies as possible, and to hold their attention for as long as possible. This is especially true for the party which is in power, which attempts to characterize itself as inclusive, and constantly strives to represent the overall interests of the general public (Satō and Matsuzaki, 1985). Here appeal and attraction refer to the kind of relationships which are centred on the election district and the business community. In the election district, politicians receive support from the electorate during an election (in the form of votes) through political support groups (kōenkai). This support is provided by local personnel who also maintain day-to-day relations with voters through courtesy activities (such as raising additional funding for the constituency, and sending gifts to Kōenkai members on the occasion of marriages, deaths and festivals) (Takabatake, 1986; Muramatsu and Itō, 1986; Takahashi, 1987; Katō, 1985). As mentioned earlier, most politicians are fairly prominent in their home districts, but in Tokyo they are mere foot soldiers. Bureaucratic institutions play a more significant role in the legislative process than politicians. The business sector also reinforces this trend by not leaving much room for politicians to intervene. Moreover, the business sector has grown more critical of the LDP as its confidence has risen with regard to the issue of political donations. Although gross levels of Keidanren political donation to the LDP have increased, they have decreased if measured in terms of their ratio to Japan's GNP (Iwai, 1990).

In addition, political candidates from the party in power must compete with other candidates from their own party in mid-sized election districts. This has a number of significant implications (Inoguchi, 1993c). First, rather than running on ideology and policy issues, conservative candidates, including LDP members, compete with each other on the basis of who can best provide favors to the electorate. Here, favor refers to generous monetary gifts on important occasions such as major holidays, births, marriages, deaths, etc. These favors are often granted in exchange for subsidy grants. In order to defeat others in the same constituency, candidates have to receive financial support, not only from the LDP headquarters, but also from their faction leaders and those who have real power in their faction. If one candidate belongs to Faction A, then the other must belong to a different faction. If we look at the distribution of Diet seats by election district, it is clear that in large districts there have usually been at least three factions represented, while in small districts politicians from two factions have usually been elected. (It should be noted that with the exception of the Amami Islands, all electoral districts have 2–5 plural seats, a large number of districts have 2–3 member seats and a small number have 4–5 member seats). From 1955, when the LDP was founded, to the early 1970s, the distribution of factions for the most part followed this pattern. Faction leaders have always had very clear ideas about which of their faction supporters should have portfolios in new cabinets. Ultimately, the formation of a cabinet has been based on balancing interests in terms of LDP factional politics. In the twenty year time period previously mentioned, it was common practice to have two to three major factions sharing cabinet positions, while other factions were regarded as anti-mainstream and excluded from the cabinet. This follows closely the principle of a 'minimum winning coalition' and it is also why the LDP government has been referred to as a 'coalition government' (Leiserson, 1968). – It is important to note that even within the same party considerable tensions have existed.

Since the mid-1970s, however, factors such as the bureaucratization of political parties have caused factional dynamics to undergo some major changes. As the era of economic chaos and political storms came to an end, and was replaced by stable economic growth and orderly politics, tolerance of anti-mainstream activities decreased, even within the confines of the LDP. Gradually, achieving entry to the party bureaucracy through the traditional channels became the central concern for most politicians. The organizational dynamics of the ruling party became more systemic. Differences between factions were still important when studying competition within individual election districts, just as experiences within the party and the representation of factions in cabinet positions continued to be important. This led to the expansion of the largest factions, such as the Sato (Eisaku) faction, followed by the Tanaka (Kakuei) faction and the Takeshita (Noboru) faction. When a cabinet was formed, cabinet positions were distributed to all factions, thus following the 'wall-to-wall coalition' principle. Even when Tanaka Kakuei was arrested in the Lockheed scandal, he still relentlessly pushed to expand his faction in order to resist investigation. When a former Prime Minister continues to head a faction which has trouble producing another Prime Minister, that faction must possess overwhelming resourcefulness in order to survive and prevent other factions from taking control of the government. To substantiate this claim, it is instructive to compare the factional backgrounds of Prime Ministers, firstly in the period from 1955 to 1974 and secondly in the period from 1974 to 1993. It is clear that in the first period the leaders of all the large factions, with the exception of Ishibashi Tanzan (who led a small faction and held this office for three months in 1957–58) were Prime Ministers. By contrast, in the second period, those who assumed the office of Prime Minister were, with the exception of Takeshita Noboru (1987–89), leaders who did not come from large factions.

Tanaka Kakuei's ability to raise funding attracted many candidates to the Tanaka faction. Dividing 350–400 LDP Diet members into five factions, there were, on average, about 50–100 in each faction, but at the peak of the Tanaka faction's popularity, it had 140 members. Despite its relative decline, the Takeshita faction still had 100–110 members until a series of incidents, known as the Recruit, Sagawa Kyūbin and Kōminto scandals led to its breakup. Two important factions emerged from the collapse of the Takeshita faction, the Obuchi faction (more than sixty members), and the Hata faction (more than forty members).

There was also a potential problem with the internal structure of the LDP which, although an inclusive party, maintained a very long period of dominance as the ruling party. If this political party of factional coalitions could keep its competitive structure, then it would be easier to expose corruption when a new faction took office. The effect would be similar to that of having a new party take office (Inoguchi, 1992c). However, when the single largest faction is able to sustain its own power, and finds itself in a position to manipulate the Prime Ministership, corruption could then easily occur. Like the other factions, the biggest faction also needed funds to operate. Although the Takeshita faction was very adept at raising money, the business sector's political donations began to decline. When funding was difficult to secure, it was often the case that money came from upstart enterprises or firms that had political ambitions (Asahi shinbunsha yokohamashikyoku, 1988). Max Weber made the analogy that US politics was like a horse race: in the process of an election campaign between presidential candidates, political donations went to the most hopeful, and the candidate who received the most political investment would then usually go on to win the race (Weber, 1980; Ferguson, 1983; Ferguson and Rogers, 1983). When the business sector, which represents the overall interests of enterprises, shows greater restraint in its general political investment, particular political donations become more significant. In the case of the Lockheed incident it was All Nippon Airlines which was desperately trying to keep up with Japan Airlines, which at that time monopolized most of the international routes. It was Marubeni who was trying to catch up with other large commercial houses, and it was Kodama Yoshio, a behind-the-scenes right wing supporter of the LDP, who was involved from the very beginning. In the case of the Recruit scandal, NTT and Recruit found themselves being squeezed during the process of deregulation and the stimulation of private investment. In the case of the Sagawa Kyūbin/Kōminto incident, the players came from extreme right wing forces. Kōminto and the criminal gangs (Inakawakai) were angry at being forced into a corner by a stable LDP order, especially having just recovered from the demands of stimulating private investment. Sagawa Kyūbin, on the other hand, tried to take advantage of deregulation and the stimulation of private investment.

The LDP was largely successful in driving its potential adversaries to the margins of society. In the early postwar period, the conservatives succeeded in creating the impression that the Socialist and Communist parties were not suitable to govern. They also convinced the supporters of opposition parties, which included the socialists and the communists, to seek their interests not in the political realm but in the economic realm. This led to the increased economism of trade unions, where the enterprises are the opponents and opposition supporters focus on fighting for wage increases and shorter work weeks, rather than trying to address their concerns through the political process of competing political parties. While this consolidated the LDP's position as the ruling party, the degree of support for its left wing opposition weakened as the income levels of workers gradually increased due to Japan's rapid economic growth (Tanabe, 1988, 1989).

In order to expand their social base in the 1940s and the 1950s, conservative forces in the government passed legislation providing subsidies to once radical farmers and the self-employed. When the environment and social welfare were neglected in the era of high growth and criticism arose, the LDP responded by adopting ideas from opposition parties and social movements, passing relevant legislation, and then taking credit for the results. This further enhanced the support base of the LDP. In dealing with the anti-Vietnam War movement and the student movement, the LDP utilized both carrot and stick at different times. To separate these anti-establishment social movements from the arena of public support, the LDP depicted the forces behind these movements as radical.

When the oil crises of the 1970s led to a period of low growth, the LDP again displayed its political deftness by quickly providing a psychological security blanket for the so-called 'new middle strata' by emphasizing 'safety, security and stability' (Inoguchi, 1990a) The new middle strata is composed of those who abide by the rules, have no superfluous desires, and are consumed by their own personal lives. As Kurihara Akira observes, devotion to one's private life is one of the four pillars of a Japanese-style managed society. The other three pillars are productive forces, centralized authority and a national Japanese religion (Kurihara, 1985). By continuing its protection of farmers and the self-employed even against a background of market liberalization, the LDP continued to receive support from these groups. The LDP also worked hard to maintain the support of taxpayers. The prospects of an aging society and further internationalization created pressure to raise taxes, and in response the LDP government managed to limit tax increases by extolling the virtues of the traditional family structure, and mobilizing nationalistic feelings.

In these ways the LDP was able to sustain itself as an inclusive party, based in a political framework that reflected and responded to social and economic change. The bureaucracy, in contrast, regarded itself as an administration that could represent general public opinion, but which could also transcend party politics by representing the general public interest. But even this bureaucratic vision helped to further strengthen the LDP. Ultimately, it was the inclusive political strategy of the LDP that successfully sustained one party dominance, but success was also accompanied by certain tradeoffs. Moreover, this success was proof that certain positive structural elements existed.

One of the most significant tradeoffs has been the hollowing-out of party politics. This hollowing-out has three aspects: the dynamics of mobilizing party support; the reduced significance of political parties in Japanese domestic politics, and, lastly, the turbulence created by various interests which span national borders. First of all, the LDP, as an inclusive party, must make strenuous efforts to absorb different social groups, especially those which have not been completely integrated into the current system. But when a variety of social groups belong to the system, the overall sense of loyalty tends to decline. A group's loyalty to the LDP will only increase when it sees itself as being different from others and receiving special treatment. If everyone receives the same treatment, it is difficult to generate loyalty and just as difficult to expect loyalty. For instance, there has not been much change in public expenditure over the past decade (Asahi shinbun, 1992). The Finance Ministry's policy has been to cut spending for as long as the fiscal deficit persists. However, with each budget LDP Diet members fought against the cuts and if anything the fact that large scale cuts were not made was mostly due to the efforts of these LDP Diet members. For those who benefited from public expenditure, including the voters, it became a standard feature of the budget: it was almost automatic for the budget to contain public expenditure, but when it did not, the Diet member from the affected district simply refused to vote for it. Occurrences such as this have become a standard feature of public policy during fiscal deficits, creating an environment that is difficult to manage, and in which rebellions by loyalists are to be expected.

It was in this context that the rebellion of extreme right wing forces such as Sagawa Kyūbin and Kōminto took place. But this is only part of the explanation for these events. The main reason, according to some, is that it was felt that the LDP did not sufficiently favor the extreme right, which had been a substantial pillar of conservative support. In addition, those members who entered the party structure through rather obscure processes began to make conspiratorial moves in an attempt to gain promotion from the grassroots level. Policy changes implemented in the period of high growth had a calming effect on Japan's welfare related social movements, but their concerns were reactivated by budget cuts and predictions of continuing cuts, despite the existence of an aging society. The once fragmented environmental movement revived itself with encouragement from the growing international environmental movement. Disenchantment with the LDP also grew among farmers and self-employed merchants and manufacturers. These people had been weakened and slightly reduced in number, as they were forced to endure a drastic restructuring process that arose due to mounting pressure for international economic integration, market liberalization and a greater concentration of business activity in the Tokyo area. Farmers faced the liberalization of rice markets during the GATT Uruguay Round, while self-employed merchants and manufacturers had to deal with concrete market liberalization measures in the fields of distribution, construction and transportation. Although the LDP did offer an umbrella of regulations and protection, in practice farmers and merchants had more and more difficulty in securing protection from the LDP and bureaucratic institutions. As this trend became clearer, people in these sectors became increasingly unlikely to support the LDP. Finally, in the face of a collapsing bubble economy, the emerging reality of reduced wages and layoffs, and the corruption of politicians as revealed in the Sagawa Kyūbin and Kōminto scandals, income earners, who constitute the largest voting bloc, grew increasingly disillusioned with the LDP government. At the time this was a great shock for the LDP, even if it later proved to be a temporary phenomenon.

The second aspect of the hollowing-out of party politics has been the reduced role of political parties. As mentioned earlier, the diminishing role of political parties is a universal phenomenon. The private sector has grown steadily in proportion to the public sector in the second half of the twentieth century. This entails a reduction not only in the role of government, but also a weakened bureaucracy, which in turn means a weakening in the position of political parties. Why is this the case? The purpose of political parties is either to organize or oppose government on behalf of society, but the private sector is able to sustain itself without depending a great deal on government. The less state-dependent the private sector is, the less inclined it is to look to the party in power for support, much less the parties in opposition. Political parties should represent the interests of social groups. The reality, however, is that some enterprises which have only a limited number of board members and account for only a very small portion of the electorate, have an overall power that is highly formidable, in terms of their economic strength and their contribution to the state.

In particular, when a society is systematically organized around corporate principles and company-centric enterprises, as in Japan, the institutionalized principles of these enterprises assume a dominant function in society at large. The pervasiveness of this culture of corporatization comes in the form of guiding principles which penetrate the entire society (Yamazaki, 1991). A clear example of this is the economism that structures the interactions of unions and management in all business organizations. Even though Japan's economic growth slowed, it still led other advanced industrialized countries. Although a downturn in the economy conventionally presents a window of opportunity for opposition parties to represent the interests of the workers, in Japan the opposition parties remain weak in the political sphere. Hence, the demands of workers from different industrial sectors during wage negotiations focused on wages, working hours and welfare benefits in the economic sphere. As long as workers from different enterprises and different sectors share a preoccupation with economism, the role of opposition parties in the formulation of economic and social policy will remain weak. Rather than being qualitatively different from each other, the ruling party and opposition parties distinguish themselves in terms of quantitative measures, as reflected in the allocation of resources in government budgets. In this situation, the only way in which opposition parties can meaningfully differentiate themselves from the party in power is on the issues of defence and patriotism. But public opinion tends to be extremely polarized on both of these issues. This again works to the advantage of the party in government, by giving it the opportunity to label its opponents as irresponsible or unrealistic.

What one might refer to as 'corporation worship' is the second indication that corporatization has permeated Japanese society. There are even differences between American and Japanese stock corporations. In the US the most important task for managers is the distribution of profit to shareholders, whilst in Japan this is not the case (or at least has not been since the 1920s). In Japan, the enterprise itself has become the purpose, and its survival and prosperity the ultimate goal for both its managers and workers (Sadaka, 1992). There are not many differences between managers and employees, in that the difference between their dining halls and wages is not that significant when compared to the disparities that exist between their American counterparts. Japanese enterprises attempt to create their own small but independent worlds, as do whole Japanese industrial sectors. As enterprises and sectors attempt to do this, they become less and less dependent on political parties, although that does not mean they do not need them. For instance, the commercial, industrial and business sectors strongly protect their own interests on issues such as corporate tax increases, anti-pollution legislation, energy supply and rising wages. This should be viewed not as a dependency on political parties, but rather as enterprises communicating their interests to bureaucratic institutions, political parties and the public, whilst striving to influence the formation and implementation of relevant policies.

Corporate handling of interactions with the extreme right or *yakuza* provides evidence that enterprises are creating their own independent world. When the extreme right or *yakuza* discover a potentially embarrassing weakness in a manager or in one of the workers of a particular enterprise, there is a tendency to negotiate without informing the police and to settle the problem with money. Enterprises, in comparison with bureaucratic institutions and political parties, have become much stronger organizations through the obligation to keep secrets. This leads to a form of organizational idolatry. An enterprise does not separate the faults of one manager or one worker from those of the organization, but instead considers him to be a part of a broader totality, and is extremely concerned about the potential that individuals might have to sully the company's reputation. One example is to refuse outside support during a management-labour dispute. In such situations, the restrictions on employees can become severe. Once the social organizing principles of enterprises have penetrated every level of society and in the process become dominant, their influence goes far beyond corporations and imposes itself on individuals and other non-corporate organizations. Political parties are not an exception to this generalization.

The third aspect of political hollowing-out is that as a result of extensive international interdependence, the corporatizing forces at work with Japanese society are comparatively vulnerable to external pressure. Technological progress has made it very difficult to maintain a closed national economic system, as the world economy becomes increasingly integrated. The era when external interference could be resisted, and the national economy protected, is over. Today, Japan's national economy is deeply integrated into the international system. It can be rapidly and profoundly affected by turbulence in the world economy. Therefore, conceptualizations of group interest have become more sophisticated and adaptive than before. As long as the Japanese political system is configured to reflect the interests and concerns of the domestic electorate, politics will inevitably reflect this strong preoccupation with domestic issues. However, through the process of international economic integration, the stronger the momentum, the more thorough the corporatization of the domestic economy will be, as it becomes increasingly affected by changes in the structure of global markets, in the mid- to long-term. If one considers comparative advantage from a global perspective, the structure of Japan's domestic economy will change. According to the theory of comparative advantage, the conceptualizations of self-interest which are advanced by social groups within societies will also undergo significant change. What this means in concrete terms is that when comparative advantage declines in a given sector of an economy, decision-makers within that sector are increasingly likely to support protectionist and regulatory economic policies. At the same time, when comparative advantage increases in a particular economic sector, that decision-makers within that sector are correspondingly more likely to advocate free trade-oriented and market-centred economic policies. If a given domestic economy is closely related to the world economy, such adaptations are natural.

For instance, the American auto industry became prosperous in the 1920s, enjoying its golden age in the 1940s and 1950s. Throughout this period, the US possessed a comparative advantage not just in the auto industry but in most manufacturing industries. As a consequence the US was, unsurprisingly, a champion of free trade. However, in the 1970s and 1980s, when auto industries in Japan and other countries began to develop a strong comparative advantage by producing smaller, more energy-efficient automobiles, the US auto industry effected an abrupt *volte face*, and advocated protectionism. At this time, and in a similar fashion to the auto industry, many other US manufacturing industries were losing their competitive edge, and subsequently added their voices to the protectionist movement. Yet, with a new cycle of technological innovation, the US auto industry was able to strengthen its comparative advantage in the production of large vehicles and luxury cars. As this happened, Japan's auto industry faced two problems: a saturated domestic market of sixty million automobiles, and the large scale investment it had made in the US market in the 1980s, which had made it impossible to increase profits. As the bubble economy burst at home, Japanese automakers began to quietly withdraw from the US market. These automakers started to explore emerging markets in developing countries and former socialist countries.

Rice is another high profile commodity which featured strongly in trade liberalization talks involving Japan. Japan's rice production industry possessed a comparative advantage up to the end of the Russo-

Japanese War. Since then the Japanese rice production industry has gradually declined in competitiveness, leading to a whole century of protectionist policies. The voice of protectionism would have been much stronger, had farmers who depended solely on rice production for their livelihood occupied a larger portion of the electorate. But in the late twentieth century, rice farmers account for only a small percentage of voters. Rice farmers fighting against rice liberalization were happy to compromise Japan's overall free trade position, even though this had negative ramifications for the rice farmers themselves. But it should be remembered that rice farmers are also consumers. If most of their consumer goods were to be produced domestically, then higher living costs would be the price of such a protectionist stance.

Even setting aside the extreme case of rice, the question of whether to adopt free trade or protectionist policies complicates the way in which voters perceive their self-interest. It has in fact been quite common for countries simultaneously to pursue both free trade and protectionist policies in different sectors of their economies. However, to comply with GATT/WTO guidelines it has been necessary to implement policies which facilitate the development of trade reciprocity and multilateralism. Countries must maintain similar tariff or non-tariff barriers to each other. Neither are any two given countries entitled to determine tariff levels exclusively between themselves. Rather, all countries should strive towards a level that is suitable for all GATT/WTO members. However, although many countries are rhetorically committed to the spirit and principles of free trade, it is inappropriate to assume that this commitment is consistently reflected in their trade policies. Japan is a good example of a country which has found it necessary to continuously modify economic activity in accordance with the free trade principle. Japan has domestic shortfalls in food production and energy generation, and as a result, exports manufactured goods in order to obtain foreign exchange, which is in turn used to import food and energy. Recently, this economic strategy has not been particularly successful. To make this strategy work it is economically imperative that Japan can sustain a comparative advantage in the world market for its manufactured products. Given these circumstances, the issue then becomes the extent to which the business sector should emphasize its own special interests (Inoguchi, 1990b).

Perceptions of self-interest are further complicated by other factors, one of which is security. Regardless of whether a country pursues free trade or protectionist policies, the basic unit which it defends and promotes is domestic society. It is often the case that countries find their national security under threat in the international system. Under such conditions, the concept of national security is introduced. According to this concept, even though a country is committed to free trade, it should still be able to secure food and energy supplies in times of national emergency. It is also necessary to possess a military contingent of a certain size in order to deter or deal with aggression from other states, or to address other urgent threats to the maintenance of order. Considerations of comprehensive national security have created circumstances in which the proportion of domestically produced food is not determined solely by the principle of comparative advantage (Nōrin chūkin sogō kenkyūjo, 1993). For example, Switzerland pursues a policy of wheat self-sufficiency. It also supports wheat production with very high subsidies. In preparation for an emergency, flour is stored and consumed in such a way that older flour (milled three years earlier) is used first. As a result, the bread is not as tasty, and although this policy runs contrary to the principles of free trade, the Swiss have decided that there is no superior alternative policy.

In Japan, despite the fact that petroleum and coal are the main sources of energy, there has also been experimentation to investigate the potential of nuclear power as an alternative energy source. After the first oil crisis, both France and Germany attempted to develop plutonium-based nuclear energy capabilities, but discontinued their projects because of the high costs and the levels of danger which were involved. Japan, however, persevered. The Japanese government was convinced that, from a long-term perspective, the future demand for oil would continue to increase. It would therefore have been irresponsible, Japan argued, to base energy policy on the mistaken premise that, simply because oil is often relatively cheap, this will always be the case, as a result of which it would always be acceptable to depend on imports (Tsūsho sangyō kōzō shingikai, 1982). This rationale for Japan's attempt to develop alternative sources of energy has increased international suspicion of Japan's motives with regard to the development of nuclear weapons. Levels of international distrust for Japan's motives are high, and this in turn weakens Japan's position. Ironically, Japan's energy policy, its attempt to articulate and implement a concept of comprehensive national security, may end up undermining the very national security which it was designed to protect.

The concept of international security has also grown in significance as international economic interdependence and integration have increased. It is no longer the case that individual countries can depend exclusively on their own capabilities to provide for their own security. Technological progress and the increased sophistication and power of contemporary weapons (their destructive force, speed and range) have made it impossible to conceive of international security in such a traditional manner. The idea that security can be managed by fostering international cooperation and developing international institutions has, meanwhile, been gaining momentum. For instance, a series of nuclear disarmament agreements between the United States and Russia (the former Soviet Union) were motivated by this conceptualization of international security as collective security (Steinbrunner, 1988). The common goal was to have not one, but two strategic nuclear powers, working together to maintain international stability whilst simultaneously reducing their respective nuclear arsenals. The European Conventional Armaments Reduction Treaty was another attempt to maintain a stable balance whilst reducing armaments levels as far as possible. Such initiatives were instrumental in ending the Cold War, and are important examples of cases where the overriding principle was the promotion of international security through collective security.

The idea of international security further complicates the way in which social groups perceive their self-interest. When Iraq invaded Kuwait, the US organized a military intervention based on the concept of international security. The concern was that if Iraq succeeded in its military intervention in Kuwait, this would set a bad precedent suggesting that the use of force could be an effective way to achieve foreign policy objectives. Also, Iraqi success would have given it hegemony among oil producing countries, and the interests of the US, Britain, France and other advanced industrialized countries, as well as oil importing countries in general, would have been damaged. Japan wanted, in lieu of military participation, to demonstrate its support by financing a substantial portion of the operation. However, world opinion was lukewarm towards this foreign policy initiative. Conversely, many people in Japan thought that rather than participating in the military confrontation with Iraq, Japan should instead have striven to maintain friendly relations with all oil producing countries, as this is the best means by which to secure Japan's oil supply. Interest groups who hold such opinions place a premium on the significance of free market mechanisms (Inoguchi, 1991a).

To sum up, the first feature of political hollowing-out is a realization on the part of a majority of the electorate that the relationship between the LDP and certain sectoral interests had become too heavily institutionalized. The second feature of political hollowing-out is that the significance of political parties has declined relative to the bureaucracy and the private sector. The third feature is the impact which increased economic interdependence has had on the way in which domestic groups perceive their self-interest. It should be pointed out that in discussing these three aspects of hollowing out I have focused exclusively on negative aspects of Japanese politics, but this is not to deny that the problems are real. This hollowing-out signifies that the Japanese political structure does not have the flexibility which is required by the political parties, the Diet and the electoral system, in order to effectively address all of the issues which relate to changing domestic and international circumstances. The key traits exhibited by the Japanese political structure are: adherence to market principles; a calculating bureaucratic administration and institutions; and a mixture of constituency and public opinion-oriented politicians. We must remember that the Japanese political system is designed primarily for the purpose of implementing pragmatic public policies .

In this chapter I have discussed what I have referred to as the hollowing-out of Japanese party politics. To the extent that I am correct, it is possible to argue that the Japanese political system has not yet fully developed into a system of representative democracy. However, it is important to note that Japan was not really influenced by eighteenth and nineteenth century European political thought, but instead developed its own indigenous representative democratic politics. The bureaucracy saw itself as a supra-party organization that represented the overall interests of the people. It administered through the use of policy monitoring devices and flexible management. From a state-society standpoint, and from a mid- to long-term perspective, the bureaucracy remains, to a certain extent, a critical agent in the monitoring, measurement and absorption of public opinion (Inoguchi, 1983). As long as the view of a state-society community predominates, not just politicians and bureaucrats but also enterprises will be sensitive to public opinion. All these groups have to limit the scope of their activities, lest they become the target of adverse public opinion. Enterprises, for example, are initially hesitant, but once a trend which requires a response emerges clearly, they firmly implement the necessary measures.

6 Reclaiming nationalism

Introduction

By the early 1990s, over half a century after the end of the Second World War, Japan had begun to regain its self-confidence. Nationalism re-emerged as a backdrop to the politics of economic superpower. This manifested itself in a number of different ways: in attempts to move beyond the humiliating experience of the war, as an expression of self-confidence from a technologically advanced economic giant, in efforts to protect and cultivate traditional Japanese culture, and even through the promotion of a vision with which to lead the world into the twenty first century. Japan wanted to remove the 'enemy country' clause from the UN Charter; this was a legitimate attempt to mitigate memories of its own wartime humiliation. Ishihara Shintarō wanted to limit American demands for restrictions on the Japanese export of semiconductors; this was an expression of self-confidence from a technologically advanced economic superpower (Ishihara and Morita, 1990). Japan opposed the liberalization of rice importation, arguing that the natural environment, an integral part of Japanese culture, would be destroyed. This demonstrated the complexity of Japan's nature-loving culture (Inoue, 1992). In the futuristic comic, *The Silent Navy*, the Japanese stole a nuclear submarine and used it to build a global nation, to achieve world peace. This reflected Japan's hidden desire to promote a vision of the future (Kawaguchi, 1988; Tokio, 1993). These examples all demonstrate that the re-emergence of Japanese nationalism has clear implications for the nature and process of Japan's internationalization.

Starting in the postwar period, Japan pursued what would later come to be referred to as the Yoshida doctrine. There were two major components to the strategy embodied in this doctrine: economic reconstruction and the adoption of a low profile in international political and military affairs. In Yoshida's view Japan's unconditional surrender and status as a defeated country gave it little opportunity to shape the emerging postwar order. It was therefore necessary for

Japan to adopt an uncontroversial position in international affairs that was not offensive to western nations, so that the Japanese people and government could be free to concentrate on the reconstruction of their country. Tokyo emphasized that it would prioritize economic reconstruction, adopt a low profile in the international arena, acquiesce in debate, and generally not stand out from other western states on issues of foreign policy.

Over the decades the Yoshida doctrine has been quietly set aside. The doctrine prompted Japanese citizens to focus on economic reconstruction, but it also encouraged them to reflect on their humiliating defeat in the war. Japan enjoyed overwhelming economic success in the postwar period. But its reliance on the United States' provision of military security not only invited American jealousy, but also provoked wider feelings of resentment. People sensed self-deception and hypocrisy in a foreign policy that extolled the virtues of pacifism, while tendering the provision of military security out to the American hegemon (Murakami, 1992). The Yoshida doctrine was initially an appropriate and pragmatic strategy for Japan to pursue. However, viewed in conjunction with Japan's subsequent economic success, there is no question that this strategy also created a perception that Japan was exploiting the negative aspects of its history, in order to claim a free ride under the US military security umbrella.

Imperial nationalism

Contemporary Japanese nationalism takes a variety of forms. Below, I identify three major streams of Japanese nationalism: imperial nationalism (a nationalism affiliated with the emperor system), nostalgic nationalism and progressive nationalism.

Imperial nationalism, as identified by Amino Yoshihiko, has three main elements: the idea of an island nation, the belief that rice farming is central to an understanding of Japanese culture, and the belief that Japan is racially homogenous (Amino, 1990; Miyata, 1990–1993). It is suggested that Japan has achieved a unique type of development precisely because it is an isolated island surrounded by ocean. Interactions with overseas cultures have been relatively limited, so Japan is unique in its development, just as kangaroos and koalas in Australia are unique, because Australia was isolated from continental evolutionary processes. This idea of an island nation includes elements that assert Japan's pureness and superiority. What might be termed 'rice farming fundamentalism' emphasizes the perceived dependence of Japan's economy on rice farming. This aspect was stressed under the emperor system, but ignored by those who subsisted by hunting and fishing. Lastly, it is claimed that from ancient times one racially homogenous group of people have lived on the Japanese archipelago, and that this homogeneity has made Japanese society pure and unique.

Amino is critical of these claims. He argues that they were for the most part advanced to facilitate acceptance of the emperor system, or at least heavily associated with the development of the modern emperor system. In refuting the first idea, Amino argues that even as an island nation, Japan's cultural interactions with other countries have been an integral part of its way of life since ancient times. In fact, not only did foreign interaction stimulate Japanese life, it was a driving force in Japanese processes of social formation. Amino further argues that support for rice farming fundamentalism reflects an anti-industrial view of the nation. Such views were held in the past by the ruling class, who attached importance to those farmers living on the plains, and neglected those who were engaged in commerce, manufacturing, fishing, forestry, and hunting. As for the belief in racial homogeneity, Amino argues that in ancient times the forefathers of the Japanese were descended from many different races, who came to Japan and lived and interbred together. Amino contends that this belief in racial homogeneity was promoted for the express purpose of building a modern Japanese nation-state, in response to the rebellions and conspiracies which were common in ancient and medieval Japan. This indicates that there have been processes of conquest and integration when groups have come into conflict. Such processes are comparable to those which occurred in medieval France when the Kingdom of Burgundy experienced repeated defeat, and was eventually incorporated into a kingdom that later became the core of modern France.

There are also some modern versions of the argument that Japan is an island nation with a unique culture. According to one such highly idealized example, the Japanese have lived in peace and harmony, building consensus in a natural environment characterized by evergreen trees on the land, and the meeting of warm and cold currents in the ocean. Umehara Takeshi's writings focus on ancient Japan, but can be considered a variation on this theme (Umehara, 1991). Support for rice farming fundamentalism has also resonated in contemporary Japanese trade policy, and in the arguments against the liberalization of Japan's rice market. It is argued that Japan can not sacrifice rice farming for the sake of international cooperation, because this particular form of agriculture lies at the core of Japanese culture. This argument is a combination of environmental concern and Japanese nationalism. It contends that rice farming, through its use of irrigation, contributes to the protection of the natural environment and the preservation of the Japanese landscape. The writings of Inoue Hisashi also reflect these values and ideas (Inoue, 1992). The belief in a racially homogenous nation is closely related to the theory of a homogeneous society, and is often said to be central to how the Japanese see themselves today. From this belief comes the argument that it is precisely because Japanese society is homogeneous that the crime rate is low, and conflicts can easily be resolved in harmonious fashion. Added to this explanation of Japanese society, Japanese believe that their high scores in IQ tests account for their high productivity, which in turn accounts for their high degree of competitiveness in industrial production. Some of Nakasone Yasuhiro's views derive from this type of thinking (Nakasone, 1986, 1992a, 1992b).

Such imperial nationalism was emphasized during the formation of the modern Japanese state, initially to promote the attainment of national goals such as economic development, and later, to promote wartime mobilization of human resources. This type of nationalism also resurfaced more recently in response to the liberalizing social and economic forces generated by the processes of international interdependence. For example, the Ministry of Education's curriculum guidelines were revised in 1989 to encourage schools to re-introduce the singing of the national anthem and the hoisting of the national flag in compulsory education. The revisions of 1989 made it clear for the first time that the Ministry wanted to formally 'guide' schools in this respect. These revisions included changes such as the abolition of social studies and the introduction of life studies to the curriculum of the lower grades in primary schools. Streaming and elective classes were introduced in junior high schools, and social studies were divided into geography/history and citizenship studies, with a view to promoting a better understanding of the emperor system and the Self Defense Forces (Sakamoto and Yamamoto, 1992).

The Japanese were deeply moved by the many ceremonies associated with the emperor system that were performed with the passing of Emperor Showa. The emotional response stemmed from the belief of a large number of Japanese that the Showa Emperor was an ardent supporter of modern Japan, especially during the period when Japan went to war, and during the period of reconstruction after defeat. This factor contributed significantly to the re-emergence of imperial nationalism (Kurihara, 1992). Of course, the Emperor's death also raised a number of questions with regard to his responsibility for the war. Critics contend that Emperor Showa should have acknowledged his responsibility to the Japanese people, almost all of whom cooperated with the war effort up to the very end. Many felt that some form of brief statement prior to the Emperor's death would have been appropriate, perhaps to the effect that he had wrongly led Japan into war, wrongly guided the war, or had been too slow in declaring Japan's surrender (Bitō, 1992).

Nostalgic nationalism

Nostalgic nationalism is premised upon an attempt to mitigate the shame of military defeat. Nostalgic nationalism attempts to rationalize and justify Japan's actions in the period up to the war by placing them, with greater historical care, in the context of Western domination in Asia. Starting in the mid-nineteenth century, Japan had been forced by Western powers to open its borders, had narrowly avoided colonization, had striven to catch up with the Western powers, and in the end had been driven into a war which shattered the Japanese nation and people. Explaining the historical context is necessary, because a country must be able to confront the implications of its own national identity. Accounts of Japan's history which do not do this misrepresent the spirit which lies behind its national identity. Proper self-understanding is psychologically necessary at both the individual and national level, but Japan has officially regarded its activities in the period leading up to the Second World War as aberrational. The problem with this approach is that it entails a denial of modern Japanese history. If Japan's historical conduct can be explained and justified rationally, so the nostalgic nationalist argument goes, then it is easier to give a more honest and consistent account of the continuities in Japan's expression of national identity. It is therefore easier for Japanese to understand their national identity as a consistent historical narrative stretching back over centuries. In other words, this is an approach that identifies the significance of nationalism in the construction of contemporary Japanese identity. Two authors who have explored this line of thought are Hayashi Fusao, who wrote *An Affirmative Theory of the Greater East Asian War* during the period of high economic growth, and Irie Takanori, who wrote *The Postwar Period of the Defeated*, during the period of economic superpower status. But nostalgic nationalist texts are not the exclusive preserve of conservative thinkers. There are writers on the left who approach the subject of nostalgic nationalism from alternative perspectives. An example is *'The Pacific War' and another 'Pacific War'*, written by Shinobu Seizaburō (Hayashi, 1964; Irie, 1989; Shinobu, 1988; Thorne, 1985),

I will briefly consider three narrative strands that contribute to this idea of a nostalgic nationalism. The first identifies modern Japanese history as unfolding against a backdrop of conflict between Asia and Europe (Inoguchi, 1991b). Modernization inevitably entailed a substantial degree of Westernization, which posed problems for the Japanese, who are racially, geographically and culturally part of Asia. There are historical parallels with the situation in Russia, where the process of modernization since Peter the Great have resulted in conflict between those who conceive of Russia as a Western power, and those who conceive of it as an Eastern power. Another related example is Singapore, where the government encouraged Singaporeans to revert to speaking Chinese instead of English at home. The government discovered that its decision to make English the official language had created a distance between itself and Asia, and had an adverse effect on efforts to promote Singaporean understanding of the Confucian values of family, discipline and harmony. Singaporeans were sensitive to the reactions of other Asian countries. But national identity has been an important issue for the Japanese regardless of the opinions of other Asians. Some believe that the Pacific War was a total war in which the Japanese tried to stand up against the racial discrimination and power of the Western nations. Hayashi Fusao, for example, argues that the Pacific War was a holy war to liberate Asia.

The second strand is a conspiratorial and realist narrative of international politics which conceives of the Pacific War as a trap set by Europe and North America, in which Japan was caught (Nihon kokusai seijigakukai, 1987–1988). The main problem in international politics in the first half of the twentieth century was that there was no dominant global power to replace Great Britain as it began to lose its hegemonic status in the early twentieth century. This became increasingly apparent after the First World War. In this environment, the United States, the USSR, Germany and Japan each considered themselves a possible candidate to replace the declining hegemon. Many states responded to the Great Depression by forming economic blocs. This economic reshaping of the world, in conjunction with racism, motivated the United States, Great Britain, France, the

Netherlands and others to contain Japan with economic sanctions. This effectively forced Tokyo to choose between a withdrawal from China and a full-blown war against the United States. This characterization of Japan's descent into war has clear parallels with A.J.P. Taylor's account of German foreign policy during the same period. Taylor understood Germany's participation in the Second World War as part of the conventional narrative of power politics: according to this 'realist' view, participants had no moral constraints and disregarded underlying ideological and racial considerations and prejudices (Taylor, 1961; Thorne, 1978). Another view offered by John Lukacs characterizes twentieth century international politics as the last dramatic series of convulsions before the fall of the Westphalian system of international relations. From this perspective, the twentieth century has been a tumultuous period with international politics testing the limits of a system developed in the seventeenth century. Viewed in longer-term historical context, the twentieth century should be understood as an age of extremes, and it could be argued that Japan was but one more of the extremists testing the limits of this increasingly obsolete system.

According to the third narrative strand of nostalgic nationalism, in view of Japan's postwar successes it is possible to argue that the Pacific War served a meaningful purpose. Yet, even while recognizing the advantage of a fresh start, this narrative still emphasizes the merit of retaining old institutions such as the emperor system, and preserving the Japanese political and economic system (Dower, 1990). This narrative places a special value on the preservation of the emperor system, arguing that Emperor's decision to commence the war ended the conflict between the army and navy, and averted a very possible coup d'etat and the bloody civil war that would certainly have ensued. (However, speculation about what kind of bloodshed a coup d'etat and civil war would have entailed, and what kind of political and economic system might have resulted, is academic. It is not possible to compare the costs and benefits of coup d'etat and/or civil war with Japan's decision to engage in interstate war, since it is impossible to estimate the cost of the former.) According to this narrative many Japanese leaders, even though they anticipated defeat, decided to go to war because they realized there were no other options. The likelihood of defeat made the conditions of surrender more generous and easier to accept than otherwise would have been the case, and made it possible for Japan to continue its existence.

Progressive nationalism

In the twentieth century, those societies which are perceived to be the most successful enjoy high levels of technological development, and possess adaptive economies and vibrant cultures. Technology enhances societal vitality and increases productivity. This trend will become more pronounced in the twenty-first century, as societies that consistently fail to innovate will deteriorate in efficiency and forsake opportunities for growth. In the twenty-first century, the global economy will become increasingly integrated, and each nation will face the challenge of correctly positioning itself in the global market and adapting proactively to the emerging trajectories of the global economy. The more closely integrated the global economy becomes, the more important culture becomes in providing a focus and rationale for economic activity. A vibrant culture values its own language, social values and social relations, and tries to harmonize these features with technological innovation and a strong economy. In the twenty-first century society will place less significance on the ability of leaders to appeal to the public. In the nineteenth and twentieth centuries this quality was necessary to provide charismatic political and diplomatic leadership in countries with a strong military capability. But in the new century continuous self-improvement, the quiet adjustment of interests, and a strong national identity will be the most critical factors (Nakasone, 1992b). These factors are recognized with some pride by Japanese as having been at the core of Japan's postwar success. There are high expectations for Japan, given its demonstration that it possesses these attributes in abundance, and is capable of further developing them in the future.

Karatsu Hajime is very positive about the future of Japanese technology. He believes that Japan should base its economic strategy on the pursuit of technological superiority, and that this is the way in which Japan can lead the world (Karatsu, 1990). Opinion polls overwhelmingly demonstrate not only that Japan's technological capability is a source of public pride, but that it is also considered the source of the nation's comparative advantage in competitive global markets (Hakuhōdō sogō kenkyūjo, 1992). In a similar vein, Iida Tsuneo, in *The Rediscovery of Japanese Strength*, states that continuous adaptability is the quality that has given the Japanese economy its edge (Iida, 1979). It then follows that the more the Japanese appreciate the degree to which their resource-poor economy is dependent on the stable development of the global economy, the more effective they will become at orienting their products towards the global market. In this regard Japan has an advantage because it has already had one such Industrious Revolution, during the Tokugawa period, in which it used technological innovation to overcome the traditional physical constraints imposed on the expansion of farmland by mountainous geography (Hayami, 1973, 1977, 1988; Hanley and Yamamura, 1977). During the Tokugawa period, Japan was able to nurture and reinforce its cultural foundations as a result of its relative isolation from the rest of the world. This was possible because basic needs were generally satisfied, and the government of the day was practical, opportunistic and stable in nature (Mizutani, 1992).

Contemporary Japan's national culture was formed by placing the achievements of the modern nation-state since the Meiji period atop the foundations which were laid during the Tokugawa period. From the Meiji period onwards, the mythology of the Japanese state, that is, the idea of an island nation, the belief that rice farming is central to an understanding of Japanese culture, and the belief that Japan is racially homogenous became accepted as the emperor system permeated the public sphere. This not only enhanced the legitimacy of the emperor system but added political stability and social resilience, which in turn created the basis for economic development. During the building of the modern state, many nationalist myths were promulgated. Elements drawn from these constructs, such as ideas of racial purity and superiority, had devastating results such as war, oppression and discrimination. But they also contributed to the successful creation of a national identity, something that had previously been absent. Such an identity, according to Nakasone Yasuhiro, is a *sine qua non* for a nation trying to maintain stability and prosperity in a turbulent and highly politicized international environment (Inoguchi, 1987b). In order not to be swept away, a country must discern and respond effectively to shifts in market and military forces.

Japan should be capable of such responses, but to make these responses meaningful, they must be articulated in support of an appropriate ideal of national identity. Japan's emerging progressive national identity is predicated on consultation, compromise and cooperation, in promotion of its technological innovation, economic adaptiveness, and cultural vibrancy (Inoguchi Kuniko, 1987). Initiatives in international politics have historically taken the form of attempts at military or economic hegemony. But Japan's emerging nationalism is novel in its progressive attempt to manage and lead international society more harmoniously. This progressive nationalism serves two functions for the Japanese; as a normative ideal of what a twenty-first century society should be, and a comforting reminder that Japan itself is already a successful prototype of such a society.

Reclaiming nationalism

In which directions have these types of nationalism lead Japan? Imperial nationalism, nostalgic nationalism, and progressive nationalism blend subtly, sometimes in harmony and at other times in disharmony. To develop this point, I examine tensions between these types of nationalism which came to the surface in the context of three issues: the liberalization of rice importation, the Emperor's visit to China, and the 1991 Gulf War.

The liberalization of rice importation

Many issues were addressed during the Uruguay Round of the GATT (General Agreement on Tariffs and Trade) negotiations, in particular agricultural trade protectionism and intellectual property rights. The liberalization of agricultural trade remained incomplete due to strong resistance from major agriculturally protectionist entities such as the United States, the European Community, and Japan. It was only at the end of 1992 that the US and the European Community started moving towards agreement on subsidies for oil seeds, which was a first in agricultural trade talks between these two political actors.

Until the Uruguay Round, Japan had been able to maintain a low profile, even with regard to its agricultural Achilles heel, the liberalization of rice importation. The objective of the GATT negotiations was to conclude agreements on tariffs affecting all kinds of goods, including rice. Japan had long been opposed to setting limits on tariffs, realizing that once rice trade was liberalized, Japan would face the risk of eventually halting its domestic rice production. Japan realized that it would face escalating demands to reduce its tariff levels, even though such tariffs could initially be set as high as 300 per cent (Saeki, 1990; Kojima, 1992). The Ministry of Agriculture, Forestry and Fisheries, together with agricultural organizations that benefited under the old tariff system, were strongly opposed to the liberalization, and were locked in conflict with the Ministry of Foreign Affairs and the Ministry of International Trade and Industry, which favored the liberalization of rice importation.

There were a variety of arguments for and against liberalization. One opposing view argued that Japan should not submit to international pressure because rice farming is a symbol of Japanese culture. This view is clearly related to a defence of the emperor system, which placed a great deal of importance on rice farming, and whose supporters do not believe in political concessions. According to another argument the protection of Japanese culture is related to the protection of Japan's natural environment. Inoue Hisashi took such a position, as did a number of environmentalists. Some rice farmers further argued that the government should only begin discussions on liberalization after a comprehensive and financially viable strategy had been developed, to help rice farmers adapt to alternative types of farming, or even to leave farming altogether. This position was held by many agricultural organizations, in particular the Central Committee of the National Agricultural Co-operatives. They were opposed to liberalization for as long as they believed that the government did not have a comprehensive agricultural strategy to which it was genuinely committed. Some opposed rice liberalization from a national security perspective, arguing that rice is a staple food for the Japanese. When Mori Ōgai, a novelist and medical doctor for the Imperial Army, inspected the food supply of soldiers on the front line for the first time, he identified rice as the most essential foodstuff. In 1992, when the SDF was part of the United Nations Transitional Authority in Cambodia, vacuum-packed rice was again identified as the most important food for Japanese soldiers.

On the other side of the debate, some private researchers advocated radical liberalization measures (Hayami, 1988, 1986; Kanō, 1984). This radical approach had some support in government ministries, with the exception of the Ministry of Agriculture, Forestry and Fisheries. For example, Hayami Yujirō insisted that radical liberalization was the only way to revive Japan's agriculture, and that this was eminently feasible. Kanō Yoshikazu promoted the idea that rice farmers should transform themselves into firms or stockholders, capable of effecting technological innovation both through large-scale capital investment, and the use of advanced technologies. The ultimate goal was and remains for Japan to have an advanced agricultural sector comparable to those in the Netherlands and Denmark. In fact, horticulture in the Netherlands and meat and dairy product industries in Denmark were established under poorer soil conditions than those which obtain in Japan. These societies have high levels of real income that are comparable to Japan's. Their experiences lend a considerable degree of support and confidence to those who argue that Japanese agriculture could also prosper through the pursuit of appropriate initiatives.

Given the trend towards regionalization in North America and Europe, and the prospects for growth in the Asia-Pacific, there were tentative plans in the early 1990s for the regionalization of the Asia-Pacific economies. There were also discussions within Japan as to how this incipient regionalism might contribute to Japan's attainment of complete regional foodstuff self-sufficiency. These plans entailed an improvement in the supply of rice, vegetables and fish from China and Southeast Asia to Japan. Both were developing rapidly, and sectorally appropriate reciprocal efforts to maintain and strengthen the universal free trade system were suggested. Moreover, a plan to grow Japanese types of rice in China and Southeast Asia was developed, particularly in Vietnam. Technology transfer took place under the auspices of official development assistance and the pursuit of joint private ventures. It was agreed that the rice produced through this system would be exported to Japan in times of need. Such plans led to further incremental initiatives to extend the scope of regional self-sufficiency to energy and industrial products, in cooperation with Australia and Indonesia with regard to the former, and in cooperation with China and ASEAN countries with regard to the latter. This is a progressive method of ensuring that food supplies are maintained, even as agricultural trade liberalizes and the universal free trade system continues to develop. But it is important to note that a number of nationalist considerations featured in the debate on the liberalization of rice importation.

The Emperor's visit to China

Emperor Showa reputedly very much wanted an opportunity to visit China, because of his involvement in the Sino-Japanese war and the indescribable pain and suffering inflicted by Japan on the Chinese. But when he died in 1990 his wish went unfulfilled. Japan's current Emperor was only able to visit China in October 1992. This was an historic occasion, as a Japanese Emperor had never before visited China. In the period leading up to the visit, many opinions were voiced, both in support and opposition (Asahi shinbun, 18 August, 1992). Few issues have divided Japanese opinion as sharply as that of the Emperor's potential visit to China. It must also be acknowledged that Japan's national self-respect and sense of place in the world were the fundamental issues which were at stake with regard to the visit. Opposition to the visit manifested itself in a number of ways:

1. It was customary, from ancient to medieval times, that when Japanese visited China, in both official and private capacities, it was to pay tribute. Those who opposed the Emperor's visit argued that the visit could give Beijing the impression that this tributary relationship was being revived.

2. Because the Japanese had inflicted an enormous amount of pain and suffering on the Chinese during World War II, there was extensive discussion as to whether the Emperor's visit should also entail an apology. It was eventually decided that this would be unnecessary, since the Peace and Friendship Treaty had been already signed.

3. The visit could have given the impression that Japan accepted or endorsed China's suppression of human rights and democracy, as demonstrated by the Tiananmen incident. Commentators who made this objection noted that, according to the constitution, the Japanese Emperor is not allowed to play a political role.

4. As the war was fought on Chinese soil, it was argued that the Emperor should address his 'royal words' not only to mainlanders, but also to Taiwanese people who left the mainland after the conclusion of the war. Opponents insisted that the visit would ignore the claims to legitimacy of the Taiwanese people. Those opposed were especially against the Emperor visiting the part of China currently ruled by the Chinese Communist Party, as it played a substantial role in Japan's defeat.

5. There was a danger that the visit would be interpreted as a signal that Japan was willing to expand the amount of official development assistance and direct investment needed by China to sustain and accelerate its rapid economic growth. It was felt that such rapid social and economic change could trigger political instability.

6. The Emperor's trip might be misconstrued as Japanese acceptance of China's military expansion. This was particularly worrisome given that China was willing to support its claim of sovereignty over the Nansha Islands with military reinforcements.

7. The Emperor's visit could convey the impression that priority was being given to Sino-Japanese relations at a time when the Japan-U.S. relationship was stagnating and Russo-Japanese relations were frozen. It would be to Japan's detriment to convey such an

impression in the post-Cold War world. In particular, some were opposed to the visit because it might heighten existing Western concerns that Japan was attempting to develop an alternative international role for itself, premised on the development of pan-Asian solidarity.

Thus, issues relating to Japan's national self-respect and sense of place were critical to the deliberations of those who were opposed to the royal visit to China. It was also natural for opinion in favor of and against the visit to be split roughly evenly. This is because, in addition to issues of self-respect and place, Japan also had to consider how Sino-Japanese relations should be characterized in a rapidly changing international environment. Moreover, since it was the Emperor who would visit China, the issue of the emperor system itself also became a major focus for debate. This is not to say that the debate on the Emperor's visit provided evidence of a re-emergence of nationalism centered on the emperor system; the opinions which were expressed related more to strategic considerations of how the status of the Emperor would impact in the diplomatic realm.

In order to hear the full range of informed opinion on the matter, then Prime Minister Miyazawa held approximately twenty interviews, with a diverse group of accomplished individuals, between the spring and summer of 1992. It is important to note, as we saw above, that opposition was presented from a variety of viewpoints. This willingness to express such a range of opposing opinions is, in itself, culturally rare. This can perhaps be attributed to the significance which the Ministry of Foreign Affairs traditionally attaches to Japan-U.S. relations, as well as the profound range of far-reaching diplomatic considerations at issue.

It was also clear that Prime Minister Miyazawa had his own ideas regarding Japanese diplomacy toward the United States. At that time, he gave serious thought to strengthening, albeit relatively, Japan's relations with other Asia-Pacific countries. But out of consideration for the United States, the Ministry of Foreign Affairs did not want to convey the impression that Japan was leaning towards Asia, or moving towards a new Sino–Japanese treaty. It sought to re-emphasize the value which Japan placed on cooperation between itself and the US, and on the diplomatic course established by the Japanese–American treaty. The Emperor was scheduled to visit China in the fall of 1992 and Prime Minister Miyazawa's visits to ASEAN countries were planned for the beginning of 1993. This meant that instead of visiting the US, which is customary when a new administration takes office, Miyazawa would instead visit ASEAN countries. In spite of the diplomatic ramifications of public opinion, a large proportion of which was not necessarily favorable, the Japanese government wanted to impress upon China its desire to overcome these obstacles, and its commitment to realizing the Emperor's visit. But it should also be noted that the nature and extent of opposition to the visit within Japan actually made it easier for the Japanese government to reassure those who were opposed to it. Given such widespread domestic opposition, it was easy for Japan to argue that it was clearly not about to embark on a new Asianist policy, to the detriment of its existing diplomatic ties and commitments to the US. The domestic political climate in response to the visit gave further credibility to Tokyo's reassurances that the foundations of Japan-U.S. cooperation were unshakable.

The Gulf War

Iraq's invasion and subsequent annexation of Kuwait in August 1990 also created a substantial foreign policy dilemma for Japan. This event brought the tensions in Japan's energy policy into sharp focus. Japan's first priority was the maintenance of friendly relations with both the American oil companies that have controlling interests in Gulf countries, and the American government, which protects these companies. A second priority was the maintenance of friendly relations with the Gulf countries themselves, and also with other oil producing states. It is clear that with regard to the issue of the Gulf War these two priorities were in conflict (Itagaki, 1991). Japan also had two further objectives with regard to energy policy; it needed to secure a more diverse portfolio of suppliers, and also to increase the proportion of energy which it produced domestically. For Japan, both the Gulf States which operate under American hegemony, and the other oil producing states such as Iraq and Iran are important. When the latter confront the United States, it is not, therefore, in Japan's interests for confrontation to lead to military conflict. However, Iraq's military invasion of Kuwait prompted the United States, acting under the banner of the UN and in accordance with Security Council Resolutions, to organize a military alliance with the twin aims of defeating Iraq and liberating Kuwait. It is here that Japan's dilemma began.

Since the Second World War the Gulf countries and Israel have been the key to American foreign policy in the Middle East. The former have oil, and the latter is a symbol which is vital to Jewish-American interests. The Gulf countries were founded by the British, and Saudi Arabia, in particular, is a large oil producing country that has friendly relations with the United States. American capital and mass media are very influential in Israel, and the Jewish diaspora wield substantial political and economic influence in the US. American Middle East policy had two aspects. Firstly, the US sought to forge protective alliances with selected Gulf countries who could guarantee predictable oil supply. Second, the US sponsored balances of power which would constrain states that aspired to a regional hegemony which could potentially disrupt the flow of oil to America from such friendly states. For example, when Egypt was the leader of the anti-Israeli Gulf countries, the United States tried to protect the interests of the other Gulf countries by concluding a treaty with imperial Iran. Similarly, when Iran became a revolutionary state and threatened the Gulf nations, the United States forged a *de facto* alliance with Iraq, and gave it substantial military aid. It is also suggested by some that the US induced Iraq into attacking Kuwait in order to give itself a pretext, under UN auspices, to crush Iraq's potential threat to regional stability (and to America's oil supply). Just prior to the conflict, the American ambassador sent the Iraqis a communique that could have been interpreted to mean that the US would tacitly accept Iraq's annexation of Kuwait. The resulting Iraqi invasion led to the eventual American liberation of Kuwait and subsequent invasion of Iraq, and American forces advanced to within a relatively short distance of Baghdad. Prior to the conflict, as the US mobilized support for the Gulf War, Japan became the target of significant international criticism.

The re-articulation of Japanese nationalism can be seen in Japan's perception of and response to the Gulf War. Three principal motives conditioned Japan's response (Inoguchi, 1991a). The first was concern with regard to the prospects for international order in the post Cold War world. The second related to the lessons which Japan had learned from its own history, and the third was Japan's confidence in its economic power at this time. These three sentiments all reflected Japan's reemerging nationalism in different ways.

Japan's concern with regard to post-Cold War international order derived from its perception that the emerging order was rather chaotic. On a worst-case scenario Japan believed it to be possible that the foundations of its postwar international peace and prosperity could be undermined. It should be remembered that at this time there was legitimate concern about the future of the Japan–U.S. Security Treaty in the post-Cold War world. Japan was also concerned at the possibility that the United States, the global hegemon and Japan's most important ally, might prematurely lose its influence, before another responsible and willing hegemon emerged. Japan's concerns stemmed from America's failure to reduce fiscal and trade deficits, its decline in manufacturing competitiveness, and its loss of momentum in the field of technological innovation. Another issue at this time was that of 'Japan-bashing'. This issue obviously related to Japan's role and identity in the international economy and provoked a strong Japanese response. Japan-bashing was seen as a manifestation of international jealousy and resentment at Japan having joined the ranks of the powerful and developed countries. Against this background of uncertainty and criticism there was a lively debate within Japan on how to manage the issue of re-asserting national identity. Some insisted that Japan should continue to adhere strictly to its policy of pacific constitutionalism, and continue to promote the ideal of peaceful international conflict resolution. Others advocated disengagement from military conflicts such as the Gulf War, a view based at least partly on anti-American sentiment. It was also strongly argued that Japan should practice a policy of absolute isolationism, and seek to distance itself altogether from intractable international issues.

Of the many things that Japan has learned from its history, three primary lessons stand out from all the others. The first is considered skepticism about the effectiveness of projecting military power abroad for prolonged periods of time. This lesson is based on Japanese military experience since the Meiji period; Japan's previous military adventures have ultimately only brought comprehensive defeat and necessitated major reconstruction. In contrast, Japan's exclusive postwar focus on economic development has brought peace and prosperity. The second principal lesson is a debt to history, that is, a sense that Japan bears a heavy burden of responsibility for the devastation it wrought in other Asian Pacific nations during the Second World War. Japan is reluctant to involve itself militarily in international affairs in recognition of this historical debt, and this reluctance intensified as nations from the Asia-Pacific voiced their concern at Japan's potential re-militarization in conjunction with the Gulf War. The final lesson is that of anti-colonialism. It might appear contradictory that Japan should advocate anti-colonialism, since Japan has itself embraced such practices in the past, and indeed continues to be accused of 'neo-colonialism' by the radical left. Seen through some Japanese eyes, however, Japan's actions were defensive, and conceived in response to Western colonialism.

In the postwar period, anti-colonialist and anti-expansionist sentiment has also intensified. Postwar anti-colonialism has partly emerged in tandem with Japan's relationship with the United States. The American occupation of Japan and the ongoing American military presence under the auspices of the Japan–US Security Treaty have often generated anti-colonialist sentiment among Japanese. Such sentiment is especially palpable when Washington attempts to impose its views and policies on Tokyo. With regard to the Gulf War, for example, the Japanese readily acknowledge that Iraq's actions were reckless and barbaric, but they also wonder if the punishment exceeded the crime. Such a sentiment has foundations in Japan's perception of its own historical experience at the hands of US power. Moreover, this sentiment is not exclusively Japanese: it is shared by all Asians.

Japan's economic confidence may appear to be at odds with the insecurity and concern which I identified above as an aspect of Japan's response to the Gulf War. However, Japan was confident because it had already successfully adjusted to two previous oil crises, and believed itself to be capable of dealing with the problems generated by the Gulf War, which effectively amounted to a third oil crisis. The US tried to persuade Japan to participate militarily in the Gulf War by reminding the Japanese of their dependence on Gulf oil. Japan's response was that a stable supply of oil could be attained through market mechanisms, rather than through military intervention. Japanese Consulate-General in New York Hanabusa Masamichi expressed such views in a speech, and he got a certain degree of criticism from the Americans. Japan was at this time generally confident of its economic competitiveness. To this extent it was natural to advocate a 'wait and see' policy, rather than send in the troops to secure oil, because the Japanese realized that there was a high level of uncertainty in world politics. This confidence encouraged Tokyo to articulate its own view of the optimal balance between cost-sharing and human sacrifice, with the government eventually opting for a policy of non-military participation. We can also say that Japanese confidence was based on nationalistic feelings which intensified as Japanese self-respect grew and as foreign criticism of Japan increased. In such an environment, it was inevitable that opposition with a basis in national self-reassertion would be the response to America's call for Japanese military participation in the Gulf War.

Thus, when we look at issues such as the liberalization of rice importation, the Emperor's visit to China, and the Gulf War, we find that nationalist sentiments were being expressed increasingly clearly. Imperial, nostalgic and progressive nationalisms have for the most part been articulated in combination. The ultimate form and trajectory of Japanese nationalism in the twenty-first century will have a substantial impact, not only on the Japanese political system, but also on international relations. This is a result of Japan's increased assertion of its cultural characteristics and sense of uniqueness, in tandem with and in progressive response to globalizing world trends. It is not yet clear whether these processes will lead to the realization of a progressive or more traditional variant of nationalism, but, whichever form comes to predominate, nobody will be able to ignore the implications of Japan's re-assertion of self-identity. As we can see from the examples which I have discussed above, three forms of nationalism have been partially articulated at both governmental and societal levels. As yet, no single form has emerged to predominate and serve as the exclusive basis for the re-assertion of Japanese national identity.

7 The contemporary Japanese political system: a comparative analysis

Introduction

There are two primary weaknesses in the approaches of those who study the contemporary Japanese political system (Inoguchi, 1994b). One weakness is that they seldom make use of historical understanding and insight. They approach the Japanese political system as if history began in 1945. This approach sometimes shares elements with the study of German history. For Maier, for example, 'All German history is about the history of the Third Reich, and that is the end of it' (Maier, 1988). The other weakness is that in comparing the Japanese political system with others, they tend to use an idealized conception of Western politics as their benchmark. This conception emerged in eighteenth to nineteenth century Europe and North America, but it is important to note that at that time it only applied to the activities of small sections of the populations of these countries. However, instead of using political reality in these countries at that time as a benchmark, scholars often seem to abstract the political philosophy that underpinned the activities of this small elite from its context. This ideal is then appropriated as the basis for analysis and criticism of Japan's contemporary political reality. It can sometimes seem as if the sole task of Japanese political science is to engage in this activity. In all fairness Western political theories, due to their long tradition and richness, could serve Japanese political scientists well if they use them as stepping stones to reach a new level of analysis. In the 1980s and the 1990s, it appears that the analytical frameworks used by Western scholars have been adapted in Japan with only limited difficulties and changes. The bottleneck to theoretical progress in Japan is due to a lack of effort on the part of Japanese scholars.

First, despite the existence of a substantial literature on pre-war Japanese history, specialists in Japanese politics tend to limit their studies to the postwar period. Moreover, they assume that Japan's response to its defeat in the Second World War created a watershed in the organization of the Japanese political system. As a result, there has been a division of labor in academia: historians study prewar Japan, and political scientists study postwar Japan. Unfortunately, it appears that the political scientists have learned little from their counterparts in historical studies. This shortcoming could be attributed to the traditional vertical division of labor among Japanese researchers, or it could be a byproduct of the sentiment that Japan is 'leaving Asia and joining Europe.' Whatever the reasons, until recently it was relatively uncommon for political scientists studying Japan to adopt an historical perspective. For example, it has been rare for discussion of the contemporary Japanese political system to be conducted from an historical perspective that extends to an analysis of the Tokugawa period (Mizutani, 1972).

Second, until recently research in comparative politics has been very weak in Japan. The major objective of comparative politics has been to describe political conditions within foreign countries. This is in part due to the Japanese tradition of producing quasi-bureaucratic country studies to facilitate a state-led accumulation of information on the world outside. These studies are premised on the collection and detailed description of facts. In the tradition of country studies, law and economics are considered principal areas in civil servant examinations, while history and foreign languages are treated as supplements in general education, with political science belonging to the latter category. Even now, comparative specialists do not conduct comparative political analysis as such but, rather, engage in more descriptive analyses of foreign affairs. Comparative politics, as an aspect of the study of international relations or international politics, is mostly a general study of foreign policy or regional studies. This descriptive tendency may be due to the strong influence of Ranke on Japanese academia. This more nuanced consideration of historical particularity and empirical detail is also, in part, a reaction against the abstract, systematic yet highly politicized dogmas of Marxism, which was highly influential in Japanese political science from 1917 to 1989. Based on the perspective provided by the sociology of knowledge, this emphasis on description might also be the outcome of Japan having always occupied a marginal position in the world. Japan has never led the world militarily, economically, or intellectually.

Effective intellectual leadership requires two things: one must be prepared to make assertions that one believes to have universal validity, and also have the cultural confidence to do so. The assertion of universality entails a belief that one's own thinking is valid throughout the world. Cultural confidence entails a strong attachment to the values, thought processes, and forms of cultural expression which constitute one's group. Japan has seldom made claims which it believes to have universal purchase. 'The whole world under one roof' claim, made during the war, may sound universal in intent, but was in fact geographically limited and impractical. Furthermore, although the Japanese undoubtedly possess cultural confidence, they have not articulated this confidence in a fashion which has engaged or impressed other cultures. Leadership and cultural confidence rarely occur together, and general intellectual leadership, on an international scale, has not been thoroughly investigated in the social sciences. It is difficult to find an intellectual framework for Japanese political science that is equivalent to that which emerged in the United States and gave birth to comparative politics at the peak of Pax Americana in the 1950s and 1960s. Pax Americana entailed the view that the American ideal of a free and democratic society should be promoted worldwide (Ricci, 1987).

I have suggested that it is necessary to position the modern Japanese political system in a more appropriate historical context, and distance ourselves from a research methodology that compares the Japanese system with an idealized and historically decontextualized political conception based on North American and European political experience. This chapter attempts this by deploying an East Asian comparative historical perspective. Such an attempt will highlight both the light and dark sides of the Japanese political system. So far most studies of the Liberal Democratic Party, which for a long time remained the single party in power, have compared the LDP with similar Western political parties. I also think it is important to compare these similar parties, and I have taken the same approach in my research. My point however is that we must not limit ourselves to such a specific way of thinking. Unless we have sophisticated viewpoints, we cannot have a deeper and sharper understanding of the Japanese political system. As an example of the former case, see Pempel (1990).

The political economy and political culture perspectives

How should we go about constructing a framework for the comparative political analysis of East Asia? Here, we want to adopt a framework that integrates an analysis of political economy with an analysis of political culture (Inoguchi, 1988). An integrated theory is needed to understand state-society dynamics, and the dialectical relationship between ruler and ruled. Political-economic and political-cultural perspectives allow us to identify two critical elements of a political system.

The first element is the accumulation of social surplus (Offe, 1984, 1985). As long as the public sector remains separate from the private sector, a state must raise a surplus from society in order to be able to administer its political system. In the modern world, it is very difficult to raise such amounts without collecting taxes. Exceptions include the Gulf nations and Brunei, which are able to extract substantial amounts of revenue from their oil resources. In these cases states tend to govern arbitrarily because they do not have to collect significant levels of tax from the public. Moreover, without the continuing prosperity of the private sector, it is difficult for a state to continue to exist in a healthy form. Let us for convenience refer to the public sector as the state, and the private sector as society. Of course state and society overlap in the modern world, but when it comes to taxes, these two entities have opposing goals. The state wants to collect part of the output generated by society to finance its expenditures on governance, while society is generally opposed to taxation. When state governance is widely regarded as legitimate, or when there is a national crisis, then societal opposition to taxation is comparatively low. It is common for the state to encourage and facilitate productive economic activity, as this makes tax collection easier. The accumulation of social surplus is indispensable. This aspect of politics is best examined from a political-economic perspective.

However, the dearth of political-economic analysis has been one of the greatest shortcomings in the study of contemporary Japanese politics. One of the reasons for this weakness is that the study of political science and economics has been separated, due to an unfortunate tradition of vertical isolation and segregation in the academic world. But it is not just political scientists who should be responsible for this separation. Economists, who have limited their research within the narrow confines of neo-classical economic theory, also have to take joint responsibility. Another reason is that the rapid decline in the intellectual integrity of Marxism has made it difficult for non-Marxist theories of political economy to be accepted. In addition to these factors, the preferences of the Japanese state were an important determining factor. The managers of the Japanese state were deeply concerned about the vulnerability of energy and food supplies, and anxious to secure Japan's access to the world marketplace. These managers believed that general economic management should be determined by the national interest as opposed to sectoral political pressure from special interest groups. Thus, approaches to the study of political economy which diverged from the promotion of the national interest have been quickly dismissed as extraneous.

The second critical element of a political system is the acquisition of political legitimacy (Giddens, 1984, 1985). Ultimately, governance does not endure without the trust of the people. Securing political legitimacy is a crucial issue for a state, because in the end a sum of complexly-weighted social preferences determine the nature of a society. In comparative politics, this aspect can be studied by adopting a political culture perspective. The ways in which political legitimacy is acquired, accorded and lost are all central themes in the study of political culture. The other great weakness in the study of contemporary Japanese politics is that although there is a literature on political culture, political culture has often been treated as a smaller aspect of the theory of political process or the theory of political behavior. A major exception is Kyōgoku (1983). It can sometimes appear as if the study of political culture has been incorporated within the broader study of political procedure, or the theory of political action, both of which examine how political-cultural factors impact on the political process. Such studies typically analyze support for political parties, regimes, and cabinets (prime ministers).

Many social scientists have distanced themselves from this research issue, perhaps because of the ambivalence surrounding the emperor system in the postwar period. In fact, the study of the emperor system in Japan more often deals with the historical emperor system than with the recent emperor system. Moreover, it is a subject preferred by historians, cultural anthropologists and sociologists, rather than by political scientists. This is perhaps related to the preferences of the administrators of the Japanese state, who in light of this existing ambivalence, are keen to leave the issue of the emperor system untouched. However, although the issue of the emperor system does not necessarily come to the fore, it has the potential to be radically politicized because it is directly related to the accumulation of surplus and the acquisition of legitimacy.

The accumulation of social surplus and the acquisition of political legitimacy are fundamental to the ability of a political system to sustain itself. It must therefore be possible to build a framework for comparative politics which is premised on an analysis of these two factors. We can say that Marx focused on the former element, and Weber on the latter. Marx demonstrated the central role of political economy, by examining the way in which different modes and relations of production accelerate capital accumulation and exacerbate unequal capital distribution. Weber discussed types of political legitimacy (charismatic, traditional, legal, etc.) and how one could become dominant, thus determining the nature of a political system. Obviously, the world has changed since Marx and Weber, and it is necessary to refine and extend the perspectives which they contributed. There is a strong need for a more fundamental comparative political analysis that examines the impact which political economy and political culture have on the constitution of state and society. The study of contemporary Japanese politics is burdened and impoverished by its lack of appreciation of the perspectives provided by political economy and political culture. The study of contemporary Japanese politics is also limited in scope, with an excessive focus on political systems, processes, and behaviors, all within a narrowly defined political domain.

To typify political studies of the East Asia region, Chalmers Johnson provides a political economy perspective, and Lucian Pye a political culture perspective (Johnson, 1981; Pye, 1966, 1989). Johnson discusses how the Japanese state identified industries whose protection and promotion were key to the development of the national interest. He explains how Japan developed a thoroughgoing industrial policy which entailed the provision of administrative guidance, and the channeling of financial and human resources to these targeted industries. The state also supported technological development and market exploration, and conducted market-friendly interventions. Lucian Pye uses the concept of political culture to discuss how, in China, perceptions of political legitimacy have determined the nature of the political system, led to the consolidation of power, given the holder of this power authority, and served to facilitate the implementation of the values of the ruler.

Karl Wittfogel's work on China combines the perspectives of political economy and political culture. He demonstrates how the need for large-scale agricultural irrigation contributed to the emergence of despotic rulers. Antonio Gramsci's hegemonic theory is Marxist, but the emphasis is not on economic determinism, but rather on cultural hegemony and its broader promulgation throughout society. In this regard, Gramsci also integrates the perspectives of political economy and political culture. Claus Offe has also emphasized the significance of the accumulation of social surplus and the acquisition of political legitimacy (Wittfogel, 1957, Offe, 1984). I want to position the study of Japanese politics within an East Asian comparative political framework by drawing on elements from these studies.

A theory of East Asian political economy

Many students of East Asian politics give a great deal of attention to the study of political economy. They do so mainly because they want to explain the substantial economic growth which the region has enjoyed. Political economists attempt to explain the roles which governments play in economic management. How do states promote the accumulation of social surplus and what do they do with this surplus? States are forced to finance their own activities unless the societies which they govern are able to generate a surplus through industrial and commercial activity. For example, states can generate their own surplus by raising revenue from trade and mining. In the case of the United States at the beginning of the nineteenth century, a substantial proportion of state revenue came from tariffs. The governments of Gulf countries automatically receive a fixed portion of the revenue from state-owned oil companies, whose management is entrusted to foreign capital.

States can facilitate the accumulation of social surplus by creating an unfettered environment in which profit-making and free enterprise are encouraged. This does not mean that the state remains idle. When the state sets rules and acts as an arbitrator in settling social disputes, it is effectively enabling the profit-making activities of a particular society. When a state intervenes in the market more than is necessary, it constrains free enterprise. One of the reasons that leading East Asian economies (and Asia-Pacific economies) enjoyed so much success in the 1980s was the promotion of economic liberalization and the deregulation of foreign investment.

Second, a state must collect a certain proportion of social surplus as tax in order to fund state activity. States must enjoy political legitimacy in order to collect taxes effectively. Political democratization in East Asia during the 1980s in part reflected the intention of states to strengthen their tax base. After making an initial decision that it would be necessary to increase state revenues, East Asian states utilized their enhanced financial circumstances to bolster their political legitimacy, and became more active in public policy. Moreover, when states deem it necessary, the surplus can also be reallocated to allow for military and welfare expenditure. If states are unable to deter potential foreign invaders, then they can not guarantee political stability; if states can not provide financial assistance to citizens on low incomes, then social unrest may arise.

Gilbert Rozman has provided a useful framework for the comparative analysis of East Asian political systems. He identifies three models: a Western model (a society-dominant model for Europe and North America, particularly Britain and America), a Northern model (a state-control model, applicable to countries such as the former USSR), and an Eastern model (a state-dominant model, applicable to countries such as Japan) (Rozman, 1990; Wade, 1990).

In the Eastern, or state-dominant model, whilst the state does not rigidly control society, it does play a substantial guiding role, and there is not a strong rights culture or a particularly robust civil society. One example of the difference between the Eastern and Western models lies in the notion of 'administrative guidance' (Morita, 1988). The bureaucracy tends to supervise many aspects of life in the private sector, even when there is no legislation which expressly permits it to do so. In the Western model, this kind of state behavior is unpopular and regarded as government interference, but in the Eastern model it is common. This difference in attitudes towards 'administrative guidance' explains why some western commentators consider Japanese governance to be a form of 'soft authoritarianism' (Johnson, 1986). Leaders of Eastern societies sometimes manipulate cultural ideas to consolidate their power (Pye, 1989; Van Wolferen, 1989). For example, leaders attempt to obtain the obedience and cooperation of their people by presenting themselves as role models. This is why Eastern leaders will often try to highlight the simplicity of their lifestyles. Another feature of this model is the development of bureaucracy as a critical tool for the implementation of government policies.

The current Japanese model could be characterized as comprising elements of both the Eastern and the Western models. Similarly, Maoist China comprised elements of both the Eastern and the Northern models, although elements of the Western model can also be discerned in contemporary Chinese governance. There have always been significant variations within the Eastern model, but increasingly, variations are occurring as a result of greater interactions between Eastern and Western countries. The fact that the Eastern model (a state-dominant model) is significantly different from the Western model (a society-dominant model) and the Northern model (a state-control model) becomes very clear when we think of the historical characteristics of East Asia.

As Rozman points out, the key issue in the study of political economy is the impact that state economic activity and civil economic activity have on each other. It is therefore necessary to study the impact of industrial policy, trade policy, monetary policy, and regulation policy on government-industry relations. There are two important objectives to policy-making: the first is the maximization of social welfare, and the second is the maximization of profit (Miller, 1987).

The first objective applies to situations in which policy is formulated to maximize social welfare, such as the provision of subsidies or the raising of tariff and non-tariff barriers, in order to protect industries that are losing their international competitiveness, and to prevent unemployment from becoming a major social problem. Underlying such policies is a strong belief that the maintenance of social and political stability will be difficult if preventative action is not taken. Successful developmentalist states must make it clear that they are prepared to sponsor and protect industries and enterprises which they believe to have a viable long-term future, and that they are prepared, at least to a certain extent, to underwrite potential short–term economic losses. By doing so they create a climate of reassurance and confidence.

The second objective applies to situations in which fledgling industries remain uncompetitive in international markets. Without the use of subsidies to protect these new ventures from foreign imports, and tariff and non-tariff barriers, they would be crushed in the early stage of development, even though they have long-term prospects for growth. Developmentalist states intervene and aggressively promote growth in such industries. This approach attempts to maximize national income by anticipating long-term growth for these industries. In doing so, the government demonstrates to everyone that it is prepared to support innovation, thereby hopefully stimulating entrepreneurial behaviour.

The latter objective is more prevalent in Japan than in European and North American countries. The first objective is more concerned with the present and oriented towards the weak, and the second more with the future, and oriented towards the (potentially) strong. The time frame for policy is longer in Japan than in European and North American countries, and in the past future-oriented policy planning has been one of Japan's strengths. Japanese companies are not pressured extensively by their shareholders to deliver profits. This allows the government to take a long-term approach when providing guidance to companies. However, it is apparent from time-series observations and an analysis of Japanese tariff rates that Tokyo has not consistently and continuously pursued this industrial and trade policy for the development of infant industries. Even though government interventions based on the second objective have been effective for the most part, this alone does not present a complete picture of government intervention.

In order to examine the nature of relations between government and industry in Japan more closely, I will utilize three models. The first is a bargaining model. This model demonstrates that both the government and enterprises tend to behave according to market principles (Kōsai, 1987; Samuels, 1987; Friedman, 1988). The second is a semi-command model (Zysman, 1984; Perkins, 1987). The third is a network model. Chalmers Johnson's 'Japanese economic model' is closer to this model (1986). While Johnson's approach is political-economic, Dore's approach is more political-cultural than political-economic (Dore, 1985, 1987). The semi-command model assumes that the government directs industry through the implementation of relatively authoritarian regulation policies which are accepted because there is a paternalistic relationship between government and industry. In terms of Rozman's taxonomy, which I discussed earlier, this could also be characterized as a pure state-dominant model. For example, when there is a shortage of investment funds, the government directs industries with the potential for future growth by encouraging low-interest loans via administrative guidance. In South Korea, the government uses this type of loan more often than subsidies. In Taiwan the government uses subsidies more often than loans. Economic governance in East Asia possesses attributes which are also common to command economies. In this model of economic management the two roles of government, monitoring and nurturing, are interlinked. The government provides administrative guidance by monitoring market rules and penalizing transgressors, but also plays a role in market formation and the nurturing of industry. This model helps us to understand the Japanese state and society from the 1930s to 1960s. It is also helpful because it allows us to contrast the Japanese state and society with its European and North American counterparts.

It is also possible to differentiate countries according to whether they are continental or peripheral (Bitō, 1986; Wolf and Hanley, 1985). According to this approach, continental European countries such as Russia, and continental Asian countries such as China, both have strong elements of state dominance. In contrast, countries such as Britain, France, and Japan, located on the periphery of the Eurasian landmass, have strong elements of society dominance. But Japan, compared with Britain, also has strong elements of state dominance. This arises from the coincidence of the age of extremes with the period of Japanese modernization, which has resulted in these characteristics being embodied in the Japanese political system to a much greater degree. Unlike new continental countries such as the US, those who note the similarities between Japan and Britain tend to emphasize family, blood relations, such as inheritance, and the flexible application of laws.

As its name suggests, the bargaining model assumes that both government and industry develop relationships through bargaining. According to this view, both government and industry have a mutual give-and-take relationship, supporting changes in the other's behavior as each responds to changes in the market in which both are actors. This implies that society has its own principles of behavior and sense of order, and moreover, that both government and industry are essentially equal. This explanation of the role of state and society from the mid-Tokugawa period to the 1980s and 1990s has become increasingly popular (Bitō, 1992; Mizutani, 1972). This approach emphasizes the similarities between European and North American countries. Japan is different because the age of extremes coincided with the period of Japanese state-building, as a result of which there developed a tradition of strong government control over the mobilization of social resources and the mobilization for war. Even under the bargaining model, the state's ability to organize is institutionally and legally much stronger than that of society. In comparison with European and North American countries, particularly continental European countries, the edifice of Japanese governance from the Tokugawa period to the present has not been a magnificent, well-planned building but rather a bungalow to which successive extensions have been added as it has become necessary. This has loosened the degree of state control while increasing the applicability of the bargaining model to Japan.

The third model conceives of both government and industry as members of a social network. This is based on the assumption that in East Asian societies individual behavior is largely determined by the collective principles of families, work places, and village or town communities rather than Western-style individualism. Both government and industry tend to place an emphasis on long-term relationships and self-imposed standards of conduct. There is an underlying assumption that societies form an organic whole. While the bargaining model views government and society as mutually distinct, the network model identifies horizontal communities that span both spheres. This model vividly illustrates the differences between Japanese society and its counterparts in Europe and North America, particularly the United States and Great Britain. This is because the model is premised on the view that social interactions generate a quasi-community (Murakami, Kumon and Sato, 1979; Kumon and Rosovsky, 1992). Robert Putnam's observation that strong traditions of civic community in Northern Italy have made democracy operate well is closer to a long-term and multi-dimensional approach. The traditions of civic communities are strengthened when a people behaves according to 'generalized reciprocity.' People do not think in the following way: 'I will help you because I have more power than you,' or 'If you are going to do anything for me now, I will also do something for you.' Rather, they think that 'I will do something for you now because I believe some day you may also do something for me' (Putnam, 1993). This can often be seen in corruption cases involving bureaucracy and industry, and in the role of the *zoku giin* who act as go-betweens amongst bureaucratic, industrial, and political groups. These relationships create an impression of untidiness rather than intimate cohesion. In Japan this network is more flexible and differentiated than those in China and South Korea because it is more exposed to market forces. Kinship and regional relations are much stronger in these countries than in Japan.

The pivotal element in all three models is the effective management of government-industry relations. For example, according to Chalmers Johnson, government goal-setting and policy implementation for the purposes of economic development are generally in harmony with profit maximization, stable labor-management relations, the independence of the bureaucracy, the independence of government from large firms, administrative guidance, industrial groups such as the *keiretsu* and *zaibatsu*, and the control of foreign investment (Johnson, 1986). The education system is egalitarian in nature, and this is possible because of political socialization and equal income distribution (Kabashima, 1984). Political socialization creates a labor force that is able to produce guaranteed levels of quality. Relative equality of income distribution softens dissatisfaction with the more authoritarian policy measures which the government adopts. It also makes it easier for the government to portray itself as a non-partisan guardian of the national interest, which is above party politics. East Asian countries, particularly Japan, Taiwan, and South Korea have relatively equal income distributions when compared to other countries. These factors allow governments to obtain public support for and understanding of their decision to make national security the first priority, economic development the second priority, and freedom and democracy the third priority. As income levels have increased in East Asian countries, European and North American countries have become more vocal in their protests concerning the human rights records and democratic credentials of these countries. But in many East Asian countries, influential actors advocate the continuation of administrative guidance on such issues instead of the seeking of immediate solutions. Such commentators believe that East Asian countries will naturally move in that direction when their economies reach a stage at which it is appropriate to accommodate change. Their opinions are grounded in the strong conviction that the above order of priorities is best left untouched (Inoguchi, 1989b).

A theory of East Asian political culture

It is the use of the political culture perspective that gives the study of East Asian politics a distinctive quality. Comparative politics dominates East Asian political research to the exclusion of political economy. A good example is provided by Pye's work on Chinese and Asian political cultures. However, there are some writers, such as Wittfogel, who combine political economy and political culture perspectives to discuss the relationship between Chinese despotism and the necessity of civil engineering projects. Theodore de Bary's work on Zhu-zi doctrines also utilizes both perspectives (Wittfogel, 1957; Pye, 1989; de Bary, 1988; Morishima, 1982; Davis, 1982).

Pye provides the most ambitious and comprehensive comparative framework for an analysis of East Asian political cultures. His analysis incorporates East, Southeast, and South Asia, but with a particular focus on the political cultures of China, South Korea, Vietnam, and Japan. He argues that Western authority is based on utility, and Asian authority is based on ritual. In European and North American countries, authority is legitimated to the extent that it generates practical and tangible outcomes. In Asian countries, however, authority is legitimated to the extent that it generates an atmosphere and psychological sense of satisfaction. The political culture perspective is important because it helps us to understand the nature of this psychological satisfaction.

According to Pye, East Asian political culture is mainly Confucian, and is characterized by hierarchical authority, a consistency, in principle, between the interests of the rulers and the ruled, and lastly, by rulers themselves embodying the moral values of society (Nathan, 1987). The distinction between rulers and ruled is explicit. Since the rulers are trying to protect the national or common interest, it follows that the interests of rulers and ruled are the same in principle. As a result, people tend to think of the nation as a community in which state and society overlap, instead of making a clear distinction between them. Rulers are further expected to embody the highest moral values. There is a strong perception of community, and as a result people tend to revolt against rulers who do not personify the community's moral values and principles. But it should be noted that revolutions, when they occur, tend to entail a change of leadership rather than a substantial change in the nature of the political system.

Confucianism evolved in different ways in different East Asian political systems. China's vast population and land area made it difficult to rule coherently and cohesively. This also created a large gap between ideal and reality in China's political culture. In contrast to the modern Chinese experience of being ruled by foreigners, South Korea is often held to be the most faithful and rigid practitioner of Confucian politics. For Vietnam, the process of adapting to the East Asian international environment has also entailed a strong emphasis on authentic Confucianism. In the case of Japan, separated from the continent by the sea, Confucianism has been colored by pragmatism. Pye's political culture perspective focuses on perceptions of authority and the values that have developed in specific political cultures. It also provides a theory of comparative political behavior and a theory of comparative political change.

De Bary tries to identify variations in the extent to which Confucianism, particularly the later Confucianism of Zhu-zi, has infiltrated the modern political systems of China, South Korea and Japan. He suggests that Zhu-zi is characterized by paternalistic group decision-making, thrift and industriousness in the pursuit of profit maximization, and political authoritarianism. De Bary argues that Zhu-zi impacted on the education systems of thirteenth century China, fourteenth century South Korea and seventeenth century Japan. He is not suggesting that this doctrine can explain all aspects of East Asian political economy. This depends on the process and extent of adoption. De Bary is merely suggesting that Zhu-zi has been influential. Several writers have studied China, South Korea, Vietnam and Japan using a political culture approach (Solomon, 1971; Chan, 1985; Unger,

1982; Wilson, 1970; Gates, 1987; Woodside, 1971; Henderson, 1969;
Austin, 1972; Richardson, 1974; Dore, 1973; Ishida, 1970; Doi, 1971;
Kyōgoku, 1983)

Rulers must possess political strategies and adopt political behaviors
that are consistent with indigenous political culture in order to attain
political legitimacy. To be recognized as possessing legitimate
authority, indigenous perceptions of authority must be satisfied. In
order to examine this kind of authority or power, we must utilize the
political culture perspective. However, political culture is difficult to
define since its origins vary and it changes constantly. The political
culture perspective does not hold up well under rigorous scientific
examination. According to this method the basis of a nation's political
culture is deduced from observations of political behavior within a
particular political system. Moreover, the political culture perspective
often yields an explanation that is permanent and static (Pye, 1966;
Kyōgoku, 1983). Therefore, most Western researchers who discuss
processes of political democratization in East Asia refer to the vertical
relations which permeate East Asian politics, and which are held to
provide the basis for authoritarian political systems. Needless to
say, this type of discussion does not help us explain recent trends in
democratization. When pushed we can explain how Confucian culture
encouraged economic development, and how economic development
led countries in the direction of freedom and democracy. But the
evidence to support the above cause and effect relationship is very
weak. We must also remember that the political culture perspective
does not necessarily stress the distinction between democracy and
authoritarianism.

Confucianism is generally acknowledged to have made an important
contribution to the formation of Japanese political culture. There are
some, however, who argue that the values and principles which are
embodied in the emperor system and the socialization of children are
just as critical to an understanding of Japanese political culture. In
Japanese history, the emperor system and the principles embodied in
it have twice been used to strengthen and bestow legitimacy on newly
emerging political leaders (Ishigami, 1993). The first occasion was
the period leading up to the formation of the Japanese nation, when
Prince Shōtoku was very active, and an elite group who had migrated
from the continent were expanding their control over the Japanese
archipelago. After the Ōnin Rebellion something like a modern state
– the predecessor of the modern nation-state – started to emerge. With
the samurai class in direct control of the state the emperor system again

became symbolic in its function, enjoying no real power in the political arena. Sometimes the authority of the emperor was invoked, and at other times the authority of the emperor was challenged. In neither case did the emperor system provide the normative framework for Japanese politics. The second time the emperor system was employed was in the mid-nineteenth century, when the modern nation-state was formed. Because of the threat presented by Western powers, the emperor system was held up as a spiritual, indigenous, communal, and authoritarian order. Threats from foreign navies and foreign cultures compelled Japan's leaders to mobilize something indigenous that would appeal to the Japanese people. Using the emperor system in this way also served to generate anti-colonial sentiment against the Western powers.

When the ancient nation was formed many groups and tribes with significantly different organizational principles were integrated by force. The principles underlying the emperor system were key to obtaining approval and presenting an appearance of harmony, because they placed an emphasis on the spirit of harmony and community. The principles behind the emperor system were spiritual, native and communal. At the same time, since the political system was based on the Chinese decree system, the state had formally established a system of law and administration. Moreover the state used the foreign religion of Buddhism as a means to acquire power and unite the country, and consciously harmonized Buddhism with native beliefs and rituals drawn from Shinto and other forms of animism.

It should be noted that the principles of the emperor system were highlighted in both ancient and modern times when foreign pressures intruded on Japanese political life. Foreign elements were strong during the years of state formation in the early modern period. It was during this period that the institutional inertia that characterized the emperor system in the ancient state was discarded. In the ancient period, nation-building was facilitated by realigning the emperor system. In the modern period, political inertia was cast aside once more. The formation of the modern state was based on the integration of two strategies. Unification was imposed by force of arms from above, but the social order itself was based on the agricultural village communities which had long existed at the grassroots level. These village communities, which flourished and matured during the Tokugawa period, became the cornerstone of mid-nineteenth century nation-building. Communalism and authoritarianism thus coexisted in the modern state, and were buttressed by the principles associated with the emperor system. This system harmonized the mobilization, modernization and war efforts, and was key to obtaining both public approval and political stability. To put it another way, the Japanese leadership twice mobilized indigenous cultural symbols to legitimate their authority.

The principles involved in the socialization of children are emphasized in studies of Japanese political culture. This is because the formation of Japanese culture is closely related to the mother's desire to nurture her children as intimately and closely as possible (White, 1987). In contrast to the United States, where mothers want to make their children independent, mothers in Japan want to identify themselves with their children as much as possible. These social principles produce a psychological framework of *amae*, which means taking advantage of others' indulgence, and this form of socialization has a deep effect on Japan's political culture. Even though the order is formally hierarchical, those who are in subordinate positions make use of *amae*, that is they take advantage of the benefits that come with the authority and power invested in their superiors, and appropriate it. Since those with authority and power want to identify themselves with their adopted 'children' and regard it as a virtuous act to respond to *amae*, it is inevitable that their authority is eroded as subordinates take advantage of them. When those in positions of authority and power no longer indulge *amae*, their authority diminishes. Therefore, those in authority tend to extend benefits on an equal basis to everyone. From a subordinate's perspective, it is common practice to coordinate with people in authority and power in order to negotiate conditions of indulged equality. In the industrial sphere, this exploitation of indulgence and *amae* can lead to insider agreements, media blackouts, and so on.

A practical example of such political socialization is the perceptions which political faction members have about their leaders. If leaders do not provide money for political activity, cabinet posts or important positions in the political parties, loyalty quickly dissipates; unless members of parliament bring public works projects to their constituencies, they will lose votes. With regard to international matters such as trade policy, it is considered appropriate for the government to restrict imports, if imported products are shown to have traces of antiseptic or insect repellents. The government is perceived to be behaving irresponsibly if it does not regulate imports, but chooses instead to yield to pressure for trade liberalization. In particular, environmentalists and consumer advocates demand that the government take responsibility for monitoring these chemicals and preventing their entry into Japan, rather than leaving this to the individual decisions of consumers. The principles involved in the socialization of children are also in harmony with the principles behind the emperor system, and are acknowledged and appreciated as having a mitigating effect on the harshness of Confucian hierarchical relationships.

A theory of East Asian political systems

Both the political economy and political culture perspectives are located at the periphery of a narrowly defined political science research agenda. In what follows I will offer a comparative analysis of East Asian political parties and bureaucracies, both of which are major actors in any political system. Then, we will be able to infer the extent to which selected East Asian political systems are internally inclusive and externally exclusive.

The Chinese political system has been characterized in the following ways since 1978: (1) as a Leninist system, (2) as a single dominant party pluralistic system, and (3) as a Confucian authoritarian system (Inoguchi, 1987c; Scalapino, 1992). China is a socialist country, and its political system has been characterized as Leninist, that is as a dictatorial system led by a radical party. In this system, the emphasis is on class relations, production relations, and distribution relations. The system is characterized by (a) social infiltration by party and state organizations, (b) economic management by state organizations, (c) public campaigns conducted by the state on behalf of the official ideology, and (d) control of citizens' personal information by the party and the state. Many believe that the Chinese system will continue to possess features associated with Leninism for as long as the Chinese Communist Party plays a leadership role. Nevertheless, the system is gradually softening and an example of this is the fact that individuals are gradually being granted access to the personal information kept about them by the party and state. Harry Harding suggests that the reforms implemented since 1978 have not brought about fundamental changes in the Leninist system but have mitigated it to the extent that it can now be depicted as a 'consultative authoritarian system' (Harding, 1987)

Although reform and liberalization did proceed at a considerable speed and the framework for economic operations has changed to a certain degree, the political system remains largely unchanged. The Communist Party retains an overwhelmingly dominant position. On the policy-making nexus between party and state, China displays a limited pluralism and has tended to respond emotionally rather than rationally, in both the domestic and international arenas. In the areas of transportation, energy, communications, environmental protection, resource development, external trade, finance, price formation, and wages and bonuses, pluralist patterns are sometimes in evidence. The traditional authoritarian framework is vertical and administration is rigidly hierarchical. The emergence of a convoluted system of policy-making and implementation has rendered the traditional Leninist model less effective in shedding light on the policy process. Disagreements between Chinese leaders on whether to prioritize reform/liberalization policies or price controls are a subtle indication that a complex policy-making process may be developing.

Those who study the Chinese policy-making process prefer to define China as a single dominant party pluralistic system. However, there is a tendency to focus on elite pluralism and policy competition among that elite, to the detriment of analysis of other levels of the political system. Examples of such scholarship include the work of David Lampton and Dorothy Solinger. But, as John Burns points out, pluralism also exists at the grass roots level. As evidence of this trend he notes the increased participation and influence of farmers in the reform politics that are associated with the decentralization of authority. This indicates that some power has filtered down to grass roots level. Vivienne Shue emphasizes the power of the state vis-à-vis the party in the current period of reform compared with the period of the central command economy (Solinger, 1983, 1985; Burns, 1988; Shue, 1988).

In characterizing China as a Confucian authoritarian system there is an assumption that the rulers and the ruled share the same interests and ideals. Political problems arise when this assumption does not hold. Moreover, Confucians believe that harmony will be restored once rulers understand the feelings and demands of the ruled. The Communist Party highlights the significance of stability and unity in China, and the leadership provided by the Communist Party does prevent unrest and fragmentation. Andrew Nathan writes about the similarities between Confucian political beliefs and the beliefs of Liang Qichao, who lived in the nineteenth century. He discusses the political characteristics of the Chinese democratization movement as symbolized by the 'Beijing Spring,' and claims that this clearly shows that the views held by the flag bearers of the democratization movement share elements of the Confucian view of politics (Nathan, 1987).

Does the leadership of the Leninist political system consider the possibility that what happened in Poland could happen in China? There is always the possibility that popular dissatisfaction will boil over, causing a political crisis, or that military-led political stabilization leads to a suppression of legitimate dissent. Is it possible that China will disintegrate, just as the former Yugoslavia did when its greatest threat, the USSR, disintegrated? The former Soviet Union achieved some success with its reforms until it faltered, at which point a period of stagnation set in, creating a system that was neither truly capitalist nor truly socialist in nature. Or if we consider China as a single-party-dominant pluralistic system, can we then think of a range of possible systems like that of the Liberal Democratic Party in Japan, the Democratic Liberal Party in South Korea, the Nationalist Party in Taiwan, or the People's Action Party in Singapore? In China, a considerable portion of the intelligentsia hope that the Chinese Communist Party will become more similar to the parties which are in power in Japan, South Korea, Taiwan, and Singapore.

The intelligentsias of China, South Korea, Taiwan and Singapore are interested in the fact that Japan was able simultaneously to achieve both democracy and economic development. The secret of Japan's success lies partly in the political stability offered by a dominant party which supported the profit maximizing activities of firms. The Japanese bureaucracy also possessed a strong sense of mission and pursued the national interest free from the distraction of electoral politics. This explanation of Japan's success is broadly shared by political commentators in both Japan and other East Asian countries. But in what direction are the Confucian elements in Chinese culture likely to pull it? Will China become a soft authoritarian system as Japan used to be, or adopt a rigid authoritarian system in the tradition of South Korea? Or will de facto pluralism at the grassroots level slowly manifest itself at the national level, culminating in the success of an elected legislative assembly, as in the case of Taiwan? It is also fruitful to use this framework to compare socialist Asian political systems such as China, North Korea, and Vietnam. In North Korea factors such as rigid totalitarianism, personal worship and Confucian authoritarianism are stronger than they are in China. Vietnam possesses a rigid totalitarian system, strong regionalism, and a legacy of Southeast Asian continental individualism. China does not share these attributes.

South Korea and Taiwan are the only East Asian political systems which it is truly relevant and meaningful to compare with Japan. First, both share the legacy of Japanese colonialism. Second, both were comparatively resource-poor countries which, through a successful promotion of developmentalist industrial policy, were able to export manufactured products to obtain foreign currencies, which in turn were used to import raw materials, energy, intermediate goods, and food. Third, one party maintained a dominant position for a long period in both of these countries. Fourth, the bureaucratic system has enjoyed a longer institutional history than the parliamentary system in both of these countries.

One quality which distinguishes Japan from South Korea and Taiwan is the length of time that democracy has been in place. An even more distinctive feature is the existence of political elites and institutions that promote the broader public interest in their policymaking. In South Korea and Taiwan, the degree of inclusiveness is relatively narrow in comparison to Japan, with place of birth, ideological affiliation, and class all important in establishing one's rank in the political hierarchy and one's access to the political goods generated by public policy. It should, however, be emphasized that, for developing countries, income distribution in both South Korea and Taiwan is comparatively even. Both countries will increase their degree of inclusiveness as economic development and democratic consolidation progress. Continuing the comparison with Japan, until recently both South Korea and Taiwan employed oppressive security measures. This is due to the authoritarian legacy and the intelligence activities that were condoned as both systems sought to survive and differentiate themselves from rival political systems which had been constructed by people from their own ethnic group (North Korea and China respectively). However, South Korea moved towards democratic consolidation after its 1987–88 transition and the election of a civilian president in 1992. Taiwan's transition was not as clear as that of South Korea, although it did move steadily towards democratic consolidation after 1987, making further advances in 1992 with the election of a legislative assembly.

What complicates the Taiwanese case is that the ruling group is formed around a core who came from the Chinese mainland. Democratization, therefore, naturally implies greater Taiwanization, which in turn generates more momentum for the cause of formal political independence from the mainland. The mainland, on the other hand, wants to discourage what it sees as the province of Taiwan from initiating moves towards independence. It wants to absorb Taiwan under the auspices of its 'one country, two systems' rationale. China also wants to promote its economic development through contact with capitalist systems. Although the democratization process has progressed smoothly without irritating and provoking China unduly, Taiwan continues to oppose contrived demonstrations of Chinese military strength.

Having discussed political parties, I will now discuss the bureaucratic aspects of East Asian political systems. Dependency theory is a conceptual framework which was conceived in order to analyze the international relations of Latin America and Africa. This framework has also been applied to East Asian regional politics (Hosono and Tsunekawa, 1986; Hosono, 1983). The idea of economic dependency is a key component of this conceptual framework. According to dependency theory, Latin American countries are unable to develop independent economies because they have been forced to subordinate their national interests to those of capitalists in Europe and North America. Moreover, politically, their situations have been characterized not in terms of sovereignty and independence but in terms of submission to various Western interest groups. The governments of developing countries want to promote economic development but they also have to preserve a set of domestic structures which benefit both Western and indigenous elites. To stay in power it was often necessary for governments to suppress domestic dissidence. According to dependency theory, this was one of the major reasons why military governments were prevalent in Latin American countries in the middle of the twentieth century. Developmental authoritarianism was the name given to this form of governance

In the third quarter of the twentieth century, many East Asian countries, in particular South Korea and Taiwan, were themselves pursuing a form of governance which appeared to share certain attributes with Latin American developmental authoritarianism. In order to promote economic development, a large amount of foreign investment was being introduced, and trade with foreign countries had become vital. Any indigenous suggestion that these economies were dependent was vigorously suppressed, with military and intelligence agencies assisting in the suppression of such criticism. The OECD's 1979 report on newly industrializing economies included South Korea, Taiwan, Hong Kong, and Singapore from East Asia, and Mexico, Brazil, and Argentina from Latin America (OECD, 1979). Another similarity is that most Latin American countries and South Korea and Taiwan in East Asia made great strides towards democratization in the 1980s and 1990s. Given these similarities, it has been suggested that it is appropriate to compare Latin American and East Asian states. Frederic Deyo's research is an example of such work.

However, South Korea and Taiwan differ from their Latin American counterparts. The difference lies in the strength of the bureaucratic system that is situated at the core of political economic management in the former countries. Although the concept of bureaucratic authoritarianism emerged from the analysis of Latin American political systems, it is appropriate only in the sense that these bureaucracies wanted to influence society by using force. In the 1960s and 1970s, Latin American bureaucracies were not effective. In East Asian countries, by contrast, bureaucracies are aggressive and forceful, but they also have the capacity to implement policy effectively by means of social infiltration and the ability to guide and persuade society.

In addition, Asian bureaucratic elites are much less likely to show loyalty to foreign countries. Many people from the Latin American elites have long felt an intimacy and a sense of loyalty towards Europe and North America. They have mostly been capitalists, farm owners, and trade merchants who lived in Latin America but had their hearts in Europe or North America. As a result, foreign multinational firms and national capitalists formed close relationships. The triad was later completed by domestic political authorities, according to dependency theory, as multinational firms, substantial national capital, and international loan agencies colluded. Similar international affiliations are also said to exist in East Asian countries, but the decisive difference lies in the self-discipline of East Asian countries (Kim, 1988). In these countries, although there are large influxes of capital, foreign direct investment has been placed under a variety of controls. Investment that will prevent the development of domestic industries, or force existing local industries to decline has been restricted. Ultimately, we can attribute this to strong government leadership.

In this sense, the concept of bureaucratic authoritarianism is more appropriately applied to East Asian countries. The triad in Latin American countries and the Philippines is not that strong. In these countries, Peter Evans and Gary Hawes suggest that the state is not at the forefront. Rather it is a 'state occupied by large domestic capital' (Gereffi and Wyman, 1990; Evans, 1979; Hawes, 1987; Broad, 1988). The export-oriented industrialization strategies which were boldly promoted in Taiwan from the beginning of the 1960s, and in South Korea from the middle of the 1960s, were generally success-ful. Needless to say, there are significant differences between the political-economic systems of South Korea, Taiwan, and Japan (Fei,

Ōkawa, and Ranis, 1985). In developing industries, South Korea places an emphasis on providing credit, Taiwan on providing fiscal expenditure, and Japan on providing both types of support. In South Korea, the government has provided credit to industrial groups called 'chaebols' which control an overwhelming proportion of the nation's production and profits. In Taiwan, subsidies and grants to small and medium-sized firms have been important because the number of large Taiwanese conglomerates is not high. The difference in the size and distribution of firms between these three countries is clear when we look at the number of firms listed in the American business magazine *Fortune*. East Asian firms listed in the top 100 were mostly Japanese, followed by a few South Korean firms, and only one or two Taiwanese firms. In South Korea, political merchants who started businesses in the rubble left behind after the war developed chaebols with the assistance of government credit, either in the form of low-interest loans or the allocation of import credit. In Taiwan, it is difficult for firms to become large because government-run firms are managed by those who are loyal to the government, and private firms are heavily dependent on kinship ties.

National political frameworks underlie and reinforce these differences. In South Korea, there is a definite trend towards the concentration of power in Seoul. Policy is determined at the centre through the provision of large amounts of credit. Edward Wagner, James Palais and Hattori Tamio examine this centralizing tendency in Korean politics in the period of the Yi dynasty, and Gregory Henderson reaffirms its existence in the politics of postwar South Korea. In Taiwan, by contrast, where subsidies to individual businesses or family businesses are decided at the level of the local legislature, people born in Taiwan can influence the process. Taiwan's extremely robust and vigorous grassroots politics are studied in detail by Edwin Winkler, Michael Xiao and Wakabayashi Masatake.

In each of these countries the strength of the bureaucracy varies. As Murakami Yausuke notes, the Japanese bureaucracy was founded by the samurai class, while the bureaucracies in South Korea and Taiwan were established by people of letters and scholars (Murakami, 1979). Political power in modern Japan was based on a foundation that was not institutionally solid, with local actors developing their own bureaucracies independently. From the Meiji Restoration until the early 1920s, a significant proportion of bureaucratic posts were filled by samurai, who helped establish norms and customs that are still respected in the contemporary Japanese bureaucracy.

After the Meiji Restoration the Japanese government adopted a meritocratic examination system in order to recruit people on the basis of their academic capabilities and talent. This was an attempt to break down regionalism, and by the 1920s Japan was recruiting bureaucrats on a national basis. In modern Japan the samurai class was not land-based. Because of this, they could immediately be recruited as bureaucrats and sent to provincial towns and cities, where they would not be subject to the personal influence or sectoral interests of the local landowning class. This development contributed to the emergence of the idea that bureaucrats are impartial agents of the modern state.

In Korea the situation was different. Local leaders were strongly attached to land, possession of which was closely related to social status. Political competition in the capital was a zero-sum struggle of life and death supported by the whole clan. To this extent, it was difficult for the bureaucracy to focus on interests beyond party politics. Because of the existence of this base we can observe an American-style recruitment method; preferential treatment is accorded to acquaintances and friends more often in Korea than in Japan. However, colonial subjugation and the Korean War not only interrupted the influence of the landowning class, but in the process weakened the elite's political clout. Regional sentiment is thriving, and the preferential treatment given to those from Kyongsanbukdo in the period of rapid economic growth in the 1960s and 1970s must have made the Kwangju Incident in the 1980s appear even more significant and cruel than it was. The strength of regional sentiment also dictated voting patterns in the democratic general election of 1987. Even in the 1992 presidential election, voting patterns clearly reflected regional interests, as a result of which it was difficult to argue that the winner, Kim Young Sam (Kyongsan namdo) enjoyed 'national' support. As long as the population of Kyongsando is overwhelmingly larger than the population of Cholla-do, it is inevitable that the candidate from Kyongsando will win any election. In fact, all presidents save Rhee Syngman (P'yongan-do) have been from Kyongsando, and with the exception of Kim Young Sam (Kyongsan namdo), all have been from Kyongsanbukdo.

The Taiwanese central government is more generous towards local governments than its Korean counterpart. This has been reinforced by such factors as the limited influence and control exercised by the Qing dynasty, a certain amount of respect for grassroots autonomy under colonial rule, and the acceptance of a certain level of regional autonomy from the controlling Nationalist party. In recent years democratic movements have become more vociferous on behalf of indigenous Taiwanese. However, it seems that Taiwan will probably establish a relationship with the mainland that entails close interaction and a certain degree of autonomy, thereby reducing the likelihood of any developments that could spark a direct confrontation with the mainland.

These bureaucratic differences greatly influence the characteristics of the respective political systems of Japan, South Korea, and Taiwan. The significance of the bureaucracy's role is particularly clear in Japan. In South Korea, the importance of the military and the American custom of recruiting and supplying bureaucrats gives South Korea's political system its defining qualities. In Taiwan, a substantial distinction is made between those who are members of the Nationalist party, or who came from the mainland, or who belong to the military, on the one hand, and those who do not fall into any of these categories, on the other. These distinctions give the Taiwanese political system its defining features. The extreme subtlety of the relationship between ethnic difference and politics is examined by Hill Gates and others (Gates, 1974).

Summary

I have tried to position the modern Japanese political system in the context of other countries in East Asia. Rozman has demonstrated the commonalities that exist between East Asian countries that have adopted the developmentalist model. By using the concepts of political legitimacy and the accumulation of social surplus, I have tried to illustrate the substantial differences that also exist between these countries. In Japan, it is significant that the bureaucratic system represents society at the grassroots level. The adoption of a national examination system regardless of social class, region of birth and income is evidence of this. Political parties are also sensitive to grassroots concerns because the election system makes it difficult for candidates who do not represent grassroots interests to gain election. The mass media and mass communication networks also enable social interest groups to voice their concerns. But it is also important to note that while state and society are not in direct confrontation, they are not united to the extent that they are identical and form a community.

In early modern Western Europe, absolutist states experienced sharp confrontations with indigenous populations. Democracy developed from this discord between state and society through the emergence of the social contract. In early modern Japan, absolutism was limited to the highest echelon of the state, which was effectively a union of regional state powers. After the Ōnin Rebellion, the collapse of the ancient and medieval state and socio-political system made it possible to create a new social order. Although the subsequent creation of a society based on the provincial territory as a semi-autonomous unit reproduced the structure of interaction between state and society, these interactions were now occurring in a world that was smaller, more visible, and more tangible. This was especially true at the level of local representation of the state and the village, hence adding an element of concord to the relationship between state and society.

The Meiji state, which could be characterized as a modern version of an absolutist state, was superimposed on this pre-existing social order. Threats from foreign countries provided the impetus for the formation of this modern state, and quickly reinforced the tendency towards developmentalism. Political legitimacy was acquired by invoking the Western threat. The emperor system was used in such a fashion in order to facilitate the legitimization process.

In the process of accumulating social surplus, the state mobilized resources for modernization and war. In the postwar period, these resources were mobilized for economic reconstruction and rapid economic growth. Whilst engaged in such activity, the government asserted a strong influence over the creation of fiscal and monetary systems, and made good use of them. Government leaders did not attain political legitimacy by imposing themselves upon society but instead used the system so that social feedback could be processed and internalized. Social surplus was not accumulated by increasing taxes, but by absorbing substantial proportions of citizen income through government-led postal savings and pension insurance schemes. Even though government intervention was viewed as acceptable, in the medium- and long-term, resource allocations were left to the free market.

Both the bureaucracy and political parties have been factors in making the interactions between state and society relatively close. If interaction between state and society had been completely absent, the development of each would have been more gradual. There would have been periods of political instability if policy could not have been adopted and implemented to address radical changes in population size, technological progress, and developments in economy, society, and the international environment. In the case of Japan, we can say that necessity really was the mother of invention, stimulating numerous innovations, each conceived as the need arose. These innovations were usually revisions to acts and regulations, carried out to reflect emerging realities. However, the teeth were removed from much of the revised legislation, giving a patchwork appearance to the modern Japanese political system. This is because the absolutist state was unable to develop fully in early modern Japan, while the social order experienced a rebirth in this period. Similarly, in the modern period the Japanese state was only ever pseudo-absolutist.

The features which distinguish Japan from continental East Asia are similar to those that distinguish Western Europe from Eastern Europe. East Asia and Eastern Europe constitute the core of the Eurasian continent. England and Japan are not similar to Russia and China as is evident when we examine family systems (Wolf and Hanley, 1985). According to Umesao Tadao, the Eurasian continental countries that created great civilizations, namely China, India, Islam, and Russia, are different from Japan and Western Europe. Within Western Europe, furthermore, England is quite distinct from continental Europe. Characterization of the contemporary Japanese political system will become more intellectually interesting as we expand the scope of examination to a comparison between those countries in East Asia and those in the rest of the world.

8 Revamping Japanese politics? Towards the emergence of a multi-party system

Introduction

On November 9, 2003 elections to Japan's Lower House of Representatives took place. These elections were widely seen as a significant step on the path to a genuine two party political system in Japan. The main governing party, the Liberal Democratic Party, won 237 seats, but lost its simple majority. The main opposition party made a substantial advance, winning 177 seats, an increase of forty seats on the previous election. In response, the LDP absorbed a minor coalition partner, the Conservative Party, and a couple of other independents, in order to revive its simple majority. Along with another coalition partner, the new Kōmei Party, the governing coalition now possesses a fairly comfortable majority, thereby enabling it to monopolize all of the Chairships of the Lower House committees.

The election was widely characterized as a watershed with regard to the emergence of a two party system in post-1945 Japanese politics (Kitaoka 2003; Reed, 2003). Japanese party politics has famously been characterized as a 'one and a half party system' (Scalapino, 1962) Others have noted that Japan has been subject to an unhealthy 'one party dominance'. (Pempel, 1990; Inoguchi, 1983, 1990, 1993). The French political scientist Maurice Duverger (1951) argued that if you have a system where one person is chosen from one district by means of a non-transferable vote, then a two party system is bound to emerge after a few general elections. In Japan the combination of the one person/one district system and the proportional representation system was introduced for Lower House elections in 1993. This abolished the middle-sized electoral district system, whereby multiple parliamentarians could be elected with one vote (Shugart/Wattenberg, 2003; Reed/Thies, 2003). However, if the Duverger law is to be proved to be empirically valid with regard to the case of Japan, then it is necessary for there to be an alternation

Table 8.1 Election Outcomes

Party	Seats Won	SNTV system	PR system	Pre-election sovereign
Liberal Democratic Party	237	168	69	247
Democratic Party of Japan	177	105	72	137
New Kōmei Party	34	9	25	31
Communist Party	9	0	9	20
Social Democratic Party	6	1	5	18
Conservative Party	4	4	0	9
Independents	1	1	0	5
Others	12	12	0	8
Total	480	300	180	475 (5 vacant)

Source : Asahi Shimbun, November 10, 2003.

of power in the near future. Only then can we argue that a genuine two-party system has emerged.

In this chapter, I would like to examine the Lower House elections of November 9, 2003. I will summarize trends in the evolution of Japanese party politics since 1945, and explain how contemporary Japanese politics, both domestic and international, are entering a period of substantial change. I will focus in some detail on the roles of various political parties, but also on some other key actors whose actions affect the nature of Japanese party politics: electorates, bureaucracies, Prime Ministers, and the state/society complex. In conclusion, I will consider the suggestion that the LDP is in decay, and examine four major variables which are deemed to be centrally relevant to the future of the LDP; the electoral system, the bureaucracy, globalization and American hegemony.

Political parties, electorates, the bureaucracy and the Prime Minister

Left-right contestation, 1945–1960

The immediate post-war period of party politics is normally characterized as one of left-right contestation. Japan's defeat in World War II resulted in seven years of occupation by the Allied Powers, headed by General Douglas MacArthur. The Allied Powers purged a small number of political, bureaucratic, business and military leaders from public office. But the scale of the purge was much smaller than that which took place with the de-Nazification of

Germany. The popularity of left-wing parties was predictable, because at this time Japanese society was poverty-stricken (Japan's per capita income levels were among the lowest in Asia in 1945). The traditional conservative elites had been humiliated by defeat and occupation, and the United States armed forces were stationed in Japan. Initially, the primary objective of the US armed forces in Japan was to keep 'the cap on the bottle'. However, with the intensification of the Cold War, the US aim shifted to one of maintaining Japan as a regional bulwark against communism (Inoguchi, 2002a). With this shift in policy, the de-purging of wartime leaders accelerated. A number of right-wing parties joined forces to create the Liberal Democratic Party (LDP) in 1955. This was a right-wing response to the merger of right-wing and left-wing Socialist parties, which had taken place earlier that year. The LDP was sustained by a triangular support base consisting of local notables, central bureaucracy, and big business in Tokyo. The key issue during this period was the alliance with the United States, and how it might be reconciled with the pacifist Constitution. The LDP placed emphasis on the significance of the alliance with the US, whereas the left-wing parties focused on the Constitution. The Japanese economy was still turbulent after the wartime nadir, and the very rapid demographic, industrial and sociological transformation which Japan underwent in an amazingly short span of time was naturally full of destabilizing moments. Left-right confrontation at all levels was a symptom of these various developments.

During this period, ordinary Japanese had to start afresh, as Japan rose from the ashes of defeat. Symbolic of the state of mind of many Japanese during the immediate postwar period is the fact that one of the bestsellers was 'Gone with the Wind', (Mitchell, 1974) with the best remembered quote being 'Tomorrow is another day'. Although they had to embrace defeat (Dower, 1997), ordinary Japanese were still full of vigor and ingenuity, and were prepared to endure hard times until things improved. During the Occupation a number of traditional politicians were purged, and bureaucrats were installed in their places as politicians. Once they were depurged, however, these politicians found their way into the leadership group of the LDP in a short space of time. Political leaders during this period had strong personalities, and a penchant for disregarding organizational and bureaucratic procedures. In some ways this was an understandable reaction to bureaucratic dominance of Japanese political affairs during the Occupation and its aftermath. Under SCAP, Japanese bureaucracy stood at the helm of government and played a key role.

The 'one and a half party system', 1960–1975

The Japan–United States Security Treaty was revised in 1960 to make the United States look less like an occupying force and more like an ally in the traditional sense of the word (Packard, 1967). The government income-doubling plan was announced shortly thereafter, and left-right contestation reduced in intensity. It was replaced by a form of parliamentary immobilisme, caused by the predominance of the LDP and the numerically feeble but organizationally well-entrenched left-wing parties. The LDP did not have a two-thirds majority, as a result of which it was unable to revise the Constitution. The left-wing parties did not have a simple majority, as a result of which they were unable to remove the LDP from power. During this period the Yoshida doctrine was implemented. By the Yoshida doctrine I mean two things. On the one hand, the delegation of national security to the United States, and the implementation of the Constitutional ban on the use of force in the settlement of international disputes. On the other, a concentration of energy and resources on wealth accumulation (Kōsaka, 1994). Others have referred to the Yoshida doctrine as a 'free rider' doctrine. The period during which the Yoshida doctrine was pursued coincided with the period of high economic growth. The electorate became increasingly wealthy, but also discontented with what they saw as a redistribution mechanism which did not reward them appropriately. Support for the LDP decreased steadily as its power base (farmers and small business holders and manufacturers) was fundamentally undermined by unprecedented economic and social change. The electorate offered what might be called 'atomised compliance' to the developmental state (Johnson, 1983; Woo-Cumings, 1990). Though immensely active in pork barreling for their districts, in the legislature politicians largely fulfilled the function of a rubber stamp, passing bills which had largely been drafted by bureaucrats. At this time the system verged on the bureaucratic authoritarian. At the district level, politics was very inclusionary and pragmatic. But at the highest, national level, bureaucrats were at the helm, with politicians socialized by and subordinate to the institutional mechanism of the bureaucratically-led developmental state.

The revival and dissolution of one party dominance, 1975–1990

The oil crisis took place at the height of the period of high growth, causing an economic slowdown. To the surprise of many observers, the steady decline in support for the LDP seemed to cease for a while during this period. What might be called a Downsian middle mass (Downs, 1957; Murakami, 1997) emerged. Voters had become wealthy during the period of high growth, and there was no credible alternative to the one party dominance of the LDP. As a result of these two factors, the electorate gravitated towards the Downsian center of the political spectrum. The term 'middle mass' is more appropriate than the term middle class, because the former is sociologically much more amorphous and heterogeneous than the latter. Nakasone Yasuhiro was Prime Minister for five years (1982–1987), and presided over the core of this period. He was often compared to his contemporaries Ronald Reagan and Margaret Thatcher, as a result of his belief in limited government and his patriotism (Ōtake, 1998).

During this period the developmental state partially transformed itself into a service delivery institution, focusing on pensions, health, welfare, medical insurance, and education. The Japanese state turned out to be what Ronald Dore calls a 'welfare capitalist' state, in contrast with the United States and the United Kingdom, which Dore referred to as 'stock capitalist' states (Dore, 1986). It should be noted that during this period the bureaucratization of the LDP deepened, and the politicization of central bureaucracy intensified (Suleiman, 2003). Ascent of the LDP occupational ladder was dependent on one's having secured a number of appointments within the LDP, and also having served on parliamentary committees, and in the cabinet (Inoguchi and Iwai, 1987; and Schwartz, 1998). In order to obtain a high-level appointment in the central bureaucracy, it was increasingly necessary to network extensively with influential politicians, especially compared to the immediate postwar period. The deprofessionalization of central bureaucracy also became salient during this period. Increased egalitarianism in civil service appointments and promotions made a further step forward during this period. In the Ministry of Foreign Affairs, for example, civil servants are evaluated by both their superiors and their juniors, by both elite diplomats and support staff. These evaluations have become the basis for promotion and demotion. The period ended with several scandals which hit the LDP hard and debilitated it for some time thereafter. The bubble economy, built in the latter half of the 1980s, collapsed in 1991, an event which coincided with the end of the Cold War.

Shifting coalitions, 1990–2005

The scandal-ridden and stagnating LDP experienced a large-scale exodus of members. The New Japan Party, which responded to popular demand for a fresh, clean, grass-roots based and pro-active party, took power in 1993. The LDP's postwar period of one party dominance ended in 1993. However, the New Japan Party and its successor held power for only one year. Thereafter the LDP resumed power in conjunction with the Socialists. After two years of coalition with the Socialists, the LDP regained a much more solid grip on power, but only in conjunction with shifting coalition partners. Two developments weakened the left during this period. The first was the fact that the Japan–United States Security Treaty needed adjustment, and the nature of the alliance with the US needed to be re-established. There were substantial divisions within the Socialist camp with regard to this issue, which caused fragmentation. Secondly, a number of public sector trade unions disappeared as a legacy of privatization legislation which had been passed towards the end of Nakasone's time in power (1982–87).

In response to popular distaste for the Nagatachō-Kasumigaseki establishment, the Japanese equivalent of the Washington establishment, Junichirō Koizumi gambled by sloganeering that he would 'destroy the LDP, and rescue Japan with reform'. Koizumi won in 2001. He possessed effective sound bytes and a youngish, stylish appearance. He projected the image of a good guy fighting evil, and this was generally well received. At this time, the LDP was extremely unpopular. The opposition was unanimously calling for economic recovery and reform of the whole system, especially with regard to social and defense policy. Koizumi adroitly outmaneuvered the opposition by championing himself as the leader of reform (Morris, 2001). In victory his coalition partners, as with his predecessor, were the new Kōmei Party and the Conservative Party.

When Koizumi scored a resounding victory in the LDP Presidential election in October 2003, he called a snap general election, hoping for something similar. But the electorate had become disaffected (Pharr/ Putnam, 1997). The two largest opposition parties, the Democrats and the Liberals, united on the eve of the general election. The new Democratic Party posed a formidable challenge, and strongly advocated regime change. Civil society has also been maturing in Japan (Schwartz/Pharr, 2003). As a result of all of these factors, the

LDP ended up short of a simple majority, and the DPJ made a 40-seat advance. After the election, the Conservatives were absorbed into the LDP, which also collected some independent winners into its fold, and thereby regained a comfortable numerical majority in the National Diet. However, the new Kōmei Party, currently the sole coalition partner of the LDP, has found itself more exposed to public scrutiny and criticism, especially with regard to the differences in social and defence policy which exist between it and the LDP.

The lower house elections of November 9, 2003

Having briefly characterized the party politics of Japan during the period since 1945, I will explain how the Lower House elections of November 9, 2003 were conceived, campaigned and concluded. Koizumi decided to hold a snap election following his resounding victory in the Liberal Democratic Party Presidential election, which was held on September 20, 2003. The electoral college for this election consisted of parliamentary members of the LDP and the represent-atives of local LDP chapters. The ratio of representatives in the electoral college from these two constituencies is roughly three to two. Koizumi received overwhelming support from both constituencies, and, having apparently anticipated such an outcome, decided to call a general election almost immediately. The LDP Presidency carries a three year term. The Lower House sits for four years, unless the Prime Minister dismisses it and calls a new general election. June 2004 was scheduled to be the end of the natural four year cycle. But Koizumi decided to take advantage of a number of factors which were in his favour at this time. He had received relatively high popularity ratings during the preceding year, and there were initial signs of economic recovery. Another important factor prompting Koizumi's snap election was that at that time the two largest opposition parties were preparing to merge into one large opposition party. Koizumi reasoned that, as both parties were only in the process of merging, they would be relatively unprepared to hit the ground running as a single opposition party in a snap campaign.

This election campaign marked the first occasion when parties produced election manifestos (Budge et al, 1997; Inoguchi, 1983). Previous campaigns were conducted during a two-week period during which a combination of campaign methods were used. These included newspaper summaries of the positions of the main parties on a number of policy issues (but no lengthy documents provided by the parties themselves), TV campaign speeches for every candidate, campaign posters, and campaign speeches on the street (it was not permitted to visit every household) (Reed & Thies, 2003). The legislation was passed shortly before Koizumi called the general election. Koizumi had seized the LDP Presidency three years previously with the unlikely slogan 'destroy the LDP, reform Japan'. In using the slogan it had been Koizumi's intention to attract the substantial numbers of disaffected LDP supporters back into the LDP fold. It was also hoped that floating voters could be persuaded by this sentiment. Koizumi was immensely successful. Reform became a buzzword with which to criticize and attack both vested interests and the establishment.

Reform also entailed greater transparency and accountability. One legacy of the Koiziumi reform project was the fact that during the general election campaign there was transparent debate about which policies each party would pursue if they gained power. There were substantial debates on economic, social and defence policy. Economic debate was necessary given that Japan's economic performance had been sluggish for the best part of a decade. The debate on social policy was necessary given that Japan has an expanding aged population which absorbs a high and growing proportion of tax revenue for pensions, medical insurance, and general welfare. The debate on defence policy was necessary given Japan's support for the Iraq war and its pledge to participate in the reconstruction of post-war Iraq.

The new election manifestos played an important role in making these policy debates more familiar and intelligible to voters. The use of election manifestos seemed to boost support for the DPJ, given that it was able to increase its total number of seats by 40. The use of manifestos provided the DPJ with an opportunity to document and set out with clarity the long list of popular grievances voters had with regard to economic and social policy. The LDP repeated its reform slogan, but without being able to offer convincing evidence that it had lived up to its reformist pledges since the previous election. The LDP manifesto juxtaposed many diverse policy positions and pledges without a great deal of coherence. The manifesto also demonstrated that vested interests in various sectors were being protected. Economic recovery was slow, and reform plans for road construction, and postal savings were not making progress. Medical insurance, social welfare, and other social policy expenditure were being steadily cut. Transfers of revenue from central to local government were also substantially cut, and local governments were not given new powers to raise tax revenues of their own.

The new Democratic Party of Japan repeated its demand for regime change, but without offering convincing, concrete and practical pledges to support their own economic, social and defense policies. Importantly, there was a general perception that Koizumi's slogan 'destroy the LDP, reform Japan' had lost its initial strong appeal during the campaign. Koizumi's reformist drive had faltered over issues such as the privatization of road construction and of postal services, and a reduction in the revenues made available to fund medical insurance, pension and social welfare. There was a feeling that despite his rhetoric Koizumi was more or less embraced by the familiar tripartite vested interests of bureaucracy, big business, and their legislator friends, the *zoku giin* (Inoguchi and Iwai, 1987). It was becoming clear that the lack of order in postwar Iraq would make Japan's role in the reconstruction of its war-damaged economy and society dangerous and highly problematic. All these negative issues overlapped with and reinforced a sense that Koizumi's initially refreshing leadership powers were on the wane.

In terms of electoral mobilization, however, one could argue that the LDP did quite well, despite the sluggish economy, the tightening of social policy, and impending problems relating to Japanese participation in the reconstruction of Iraq. The LDP activated its support bases in the districts, where the new DPJ did not have much time to cultivate support. Many DPJ candidates spent an enormous amount of time in the districts they would stand in, because they were painfully aware that in general they did not enjoy nearly as much grass roots support as many LDP candidates. This information emerged in a survey of all legislators, which was conducted in August 2003 prior to the general election. The survey in question was designed by this author in conjunction with the Mainichi shimbun (Mainichi, 2003b).

What was most striking about the November elections was the intensity of electoral mobilization by the new Kōmei Party. Its basic strategy was to offer electoral cooperation to parties whose candidate desperately needed substantial support from Kōmei voters. The Kōmei Party operated two complementary strategies. It abstained from fielding its own candidate in particular electoral districts so Kōmei votes could be mobilized in support of Kōmei's electoral allies. They also adopted a 'mixed voting' strategy to gain the maximum benefit from Japan's mixed majoritarian voting system. The most typical tactic was that in a small district, Kōmei supporters would vote en masse for their partner's candidate in the majoritarian vote to elect one person per district, and the partner party's supporters would vote for new Kōmei Party candidates in the proportional representation part of the vote. The new Kōmei Party has pursued these strategies for the last decade, since the new electoral law was passed in 1993. But its strategy was perhaps most successful in this last election. Kōmei now enjoys the status of a governing coalition partner. It has penetrated the LDP's support base by extending its electoral cooperation. The Kōmei Party complements these strategies with a time-tested policy whereby Kōmei supporters will often change residence, in order to maximize the significance of their vote for the wider Kōmei cause. This requires astute planning by Kōmei's electoral mobilization department, because the public office election law stipulates that only those who have lived in a district for a certain period of time are eligible to vote in elections. Kōmei has to be substantially ahead of the game with its planning. (It should also be noted that the Kōmei Party provides limited assistance to some DPJ candidates with regard to forward electoral planning).

Kōmei is a comparatively small party, with its supporters numbering some 7 or 8 million voters, less than ten per cent of the total electorate. As such, the Kōmei Party has enjoyed a disproportionate influence on public policy. Many reasonably specific and concrete election manifesto pledges were made during the election campaign by all of the parties. However, the Kōmei Party is the only party which had already achieved two of its pledges, as of 31 December 2003. More specifically, the Kōmei Minister of Health, Welfare and Labor implemented his Ministry's plan for reform of social policy by rejecting a raft of proposals which had been made by the Treasury with impressive speed. Also, Kōmei support for the LDP's policy of dispatching Self Defense Force troops to Iraq was decisive in determining the nature and timing of the dispatch. The new strength of the Kōmei Party has generated two responses. Some have suggested that Kōmei holds the electoral balance of power, and that the Kōmei Party can determine who will gain power by aligning or dealigning itself from particular parties as it pleases (Kabashima and Sugawara, 2003). Others have argued, however, that that the Kōmei Party's uneasy and opportunistic alliance with the LDP governing coalition visibly reduces popular support for the coalition government (Isao Iijima as quoted by Sano, 2003). A reduction in the level of popular support for the government is also noted and explained in the Mainichi shimbun (2003c).

Is the Liberal Democratic Party heading towards decay?

The Liberal Democratic Party briefly lost power briefly in 1993, after 38 successive years in control. But in 1994 it returned to power in coalition with other parties. Although its coalition partners have changed intermittently, the LDP has consistently been a key governing party since 1994. Four general explanations have been offered for the LDP's extraordinary electoral resilience during this period. These are: (1) reform of the electoral system (2) the politicization of the bureaucracy (3) the limited effects of globalization and (4) the American promotion of polyarchy.

Reform of the electoral system

It has been suggested that the introduction of a mixed majoritarian voting system (MMS) may be one of the major factors which has enabled the LDP to prolong its hold on power. This revised electoral system was introduced in 1993, with the aim of combining the best elements of two distinct voting systems, the majoritarian and proportional representation systems (Shurgart/Wattenberg, 2003). Under the majoritarian system, as stated, one person is elected from each district by a single nontransferable vote. According to the Duverger law, the more seats which are allotted in this way, the greater the chance of the formation of a genuine two-party system. Conversely, if more seats are allotted according to the proportional representation, the slower the trend towards the formation of a two party system. The proportional representation system assumes that parties are national in scope, disciplined, and can offer a coherent program of policies. The MMS system accords greater weight to the selection of one person from one district by means of a single non transferable vote than it does to the proportional representation system. The new MMS system therefore prioritizes the Anglo-Saxon practice of majoritarian voting. Two thirds of seats are allotted in this way, and one third according to the proportional representation system.

Since this legislation was passed three general elections have taken place, in 1996, 2000 and 2003. There are signs that a genuine two-party system is emerging (Reed, 2003). Firstly, the largest opposition party, the Democratic Party of Japan, has merged with the Liberal Party and successfully marginalized both the Social Democratic Party and the Communist Party. In doing so it has emerged as a party which is genuinely capable of assuming power, which is one of the criteria which need to be fulfilled in order that the Japanese system can be described as a genuine two-party system. Secondly, the Public Election Campaign Law was revised on the eve of the last general election to allow for the use of party manifestos in election campaigns. Although strict limitations were placed upon print, radio and television advertising, and also door-to-door canvassing, the introduction of manifestos led parties to present their policies in a more coherent, programmatic and thereby effective fashion. Third, the Liberal Democratic Party absorbed the Conservative Party shortly after the general election. Given the mixed nature of the voting system, however, it will take further general elections in order for the Japanese party system to become a 'genuinely' two party system in which power alternates between different parties. This will depend on a parties ability to (1) address local interests in order to win seats allotted according to the majoritarian system, and (2) offer a convincing and coherent manifesto in order to win seats allotted according to the proportional representation system.

The entrenched interests of politicized bureaucracy

Japan's bureaucracy has been a key foundation of its politics. As a general rule of politics, it is clear that it is easier for a governing party to survive if it can successfully accommodate the modus operandi of the bureaucracy with which it has to deal (Inoguchi, 2003). In its manifesto, the Democratic Party of Japan proposed that a substantial section of the senior bureaucracy should be politically appointable by a new governing party. This is one of the more original and distinctive policy proposals which the DPJ has come up with. It is a worrying development for incumbent senior bureaucrats, because there is the possibility that they could lose their jobs if this manifesto pledge ever became policy. The existing bureaucracy, for this and other reasons, is therefore more supportive of the Liberal Democratic Party. In the last decade or so, Japan's bureaucracy has become increasingly politicized. This is also true of other industrial democracies, but in Japan, it has been argued, bureaucratic dominance is more pronounced than most other such countries (Suleiman, 2003). The politicization of the bureaucracy can take a variety of forms: legislators can be appointed as Vice Ministers and Deputy Ministers; the power of the Prime Minister's Office can be enhanced; a new Cabinet Office can be created.

The DPJ's manifesto pledge is interesting, because it threatens currently entrenched bureaucratic interests. But in reality, whilst this policy seems refreshing, the DPJs objective would be to replace conservative bureaucrats with new bureaucrats who would reflect the interests and policies of the DPJ. The DPJs manifesto renders high level bureaucratic appointment contingent upon the approval of the governing party of the day. This is not an argument against bureaucracy per se. It is an argument against the retention of a particular bureaucracy that does not serve one's own party political interests. It will be interesting to see which bureaucratic model prevails in Japan in the coming decade. Will Japan's traditional bureaucrat-dominant political system remain, or will we see the introduction of a form of transitory political appointeeism, as mooted by the DPJ? This of course depends on how successful the DPJ challenge to the electoral dominance of the LDP will prove in the coming decade.

Ozawa Ichirō, the Acting President of the Democratic Party of Japan, has conceded that the politicization of bureaucracy is more or less inevitable and necessary. Furthermore, when one of the two largest parties wins power, the other large political party is bound to lose seats and influence. This undermines the foundations of a two party system and bolsters the dominance of the party in power. But this is also an unavoidable feature of political competition. Ozawa's argument lends credence to the view that whichever party wins, bureaucracy will prove a highly resilient influence on Japanese politics. To the extent that this is true, the incumbent bureaucracy has a clear and significant stake in the maintenance of LDP dominance.

The comparatively limited effects of globalization on Japanese society

Substantial globalization would undermine the industrial and sociological power base of the Liberal Democratic Party. However the degree and rate of penetration of Japanese society by globalizing forces has been comparatively slow. This has allowed the Japanese economy, polity and society to adapt steadily to change without experiencing major disruption (Inoguchi, 2002b). The results of an Asian cross-national survey on the impact of globalization on daily life have shown the impact to be lowest in the following ten societies: Japan, Korea, China, Vietnam, Myanmar, Thailand, Malaysia, Sri Lanka, India, and Uzbekistan (NRC, 2003).

Table 8.2 The Extent to Which Globalization Permeates Society

	Japan	Korea	Malaysia	Thailand	China	Sri Lanka	India	Vietnam	Uzbekistan	Myanmar
Family members and relatives abroad	6.7	16	17.3	14.9	12.6	30.4	18.9	36.2	46.3	16.1
More than 3 tours abroad in the last 3 years	5.8	2.9	8.4	3.1	2	6.8	2.2	1.6	16.4	0.8
Have foreign friends	9.8	3	15	8.6	9.3	17.8	11.9	19.1	46.4	6.3
Frequently watch Fuji TV programs	14.8	11.6	71.6	67.3	29.6	56.8	33.5	73.6	67.6	82.6
Routinely interact with foreign business through internet	2.5	4.5	76	2.9	9.5	7.4	7.8	10.3	7.5	0.8
Business travel with foreign business firms	5.3	3.9	4.1	2.5	5.3	4.1	2.8	4.8	12.5	0.9
Others	65.8	68.9	18.9	41.9	54.8	29.5	52.8	2.2	14.1	13.3
DK	0.8	0.9	3.1	0.3	-	0.5	0.2	0.1	-	0.1
Average number of responses	1.4	1.13	1.12	1.46	1.21	1.23	1.53	1.3	1.68	2.11 1.21

Source : Nippon Research Center, AsiaBarometer : A Country-by-Country Comparison Tokyo : NRC, Nov 2003"

Japan's exposure to globalizing forces has been comparatively moderate. Japan has a large population and a substantial economy, and this has allowed it to rely heavily on domestic markets. Within Japan, technological and economic adaptation to the pace of globalizing forces has been steady, and this is due to the way that Japanese handle industrial, financial and sociological adjustment. Japan has responded to the partial penetration of its markets by globalizing forces with what Ronald Dore has characterized as 'flexible rigidity' (Dore, 1986). By this Dore means that Japanese adaptation takes time and that unless and until the penetration of external social forces cannot be prevented, Japanese tend to tinker indefinitely with time-tested formulas and schemes. But when the threshold comes, and change can not be avoided, Japanese discard these rigidities in a rapid, highly pragmatic and flexible manner.

A comparison with Korea is useful here. During the 1997 Asian financial crisis all East and Southeast Asian economies suffered. The Korean economy was placed under IMF surveillance. Many Korean financial institutions and industrial groups, or 'chaebol' were eclipsed in the process. Korea started to recover as early as 1999. But the more structurally rooted problems persist and periodically return to blight the Korean economy. Bankruptcy and unemployment rates rise and fall intermittently. Fairly frequent labor strikes and disputes are a reflection of this. The Asian financial crisis hit Japan hard as well, but the way in which Japan adjusted to the crisis was different from Korea. Aside from the fact that the IMF did not place Japan under surveillance, Japan was reluctant to advocate bankruptcies and redundancies, as the logic of free market economics would perhaps have suggested at the time. Only a handful of banks were allowed to go bankrupt. Most others have endured hard times without firing many employees, and have improved their lending strategies and managed revenues and costs more effeciently. In the Japanese case, it was as if the primary goal of business was employment rather than profit (Inoguchi, 2002b).

Helped immensely by this gradualist Japanese mode of adaptation, the Liberal Democratic Party has been able to surf, as it were, on waves of economic and social change over a period of half a century. Its initial electoral base consisted of farmers and small business holders/manufacturers. This was the case up until roughly the time of the first oil crisis of 1973–1974. Since then, the LDP has been very successful in cultivating middle class support, on the basis of Japan's successful adaptation to global economic change, from the 1970s through to the 1990s.

The American promotion of polyarchy

Japan's increased economic competitiveness in the late 1980s and early 1990s gave rise to the suspicion in the United States and the rest of the world that Japan might be playing an unfair game, through its notorious industrial policy, its practices of administrative guidance and its keiretsu-style corporate organization. This suspicion led the United States government to make concerted attempts to unravel Japan's tightly knit business-bureaucracy nexus, through trade negotiations as well as political engineering. The latter focused on encouraging political forces inside and outside the Liberal Democratic Party which were strongly committed to free trade, free markets and liberal democracy. (Inoguchi, 2000) At around this time there were a number of high profile LDP scandals, resulting in a pervasive distrust of the LDP amongst the Japanese electorate. The US found this environment most congenial to its agenda of unraveling the Japanese state-business complex. The LDP lost power in 1993. Prime Minister Morihiro Hosokawa, head of the New Japan Party, became Prime Minister in 1993. The NJP and its successor, the New Frontier Party, believed that Japan should become an ordinary country, that is, it should embrace free trade, liberal market economics and liberal democracy, and should seek to become normal in the sense that it could use force in the settlement of international disputes. This position was forcefully articulated by Ozawa Ichirō, Secretary General and strong man of the New Frontier Party (Ozawa, 1993). During this time of domestic political upheaval in the early 1990s it was interesting to note that United States Ambassador to Tokyo Michael Armacost was not photographed with LDP politicians, but rather with NJP or NFP politicians (Inoguchi, 2000). At this time some United States observers mistakenly believed that the two main problems that the US faced after the Cold War were democracy promotion in post-communist states, and the curtailment of what was sometimes seen as Japan's quest for global economic and then political hegemony.

The New Frontier Party did not last long. The aims of its members were too disparate. All that was shared was the common objective of overthrowing the LDP and becoming Japan's new ruling party. By 1994 the Socialist Party of Japan had left the NFP and formed a coalition with the LDP which was to prove sufficient for the LDP to return to power. The economic goals of the United States government, namely market liberalization and the stimulation of international trade, were more or less achieved as the Japanese economy entered a prolonged period of stagnation, and thereby ceased to be a threat to US economic predominance. America's politico-military goal was to enable Japan to use force to counter attacks on Japanese territory. Ironically, the significant diplomatic burden of negotiating the modalities of alliance adjustment with the United States fell to a Social Democratic Prime Minister, Tomiichi Murayama. Later, in 1997, Prime Minister Ryūtarō Hashimoto of the LDP issued the Japan-United States Defense Guidelines, in which Japan is recognized as having primary responsibility for the repulsion of attacks on Japan.

The terrorist attacks in the United States in 2001 prompted it to wage a global war on terrorism, in the course of which wars have been prosecuted in Afghanistan and Iraq. As a result of these developments Japan sent its Self Defense Force firstly to the Indian Ocean, and then to Iraq itself. These events have triggered a substantial debate within Japan as to whether Japan should have sent troops or not. This in turn has reignited older debates about the need for Constitutional revision, with some arguing that the prohibition on the use of force for the settlement of international disputes, stipulated in the Constitution, should be removed. By the time of the November 2003 general election, both the Liberal Democratic Party and the Democratic Party of Japan had both concluded, for different reasons and in different ways, that the Constitution should be revised. This will make the process of Constitutional revision much easier and perhaps quicker than otherwise might have been the case. The early 1990s saw the New Japan Party and the New Frontier Party take the lead in the dismantling of government-business linkages The early and mid-2000s will see the Liberal Democratic Party adopt a leadership role with regard to Constitutional revision. In the early and mid-2000s, the United States government did not have to do much to promote polyarchy in Japan, because Junichirō Koizumi won the election on the strength of his injunction that we should 'destroy the LDP, (and) reform Japan'. This move towards polyarchy was a most welcome development for the US. The US government was also happy to see Prime Minister Koizumi steer Japan steadily in the direction of normal statehood, first by sending troops to the Indian Ocean and Iraq, and then paving the way for the revision of the Constitution.

All things considered, the November 2003 general election has proved to be a watershed in a number of important ways. There has been a substantial move in the direction of a genuine two-party Japanese political system. The politicization of the bureaucracy has intensified. Japan's decade-long economic stagnation has led it to import a massive amount of foreign capital, and to shore up or purchase weak or bankrupt firms. Japan has invested massively in the overseas relocation of Japanese manufacturing. There has been much foreign direct investment, especially in China, and this has substantially facilitated the growth of globalization in both directions, and greatly diluted Japan's once-vaunted state-led developmentalism. The unipolar nature of the US's new foreign policy has led it to seek partners rather than allies, partners who are prepared to participate in contentious joint endeavors. Japan's transition may take a decade or more. But it is clear that the *ancien regime* characterized by one party politics, the ascendancy of the bureaucracy, state-led developmentalism and rigid alliance with the United States are gone. The general election of November 2003 has ushered in a new era.

9 Japan's contemporary international relations: towards the resumption of ordinary power?

Japanese foreign policy: Adjusting every 15 years

Henry Kissinger has suggested that Japan is slow to respond to significant political developments. In the past, he argues, it has often taken some fifteen years for a decisive response to emerge (Kissinger, 2001). He cites three examples: Commodore Perry's visit to Japan in 1853; the comprehensive defeat of Japan by the Allied Powers in 1945; and the collapse of the bubble economy in 1991. It took 15 years for the Japanese to put an end to internal debate and strife and start de novo in 1868 (Mitani 2003). It took 15 years for the Japanese to firmly commit themselves to the United States, before they announced the income-doubling plan in 1960, and indicated that they would focus on wealth accumulation. It has taken roughly 15 years after the collapse of the bubble economy for the Japanese to decide how many employees to lay off and how to deal with bad loans. The Japanese economy started to pick up at long last towards the end of 2003. The substance of Kissinger's basic observation seems to ring true, even if one remains skeptical of his explanation of why the Japanese invariably take a comparatively long time to formulate effective responses to new developments.

The contest between pro-alliance and anti-alliance sentiment: 1945–1960

Bearing Kissinger's argument in mind, I have studied the basic contours of Japanese foreign policy since 1945. His argument generally holds true. This is an interesting and valuable observation, because it is often argued that postwar Japanese foreign policy has been unchanging. In fact, if Kissinger is to be believed, Japan has been making substantial adjustments to its foreign policy every 15 years. During the first period, between 1945 and 1960, there was extensive discussion of whether Japan should work closely with the United States or not. The die was cast in 1960 when Prime Minister Nobusuke Kishi passed the revision of the Japan–United States Security Treaty, despite vigorous resistance, and submitted his resignation to the National Diet (Packard, 1967). The Yoshida doctrine was effectively pursued from the day of his resignation. The term Yoshida doctrine refers to the policy of seeking protection under the US military umbrella, and focusing Japan's national energy and resources on economic regeneration, and wealth creation and accumulation (Kōsaka, 1968). There was vigorous internal debate about whether to adopt the Yoshida doctrine during the period between 1945 and 1960. Many Japanese were unable to come to terms with the humiliation of delegating national security to a foreign country. They were also concerned at the potential contradiction between the provisions of the Japan–US Security Treaty and the provisions of the Japanese Constitution. The Yoshida doctrine was only embraced after Prime Minister Hayato Ikeda announced the income-doubling plan of 1960–1970. In 1960 it became clear that no significant internal or external enemies to the Yoshida doctrine remained.

Yoshida doctrine or free ride? 1960–1975

During this second 15 year period Japanese income levels rose so steadily that Japan became the target first of envy and then of enmity. Internally, cumulative economic, social and demographic changes were undermining the political base of the governing party, the Liberal Democratic Party. President Charles de Gaulle unkindly observed that Japan was a nation of 'transistor salesmen'. This was a caricature of Japan's decision, in accordance with the Yoshida doctrine, to focus on economics rather than politics and military affairs. De Gaulle's observation attempted to strip away the valor and pride of the visionary politician, Shigeru Yoshida, and expose what he believed to be the unsatisfactorily self-serving nature of his doctrine. De Gaulle claimed that Japan was a free rider who had no sense of responsibility for the management of world politics, even though it possessed the world's second largest economy. This perception of Japan as a free rider prevailed for more or less the duration of this second fifteen year period.

Systemic supporter of the US: 1975–1990

Towards the end of the second period the oil crisis erupted, and war broke out in the Middle East. Japan wavered between pro-American and pro-OPEC positions, as the accusation that Japan was a free rider echoed back and forth from both sides. This criticism prompted Japan to shift its position slowly but steadily from that of a free rider to a systemic supporter of the United States (Inoguchi, 1986). By systemic supporter I mean an actor that helps to maintain the United States-led international system. It is important to note that Japan's support was mostly of an economic nature, as exemplified by Japan's positions on free trade and energy security. Towards the end of this period, however, Japan's support began to assume a more political and military complexion, as exemplified by Japan's support for the US on issues such as SS-20 missiles. However, Japan also highlighted the concept of 'comprehensive security' during this period. It did so firstly to emphasize its limited support for the U.S.–led system, and secondly to highlight the importance of other aspects of security when the United States focused excessively on the military aspect of security. This third period can therefore be characterized as one during which Japan played the role of a systemic supporter. Japan prosecuted this role in the spirit of Machiavelli's dictum that we should provide support to our friends, but project our neutrality to enemies. Despite all the difficulties associated with the Constitutional ban on the use of force for the settlement of international disputes, there was no shortage of rhetorical freedom. Prime Minister Nakasone Ysauhiro went so far as to characterize Japan as 'an unsinkable aircraft carrier' towards the end of this period.

Global civilian power: 1990–2005

The start of this fourth period is marked by a steady decline in the frequency of wars among major powers (Mueller, 1989) and by the end of the Cold War (Fukuyama, 1991). These developments set the stage for what have been called 'global civilian powers' to play a more significant role (Maull 1990; Funabashi, 1991). Before and during WWII both Japan and Germany had been revisionist, militarist and expansionist powers. However since 1945 both have been exemplary pacifist countries, and both Japan and Germany were delighted to be ascribed the role of civilian power after the Cold War. Germany and Japan had both suffered as a result of their quest for expansion prior to 1945, but both have emphatically relinquished this quest in the many years since (Schwartz, 1987; Katada, Maull & Inoguchi, 2004). Both are populous, large and wealthy; both are pacifist; and both are good allies of the United States. However the legacy of the past and the ban on the use of force remains a burden for both countries. Despite these constraints, it was still possible for both countries to play a significant role in post-Cold War international relations. Using the emerging concept of human security as a guide for their actions, both countries engaged in peacekeeping operations and economic reconstruction projects in many parts of the Third World. Japan in particular was very generous in offering official developmental assistance to the Third World, with a focus on health, education, agriculture, manufacturing and industrial infrastructure. Germany was creative in tailoring the operational strengths of its troops to meet the emerging and comparatively novel demands of peacekeeping operations.

During the early 1990s the United Nations, under the leadership of Secretary General Boutros Boutros Ghali played a proactive role in the promotion of these activities. However, substantial problems began to emerge in the post-Cold War Third World. Global market integration deepened the predicament of poverty-stricken and strife-riddled countries. The end of U.S.–Soviet Cold War confrontation meant that both had a reduced stake in many Third World countries. This contributed to the creation of failed states and bankrupt economies. Addressing these tasks is beyond the self-proclaimed global civilian powers, the United Nations, other international organizations, and non-governmental organizations. Under such conditions the events of September 11 took place, as if calling for the United States to make its power felt and act decisively. Such a development would end the fourth period in Japanese postwar foreign policy, during which it aspired to be a global civilian power. It would also pave the way for Japan's re-emergence as a global ordinary power.

Global ordinary power: 2005–2020

Japan has chosen to define itself as an emerging global ordinary power. It is in the process of consolidating this role for itself. It is important to stress that Japan views itself as an ordinary power that will seek to act justly. This new self-definition seems revolutionary, given Japan's supposed postwar pre-occupation with Machtvergessenheit. In order to dispense justice, one needs power, in the sense of an ability to control or influence outcomes. One can not afford to neglect power. I must hasten to add, however, that in its recent past Japan has not been powerless to control or influence outcomes, either as a systemic supporter or as a global civilian power.

Japan is becoming an ordinary power with Japanese characteristics. Firstly, there is greater support for the use of force, provided that this force is used for solely defensive purposes. To defend Japan effectively against terrorism requires a number of courses of action. In an incident which took place in 2002, the Maritime Safety Agency used force on the Sea of Japan against an unidentified vessel which fiercely resisted the Japanese coast guard's attempt to investigate its actions. Public opinion was broadly supportive of this use of force. Furthermore, the Self Defense Force already has permission to use force, more specifically rifles, once it is attacked or once it detects that an enemy is about to attack, in the context of United Nations peace keeping operations. This legislation was passed in 1991. The 2003 legislation which permits troops to be sent to Iraq also contains a permission for the Self Defense Forces to use force, more specifically person-to-tank weapons. Secondly, the non-provocative use of force needs to be developed. In other words, strictly defensive methods must be practiced. If it is necessary to use force to such an extent that this goes beyond strictly defensive purposes, then it will be necessary to revise the Constitution. Thirdly, it should be recognized that terrorism can only be reduced with international efforts to eradicate extreme poverty, to end discrimination and to enhance inclusive involvement of wider populations in the running of their own societies.

Although there have been substantial continuities in Japanese foreign policy since 1945, a closer look enables one to discern clear 15-year phases, and concomitant adjustments and shifts of emphasis to address emerging threats and conditions in world politics. These periods can be characterized as follows. The first entailed an internal battle between pro-alliance and anti-alliance sections of Japanese society (1945–1960). The second period was characterized by adherence to the Yoshida doctrine (1960–1975). The third period saw Japan tentatively emerge as a systemic supporter of the United States (1975–1990). The fourth period saw Japan attempt to pursue the role of global civilian power (1990–2005), and the fifth will see a gradual consolidation of Japan's emerging role as a global ordinary power (2005–2020). It is clearly necessary to elaborate further on what Japanese ordinary power might entail. I shall do so below. But it is important to stress that Japan has started a major transition in the direction of ordinary power.

Three models of ordinary power, Japanese style

Since WWII Japan has been an extraordinary country in the sense that it has been deprived of the ability to use force legitimately in the settlement of international disputes. Movements towards the legitimation of the use of force, such as those which I briefly noted in the previous section, allow Japan to consider a number of alternative foreign policy initiatives. I shall examine three models of ordinary power, Japanese style, with reference to the example provided by three key European allies of the United States, namely Britain, Germany and France.

It is likely that the Pax Americana will endure for some time to come, possibly a la Pax Romana (Nye, 2002; Nau, 2002). As such, any discussion of the extent to which Japan can regain ordinary power status must be located in the context of its relationship with the United States (Armitage, et al., 2000; Vogel, 2002; Ikenberry/ Inoguchi, 2003). Here, alliance has arguably been replaced by partnership (Friedman, 2002). As Francis Fukuyama (1995) argues, fundamental differences in values and institutions have vanished since the end of the Cold War. In post-Cold War global politics, trust has gained increasing salience. When trust is ascertained, then partnership can be created. Befittingly, the key theme of the World Economic Summit in Davos in 2003 was trust. When I refer to the US-Japan relationship the idea of a transition from alliance to partnership should be kept firmly in mind. I have come up with the following three models, which I hope will be of use in surveying and illustrating the range of partnerships with the US that Japan might consider. I will look in turn at the following models: (1) British, (2) German, and (3) French.

The British model

The key idea is that of a special relationship (Inoguchi 2004). Japan conceives of itself as having special bilateral relations with the United States. Slightly more than a decade ago, the US Ambassador to Japan, Mike Mansfield, characterized the US relationship with Japan as its 'most important bilateral relationship – bar none'. This phrase was often deployed as the defining concept of Japan-United States relations during the 1990s. The United Kingdom also conceives of itself as having a special relationship with the US. In policy recommendations proposed by Richard Armitage the US-UK model was recommended as the best model on which to build future partnership between Japan and the US (Armitage et al, 2000).

Japan and the UK share some significant commonalities:

1. They both conceive of themselves as distinctive and somewhat distant from their respective Continental neighbors;
2. Both have high levels of economic interdependence with the United States and are embedded in the American complex of economic relations;
3. Both have significant alliance links with the US.

Since 9/11 the United States has drawn on the co-operation of a very wide-ranging number of partners from the anti-terrorist coalition, rather than on a few close allies hitherto distinguished by their perceivedly special relationship with the US. It is true that the United Kingdom and to a lesser extent Australia have been regarded as reliable allies by the United States on many occasions since September 11, 2001. The United Kingdom and Australia are indeed qualitatively distinct from Japan, in that they can take military action without being subject to the same constraints as Japan. It can sometimes seem as if the United Kingdom and Australia act like America's mercenaries. This has provoked senior Japanese diplomats to remark that Japan is not as small as the UK (whose population size is one half of Japan's), and does not feel it to be quite as necessary to fall into line so unquestioningly (Interviewee A, 2003). Such observations suggest that the US-UK model might not be so appropriate to the governing of the US-Japan partnership. Japan was mentioned as a reliable ally a couple of times in the fall of 2001, but not after that. Rather, Japan has been lumped together with other members of the coalition against terrorism, a group in which other partners such as China and Russia loom much larger, a fact which Japan has found mildly disturbing.

Yet the prospect of American war with Iraq initially drew an ambivalent response from Japan. This is why Japan was mostly silent about the prospect of war with Iraq until after France and Germany took a very different position from the US with regard to the postponement of the United Nations inspections in Iraq. As a result of this, in a speech given at the United Nations, Japan made explicit the fact that its position was more tightly aligned with the United States (Inoguchi, Open Democracy, 2003). There is of course an element of contradiction in Japan staying out of a war which is so clearly important to America, and yet still aspiring to be recognized as its most important bilateral partner. It is true that sending SDF forces into Iraq arouses opposition at home. But sending state-of-the-art Aegis destroyers into the Indian

Ocean, if not into the much closer Persian Gulf, was also argued by some to be both a prudent and gallant strategy for Japan to adopt. There is also a contradiction between the deftness and decisiveness of the initiatives taken on the Korean Peninsula and the indecisiveness and ambivalence demonstrated over the issue of potential war with Iraq. What is more, Japan acted on the North Korea issue after little consultation with the United States. Presumably, North Korea wanted to extract concessions from Japan bilaterally while Japan wanted to create a diplomatic success domestically.

The German model

The key idea here is regional embeddedness. Germany has been concealing itself within regional and international institutions such as the European Union and the North Atlantic Treaty Organization, adroitly aligning its national interests to broader regional and international interests. With its technocratic competence, rule-based steadiness and economic surplus deployed in pursuit of higher purposes, Germany has been quite successful in rehabilitating itself within a context where it does not regenerate old security concerns. This notwithstanding, Germany is also able to take initiatives which suit its own purposes within the broader context of European governance. This can be seen in the European Union's eastern expansion and in the introduction of the single currency (Eberwein/ Kaiser, 2001).

Japan and Germany share some significant commonalities:

1. Their past experience as revisionist powers. In the words of Hans-Peter Schwartz (1985), Japan and Germany have progressed from Machtbesessenheit (self-aggrandizement before 1945) to Machtvergessenheit (an abstention from power politics after 1945). This experience, combined with significant economic strength, has rendered both significant global civilian powers (Maull, 1990);
2. Their strong alliances with the United States, sustained by a substantial American military presence;
3. Their strong economic ties with and economic embrace of their respective regional hinterlands.

Despite its firm economic embrace of Asia, at least until the Asian financial crisis of 1997 (Pempel, 1999; Noble/Ravenhill, 2001; Hagaard, 2000), Japan has not been characterized as being strongly embedded within the region. First, Japan's traditional approach has been to conceive of itself as somehow external to Asia. For 'Britain and Europe' read 'Japan and Asia' (Inoguchi, 1995a; Thakur / Inoguchi 2003). Second, China, which does not necessarily share basic norms and values with maritime East and Southeast Asia, has been on the rise, both in terms of economic might and military power. If Japan is to embed itself within Asia, then it has to reconcile itself to much deeper linkages and alignment with China. This is a possibility which Japan is not willing to consider seriously at present, given its predominant emphasis on freedom, democracy, human rights, free trade, market economics and strong alliance with the United States (Inoguchi, 1997). Until 1997 Asia could be characterized as 'in Japan's embrace' (Hatch/ Yamamura, 1995), but since 1997 can more aptly be characterized as 'lured by the China market' (Inoguchi, 2002b), albeit arguably still in Japan's embrace. China's offensive to lure foreign direct investment and conclude a region-wide free trade agreement has intensified since its accession to the World Trade Organization. Third, Japan's way of handling its historical legacy has not always been to the liking of other countries in the region. Japan's adherence to the US-certified interpretation of its modern history has been solid, but has in recent times been partially diluted, due to both the passing of time and the rise of nationalism. But Japanese nationalism should not be exaggerated. Japanese are much less likely than other Asians to conceive of national identity as their primary source of identity. 80–85% of South Koreans and Thais depict national identity as their primary source of identity, but only 60% of Japanese do the same (Inoguchi, 2002a).

In the war against terrorism in Afghanistan, Japan and Germany, like most others, did their best to support the United States. They disregarded precedents, bent interpretations and sent military personnel to the Indian Ocean and Afghanistan respectively. As the prospect of an American war with Iraq increased, Gerhard Schroeder announced that Germany would not participate. On September 17, 2002, Koizumi Junichirō visited North Korea, one of the members of the 'axis of evil', and concluded a communiqué with Kim Jong Il. In this communiqué Japan acknowledged historical issues and pledged to extend compensation once diplomatic normalization was complete, while North Korea undertook to demonstrate its peaceful intentions, declaring that it would not seek to develop and maintain missiles and weapons of mass destruction. (One month later, Kim Jong Il admitted to James Kelly, US Under Secretary of State for East Asia and the Pacific, that North Korea had been developing nuclear weapons until recently, which is quite contrary to what Kim Jong Il had said to Koizumi.) Depending on your view, the actions of Schroeder and Koizumi could be interpreted in two ways. They could be interpreted as constructive attempts to reduce tension and facilitate peaceful accommodation with axis of evil countries, or as maverick self-interested acts which undermine the focus and integrity of America's policy of seeking disarmament, and ultimately regime change, in axis of evil countries.

One should also bear in mind the fact that the greater a state's regional embeddedness, the less straightforward its process of preference ordering. This is especially so when domestic anti-militarism norms are so strong, and especially in countries where the legacy of war has played such a pervasive role in the construction of contemporary national identity. The US is mildly apprehensive that if Germany and Japan become more regionally embedded, this will push their foreign policy preference-ordering still further out of kilter with American concerns. Schroeder's flat refusal, during the election campaign, to participate in the war on Iraq, and Koizumi's blitz summit diplomacy in Pyongyang were both in broad disharmony with the evolving American campaign against the axis of evil (Iraq, North Korea, and Iran). The United States ascribes differing degrees of significance to the North Atlantic Treaty Organization and the Japan – United States Security Treaty. After September 11 the United States found Europe decreasingly problematic in terms of strategic priority. Its policy towards Europe has become more benign, if only because of the lack of threat from Russia and from its strategic nuclear forces. Instead the United States finds the Middle East and East Asia much more problematic and volatile, with each region having the potential to destabilize the peace and stability of the entire world. For this reason Germany has more latitude to pursue policies of which the US does not approve. East Asia has greater strategic importance to the United States compared to Europe. Accordingly, Japan has less latitude to adopt anti-U.S. policy than Germany, because of East Asia's greater contemporary significance for international peace and security.

The French model

The key idea here is that of autonomy. Japan is a close ally and partner of the US. But this alliance has its roots in an ultimatum, an all out war, complete disarmament, occupation, and regime change. Given Japan's economic performance since the Second World War it is only natural that it should seek more autonomy. France has also recently asserted itself against the US. It has accomplished this through Jacques Chirac's deft and adroit maneuvering in the debates surrounding the passing of UN Security Council Resolutions permitting the use of force against Iraq. This French self-assertion is something Japan is quietly envious of, but also very apprehensive about. French self-assertion divides Europe, divides the West, and renders the United Nations less effective, and the United States more unilateralist (Keeler/ Schain, 1996).

Japan and France share some significant commonalities:

1. Both are close allies of the United States;
2. Both have a strong interest in peaceful and prosperous regional relations. Japan is sandwiched by China and the United States, as is France, by the United States and the United Kingdom on the one hand, and by Germany and Russia on the other;
3. Both seek to cultivate a diverse range of diplomatic partners from outside their immediate spheres of activity, using such concepts as comprehensive security and the Francophone group respectively.

Gaullism is attractive to Japan as it essentially boils down to an assertion of autonomy. Through its tight alignment with the United States, Japan has placed all of its diplomatic eggs in one basket (Inoguchi, 1997). This excessive alignment has generated a significant body of dissenting argument suggesting that Japan should strive for greater autonomy. I will briefly note three examples of such dissent. Akira Morita and Shintarō Ishihara (1989) famously published a book entitled *The Japan That Can Say No*. Prime Minister Ryūtarō Hashimoto, in a speech in Washington D.C., suggested that converting all the Japanese-owned US government bonds back into Japanese yen might lead Americans to think again about taking Japan for granted. Eisuke Sakakibara, Vice Minister for International Affairs at the Ministry of Finance, was openly defiant when his idea of setting up an Asian Monetary Fund in the wake of the Asian financial crisis was flatly rebuffed by his American counterpart, Lawrence Summers. Summers wryly noted that he thought wrongly that Sakakibara was a true friend. When this author interviewed Sakakibara in 1997, his office was dominated by a big picture of a militant Islamic Mujahedeen fighter brandishing a sword. The alleged beauty of the French model is that, in the words of Jacques Chirac, France is a true friend, in the sense that true friends will often give you advice that you do not want to hear, before ultimately offering you their support. He also noted that sycophants will not do this, alluding perhaps to Tony Blair's United Kingdom.

The problem with the French model is that the Japanese leadership style is poles apart from the French. Japanese elites have not produced a Jacques Delor, a Pascal Lamy, a Jacques Attali, or a Francois Giscard D'Estaing. These men all exercise a strong leadership role in an articulate, aggressive and adroit fashion. The Japanese political system, as an essentially decentralized consensus-oriented system, tends either not to create, or perhaps more importantly not to reward, such a leadership style at the highest level (Inoguchi, 2003b). Potential Japanese Gaullists endure great frustration as a result. However, Koizumi's articulate message and decisive response in support of the war against terrorism, and his dramatic Pyongyang summit are not inconsistent with the French model of leadership, and the French preparedness to pursue initiatives which might upset the US.

Viewed from the United States, France and Japan are different, and as such should not be expected to attempt to achieve similar levels of autonomy from the US. The key intermediary variable is the perceived value to the United States of the roles they both play in their respective regions. France is critical to the aggregation of unity and stability in Europe, with the United Kingdom psychologically semi-detached from the Continent, and Germany hampered by the institutional and historical constraints placed on its foreign policy initiatives, especially in the absence of a countervailing Soviet threat. France is perceived to be sufficiently critical to unity and stability in Europe that the US is prepared to grant it considerable autonomy in its diplomatic affairs. However, one might also argue that the Gaullist policy of seeking autonomy not only for France but also a greater Europe stretching to Estonia and Cyprus does undermine the interests of the United States. Such a policy also undermines the interests of NATO and, to a lesser extent, those of Germany in Central Eastern Europe, the Baltic, the Balkans and the East Mediterranean.

Japan's role in East Asia is very different. Other than Japan, there is no country that the United States can count on as a key stabilizing power. China does not share core values and norms with the United States and the other leading, largely Western, liberal democracies who manage the international system. Korea is too small for the United States to count on. ASEAN is not only too small but also too fragmented and vulnerable. Hence the degree of autonomy the United States can afford to give to Japan is measurably smaller.

Overcoming legitimacy and capability deficits

Embracing defeat in 1945 resulted in two kinds of deficit which Japan must overcome as it attempts to become and behave like an ordinary power. Japan has a legitimacy deficit with regard to the use of force, and a capability deficit in using force as an instrument of defense, deterrence and diplomacy.

Japan's legitimacy deficit

This deficit manifests itself in a number of ways. First, Article Nine of the Japanese Constitution forbids Japan from using force to settle international disputes. The preamble of the Constitution also declares that Japan renounces war forever. The Constitution has played a strong role in shaping Japanese politics, and the public have been tenaciously and overwhelmingly pacifist for more than a half a century. The Yoshida doctrine, which advocated military reliance on the United States and the prioritization of wealth accumulation at home, was accommodated at the elite level with little difficulty as early as the 1950s. But at the mass level the Yoshida doctrine was not accepted during the 1950s, and anti-Americanism was an undeniable feature of Japan's domestic politics. Communists and socialists opposed alliance with the US, and the Conservatives advocated alliance with the US. Even in the 1960s when the debate had been won and lost, and the focus had by and large turned to wealth accumulation, the security arrangements intermittently triggered large-scale anti-Americanism. In other words, of the two components of the Yoshida doctrine, the military reliance provided for in the Security Treaty was not fully embraced by a majority of the public. The principal source of concern with regard to the Security Treaty for the public during the 1950s and 1960s was the possibility that Japan might be pressganged into war by the United States. The Korean War, United States nuclear testing in the southern Pacific, and the Vietnam war continued to fuel this general public concern. Elite sentiment with regard to the Security Treaty was the opposite of that of the electorate. The elites were concerned that unless Japan could demonstrate its willingness to abide by the provisions of the Security Treaty, it might be abandoned by the United States. Prevailing public sentiment was also to be a great hindrance to elite attempts to reposition Japan as a systemic supporter of the US in later years. Economic, political and military burden- sharing were all debated extensively during this period. But acceptance of the possibility that Japan could legitimately use force in observance of its commitments under the Security Treaty was slow to emerge.

Japan's rapid economic penetration of world markets led it to re-appraise its responsibilities, interests and role in the international political economy. Japan's manufactured products and financial assets were ubiquitous, and yet Japan's capacity to influence the political and military forces that affect world markets was comparatively limited. Japan decided to support the United States and voice its demands from within the US camp. This would be more effective than going it alone, and would make it less likely that the US would interpret Japanese criticism as irresponsible or hostile. However, for some the fact that Japan was making it clear that it was a systemic supporter of the US increased the possibility that Japan would be dragged into wars neither of its making nor vital to its own national security. Exponents of this position were alarmed by statements such as those of Prime Minister Nakasone Yasuhiro, who argued that Japan was an 'unsinkable aircraft carrier,' in the context of the Soviet deployment of SS-20 missiles against the North Atlantic Treaty Organization.

The 1990s saw the end of the Cold War and the further deepening of globalization. The travails of Third World countries became more salient due to the relative reduction in conventional wars between major powers. UN peacekeeping operations were a feature of the first half of the 1990s. UN Secretary-General Boutros Boutros Ghali vigorously promoted a proactive role for the United Nations in the post-Cold War world. Superficially at least this post-Cold War world seemed best suited to global civilian powers like Japan and Germany. As I explained above, there are restrictions on the right of Japanese troops to use force. As Japan assumed a greater peacekeeping role, this created a new set of problems associated with the use of force in the execution of peacekeeping operations. The newly legislated Peacekeeping Operations Law that permitted Japanese troops to participate in UN peacekeeping operations only mandated troops to carry small-scale weapons such as rifles, to indicate that their involvement in peacekeeping was not aggressive in intent. This legislation also stipulated that weapons could only be used when troops were attacked, or were about to be attacked, in the judgement of a troop leader. Because Japan conceived of itself and promoted itself as a global civilian power, it was necessary to address such operational matters. Japanese have invested a vast amount of time and effort, both inside and outside of the National Diet, to ensure that the participation of Self Defense Force troops in United Nations peace keeping operations has been constitutionally appropriate. When this legislation was passed it was hailed as a major step towards Japan's re-assumption of the status of an ordinary power, although retrospectively this was only a comparatively minor step forward.

This legislation stipulated that the overseas dispatch of troops for peacekeeping purposes could only be mandated by an appropriate United Nations Security Council resolution. It remained necessary for the overseas dispatch of troops to be legitimated by the United Nations (Inoguchi, 1995b; Fukushima, 1999).

There were further developments in the 2000s. Japan's participation in the Afghan war of 2002 was limited to the prosecution of two tasks in the Indian Ocean. Firstly, Japan's state-of-the-art Aegis-equipped destroyers patrolled the Indian Ocean and monitored maritime traffic. Secondly, Japan supplied gasoline to the combat aircraft of the United States and the United Kingdom. It was not necessary to legitimize these support activities with a UN Security Council Resolution, because the Indian Ocean was designated as a non-combat area. The stipulation of the Peace Keeping and Other Operations Law that Self Defense Force troops can only be sent to non-combat areas was not relevant for the same reason. Japan was able to avoid incurring casualties and fatalities in undertaking these support operations, unlike the United Kingdom and Germany, which both sent troops to Afghanistan.

With regard to the Iraqi war, Prime Minister Koizumi indicated to the United States that Japan supported the war in Iraq shortly before the outbreak of hostilities in March 2003. The divisions between the members of the Security Council emerged as it become clear that the UN Security Council would not agree a resolution authorizing the use of force in Iraq. (Wallerstein, 2003). The United States and the United Kingdom wanted such a resolution, while France, Russia, China and Germany were strongly opposed. Defying the preferences of the three permanent members of the Security Council and Germany, the U.S.-U.K. Coalition forces attacked Iraq in March 2003. This complex and sensitive situation required Japan to perform a careful diplomatic balancing act. Japan justified its support for the coalition forces by referring to the fact that Iraq was in breach of numerous existing Security Council resolutions which had been passed since 1991. However, Japan did not make reference to the WMD issue in justifying its support for the intervention. By not invoking the WMD issue, Japan was simultaneously able both to sustain its argument that military action requires a United Nations resolution, and to remain a close and demonstrably reliable partner of the United States.

The legislation mandating the dispatch of Self Defense Force troops to Iraq was passed in October 2003, shortly before Koizumi announced that elections to the Lower House would take place in November. There are some problematic aspects to this legislation.

Firstly, it stipulates that troops should be sent to non-combat areas. However, the United States has clearly neither pacified the country nor eradicated militant terrorism. Second, the SDF mission is to be prosecuted within the context of a United Nations resolution that was passed after the conclusion of the war, as a result of sensible compromise diplomacy on the part of the United States. How solid and binding this resolution is remains to be seen, however. The purpose of the mission is to conduct peacekeeping operations and facilitate economic re-construction. Such objectives are appropriate for a global civilian power guided by the concept and spirit of human security. However, dissidents and terrorists continue to attack not only United States troops and troops from other coalition countries, but also the personnel of international organizations such as the United Nations and the International Red Cross. In view of the likelihood of attacks by dissidents and terrorists, it is stipulated that land troops be equipped with anti-tank weapons. It is not clear whether such anti-tank weapons will be sufficient to enable SDF troops to achieve their objectives. The plan is that Japanese SDF troops will secure water supplies to hospitals and electric power to key facilities in Mawala, a city located between Baghdad and Basra.

Japan's capacity deficit

It is clear that overcoming the legitimacy deficit is of major importance if Japan is to become an ordinary power. However, Japan's capacity deficit in the use of force is no less serious. This deficit stems from the fact that the Self Defense Force was established on the assumption that it would operate for strictly defensive purposes. When Japan's new Constitution was drafted by the occupying Americans there were two priorities. Japan should experience both complete disarmament and New Deal-style democratization. Complete disarmament was understood to mean the immediate, absolute and permanent destruction of Japan's military infrastructure. General MacArthur intended Japan to become a 'Switzerland of the Far East', by which he meant a small, agricultural and peace-loving country. New Deal style democratization refers to regime change, with Japan reverting from military authoritarianism to democratic freedom, human rights, gender equality, and extensive New Deal-style social policy. The composition of General MacArthur's staff reflected these priorities. MacArthur's staff consisted of those who were expert in military and security affairs, and those with experience of implementing New Deal reforms in the

US. Both of these priorities are duly reflected in the Constitution, which is the basis for Japan's capacity deficit in the use of force.

The growing threat of nationalism, communism and anti-Americanism in East Asia, especially on the Korean Peninsula, forced the Supreme Commander of the Allied Powers to redeploy American occupation forces from Japan to Korea. America's capacity to police fiercely anti-American elements in Japanese society was weakened, as a result of which American forces had to be supplemented by Japanese forces. The Police Reserve Forces were created for this purpose. Shortly thereafter, the Police Reserve Forces were re-named as the Self-Defense Force (SDF). The SDF's primary initial mission was to maintain internal security. (Political elites were very apprehensive about the maintenance of internal security in the 1940s and 1950s). The SDF's secondary mission was to provide assistance and maintain order during disasters. This mission was designed to make the SDF more acceptable to the public. It is very important to underline the point that the SDF's role in the protection of national security was initially tertiary. Opinion polls demonstrate public preferences with regard to these matters quite clearly:

Preferred SDF missions as revealed in opinion polls

The Constitution has effectively constrained and dictated the SDF's force structure up until the present time. It has periodically been important to stress the positive nature of the contribution which the SDF makes to Japanese society, especially at those times when the SDF's legitimacy has been questioned on constitutional grounds. While the SDF's primary function has seldom been stressed, for obvious reasons, its secondary function has been identified by the public as the most appropriate function up until the 1980s. Only in the mid-1990s has there been a general recognition that the most important function of the SDF is the protection of national security. Legal, institutional and public opinion have typically placed constraints on the kind of weapons and forces with which it has been felt appropriate for the SDF to be equipped. These constraints have contributed to the emergence of Japan's capacity deficit.

The National Diet has stipulated all manner of constraints, specifying the nature and number of weapons that can be deployed. The guiding principle has been that the function of the SDF is strictly and exclusively defensive. One problem for the Japanese government is that weapons technology is constantly evolving, and therefore even armed forces configured in an exclusively defensive manner are periodically forced to upgrade their weapons and revise their force structures to keep pace with new developments. Military configurations and threat perceptions have changed, and, as a result, so has Japan's alliance with the United States. I have already discussed this in section one.

In order to build and maintain defensive armed forces and simultaneously fulfil its duties as a reliable ally of the United States, Japan's military strategy and associated force requirements during the Cold War could be summarized as follows:

1. The SDF focused on anti-Soviet land-based defense on the island of Hokkaidō, adjacent to the Soviet Far East territories. Large-scale Soviet assaults on Hokkaidō would be countered by fighter aircraft based at the Chitose and Misawa airbases.

2. Soviet attempts to mount an amphibious landing would be obstructed by extensive mining, both in the waters surrounding Hokkaidō and on land. There would also be a strong counterattack by fighter aircraft and tanks.

3. Any Soviet occupation of Hokkaidō should be restricted to and ultimately defeated on Hokkaidō by heavily armed, highly mobile units.

4. While Self-Defense Forces hold and contain Soviet invading forces, the United States should swiftly engage in counterattacks to repulse the aggression.

It is important to note that the SDF was initially expected to be active only on and adjacent to Japanese territories. Production and procurement efforts accordingly focused on the provision of fighter aircraft, tanks and anti-submarine vessels. Until recently, the following aspects of defense were not given much consideration: a capacity for force projection, nuclear deterrence strategy, intelligence-gathering, and a strategy for countering non-conventional threats.

Within the context of perceived Cold War security needs and restrictions, the SDF built a world class army based on fighter aircraft, tanks and submarines. Even though the SDF has periodically upgraded its forces since the end of the Cold War within this context, new types of weapons and new modes of force structure have also become necessary. Acquisition of the following capabilities and weapons has been deemed necessary by sections of the mass media and the National Diet. This list enables one to understand the extent to which Constitutional and other constraints have contributed to the Japanese capacity deficit. It is deemed to be necessary to acquire:

1. long range fighter, bomber, and transport aircraft;

2. nuclear submarines;
3. aircraft carrier(s);
4. a missile defense system;
5. an intelligence gathering satellite;
6. destroyer vessels;
7. greater capacity to conduct peace keeping operations.

In response to September 11 the US government highlighted the following weapons and capabilities that it felt were necessary to address the new security environment. It is instructive to compare this list with the Japanese list above:

1. more efficient intelligence-gathering;
2. an enhanced capacity for pre-emption;
3. concerted efforts at anti-terrorism;
4. a missile defense system;
5. small weapons and light arms;
6. chemical and biological weapons;
7. precision targeting.

The events of the last decade, and in particular events since September 11, have highlighted the need for a re-appraisal of conventional national security strategy. Japan must address its voluminous export deficit. But it must also decide precisely what role it intends to play in international relations, as it gradually comes to acquire the status of a global ordinary power. This is an issue to which I now turn.

Manifesto visions of ordinary power, Japanese style

I have traced the evolution of Japan's foreign policy since 1945, and examined the two deficits which Japan must overcome if it is to become an ordinary power. The Constitutional issue remains unresolved, but in the last three decades three other important elements of Japanese foreign policy have been addressed. There has been a gradual strengthening of the SDF, a consolidation of the alliance with the US, and a more substantial engagement in peacekeeping operations and disarmament. Japan's military development has kept pace with that of other countries in the region which are seeking to enhance their military capability. Alliance consolidation has been adroit and smooth. Japan has vigorously supported peacekeeping and disarmament initiatives.

An important outcome of the November 9, 2003 general election is that a two party system has emerged. The two leftwing parties, the Social Democrats and the Communists, both lost a substantial proportion of their seats. Neither of the two major parties, the Liberal Democrats and the Democrats, articulated their foreign and security policies with any particular clarity during the campaign. What is clear, however, is that both parties support the idea of Constitutional revision in the near future.

The LDP supports a policy of *kaiken* (constitutional revision) while the DPJ supports a policy of *sōken* (constitution-creation). Prime Minister Koizumi's LDP found it impolitic to highlight the issue of constitutional reform during the campaign. Koizumi was critical of the conservative Nagatacho-Kasumigaseki bureaucratic establishment (Morris, 2002). By portraying the LDP's position as reformist, Koizumi was able to outmaneuver the DPJ, which presents itself as a champion of reform and seeks to trigger regime change. More importantly, the LDP was unable to articulate a clear foreign policy vision. It merely juxtaposed the three elements of foreign policy that I discussed above; self-strengthening, alliance consolidation and engagement in peacekeeping operations and disarmament initiatives. The DPJ was similarly unable to articulate a clear foreign policy vision. Although its election manifesto was quite ingenious in many ways, which was certainly a factor that contributed to its substantial increase in seats, from 137 to 177, the foreign policy section of the DPJ manifesto was half-baked. The merger of the two opposition parties, the Democrats (center left) and the Liberals (rightist) shortly before the campaign, meant that the new Democrats had insufficient time to forge a better-crafted manifesto on this particular issue. The DPJ's pro-UN and pro-alliance commitments were made clear, but it was less clear how these commitments might simultaneously be implemented within a coherent and practical framework.

The two minor leftwing parties lost many seats. The Communists saw their total number of seats drop from 20 to 9, and the number of Social Democratic seats was reduced from 18 to 6. This was partly due to the cumulatively felt impact of the introduction of the 'one person/ one district' system, which has been in effect in Lower House elections since 1993 (Shugart/Wattenberg 2003). The merger of the two largest opposition parties accentuated this trend. But the decline in support for these left wing parties is also due to the fact that their pacifist stances no longer appeal as strongly to the electorate. It is increasingly felt that the primarily pacifist stances of these two parties fail to address the pervasive sense of insecurity which Japanese voters feel as a result of aggressive American unilateralism, the North Korean threat and the postwar travails of Iraq. The new Kōmei party, a political wing of the lay Buddhist organization and a coalition partner of the LDP did gain gained a few more seats despite the impact of the introduction of the 'one person/one district' system. Its foreign policy manifesto is clearly pacifist, pro-UN and pro-alliance, as is that of the Democrats. But the major difference is that the Kōmei party has made clear its (highly qualified) support for the decision to send SDF troops to Iraq, as well as stating its very strong pro-UN position.

Since the LDP and the DPJ have unmistakably moved in the direction of Constitutional revision, it is necessary to discuss what sorts of Constitutional revision they might promote. The LDP focuses on Article Nine, arguing that with respect to the use of force in the settlement of international disputes Japan should revert to the ordinary status enjoyed by all other sovereign states. The LDP has already announced that it will propose a draft of a revised Constitution in 2005. In other words, it is not unlikely that this draft will be published whilst Koizumi is still in power. In justification of this position, the LDP argues that there has been a steady arms buildup in Japan's vicinity, and direct military threats have even been made. Furthermore, there is a new regional and global terrorist security threat and an ongoing need to consolidate the alliance with the United States. A number of specific incidents have persuaded the LDP to support Constitutional revision. These include North Korea's infringement of Japan's state sovereignty and human rights, and its claim to be in possession of nuclear weapons. China has also conducted frequent investigative sorties in areas surrounding Japanese territories, is involved in a steady military buildup, and has successfully launched a manned space vessel. There is an increasingly ominous terrorist threat in Southeast Asia. And, importantly, there is the ongoing need to keep up with United States global strategy by upgrading existing weapons and developing and/or purchasing new ones.

The LDP is also conducting an internal debate on the precise nature of its pro-UN policy. Specifically, it is debating the issue of whether the overseas dispatch of troops must be specifically mandated by a UN resolution or not. One study group, organized by Chief Cabinet Secretary Yasuo Fukuda, and chaired by a former United Nations official, Yasushi Akashi, has recommended that there be a continuing linkage between UN resolutions and the overseas dispatch of troops. Another study group, organized by Foreign Minister Yoriko Kawaguchi, and chaired by Prof Shinichi Kitaoka of the University of Tokyo, has recommended that the overseas dispatch of troops be delinked from UN resolutions.

To sum up, the foreign and security policy manifestos of all the political parties, especially those of the LDP and the DPJ, were insufficiently precise, coherent and practical. There are two reasons for this. The first is that legislation mandating the use of manifestos in the election campaign was only passed at a very late stage. This meant that there was an exceedingly short amount of time in which to craft a sophisticated manifesto. The second is that the foreign and security policy environments are both currently in a state of extreme flux, which makes it more difficult to keep up with events and to formulate generally relevant principles.

The emerging profile of a global ordinary power

Japan has adjusted its foreign policy roughly every 15 years. Each time, some unforeseen combination of domestic and international factors has led it to metamorphose, albeit within the broader framework of alliance with the United States and the non-use of force in the settlement of international disputes. The tensions inherent in military alliance with the United States and a Constitutionally stipulated non-use of force afford considerable space for metamorphosis. That is why it is very important to realize that Japan has been changing much more dramatically each and every 15 years than it appears at first glance.

What will be the emerging nature of Japan's ordinary power from 2005 to 2020? The legacies of pro-alliance orientation and the Constitutional ban on use of force will remain firm. Firstly, there is an emerging consensus on foreign security policy based on the three key components; alliance, pacifism, and a pro-UN orientation. The two large parties, the LDP and the DPJ, agree on these matters, and these three issues will be the pillars of Japan's global ordinary power. Differences between the LDP and DPJ foreign policy stances are likely to be a question of emphasis with regard to each pillar, rather than disputes over fundamental issues. The LDP is likely to give greater weight to the pro-alliance orientation than the DPJ, and attach less significance to the pro-UN and pacifist orientations. These three components aside, the LDP contains a bulk of legislators who talk tough on self-strengthening. The LDP is more likely to endorse the overseas deployment of troops than the DPJ, and less concerned than the DPJ about whether such a dispatch is authorized by a UN Security Council Resolution or not. The LDP would countenance the dispatch of Japanese forces to join a coalition not authorized by the UN, whereas the DPJ would not. The DPJ has been trying to differentiate itself from the LDP by giving greater weight to the pro-UN and pacifist orientations. The DPJ is more likely to come up with the line of giving a go-ahead to sending troops abroad to join UN forces, but not to join multinational forces, even with a UN resolution. It is also important to stress here that the new Kōmei party, a coalition partner of the LDP, takes its strong pacifist and pro-UN orientations very seriously. In light of its growing influence within the current LDP-Kōmei coalition, the Kōmei factor remains an imponderable with regard to the issue of the overseas dispatch of troops.

Secondly, Constitutional revisions are more likely to take place during the 2005–2020 period. If the LDP continues to hold power in one way or another, Constitutional revisions are likely to take the following form:

1. endorsement of the ordinary use of force in the settlement of international disputes;
2. greater empowerment of the Prime Minister in the direction of the 'Presidential Prime Minister' model; and an associated reduction in bureaucratic power;
3. greater restraints on the scope, nature, and expense of social policy;
4. greater inculcation of nationalism and patriotism.

It is important to note here that the new Kōmei party is unlikely to be comfortable with the first, second, and third of the four possible revisions that I have identified. The same is true of the DPJ, which would be especially unhappy about developments with regard to the third and fourth revisions, relating to social policy and patriotism.

Third, in terms of external environments in Japan's vicinity, relative calmness is expected to prevail during the period 2005–2020 if the following issues are handled deftly and cooperatively:

1. the Korean peninsula;
2. the Taiwan Straits issue;
3. China's transition to market economy and democratization;
4. North Korea's transition to market economy, democratization and re-unification.

As these are enormously significant issues, it is expected that Japan will reorient itself and respond to new contingencies as it is required to do so. Needless to say, Japan's ongoing metamorphosis into a global ordinary power is at least a partial response to the potential enormity of these problems.

10 Conclusion: Normal party politics, and ordinary global power

Japan's postwar politics were premised on one-party dominance, economic developmentalism, the military protection of the United States, and the renunciation of the use of force. Each of these premises is undergoing fundamental review and adjustment as a new period of international relations begins to take shape. Japan's politics, economics and international relations are undergoing a significant transformation. With the end of the Cold War Japan found itself under pressure to liberalize its trade and to make more of a contribution to its own defense, and there have been tensions in the alliance with the US. Although the LDP has tenaciously clung to power during most of the last decade, through a number of electoral coalitions, there has been a clear disillusionment with Japanese party politics. However, after 9/11 the international security environment has changed, with the result that there has been pressure on Japan to become more actively engaged in international politics. Japanese nationalism has also been on the increase in the 1990s, and these two events, taken together, have contributed to calls for reform of the Japanese Constitution. I conclude that it is likely that Japan will become an 'ordinary global power' in the coming years. What I mean by this is that Japan will re-assert its right to use force in the settlement of international disputes, as other states do. This would, of course, be a seismic development in the international relations of postwar Japan. I also conclude that we are witnessing the gradual emergence of a genuine two party system in Japanese domestic politics, as Japan comes to experience 'normal party politics'.

Normal party politics

The 2003 elections were widely characterized as a watershed with regard to the emergence of a two party system in post-1945 Japanese politics. The Liberal Democratic Party won but lost its simple majority, and the main opposition party made a substantial advance on the previous election. In response, the LDP absorbed a minor coalition partner, the Conservative Party, and a couple of other independents, in order to revive its simple majority. Along with another coalition partner, the new Kōmei Party, the governing coalition now possesses a fairly comfortable majority.

Many have noted that Japan has been subject to the unhealthy dominance of one party. Duverger has argued that if you have a system where one person is chosen from one district by means of a non-transferable vote, then a two party system is bound to emerge after a few general elections. In Japan the combination of the one person/one district system and the proportional representation system was introduced for Lower House elections in 1993. However, if the Duverger law is to be proved to be empirically valid with regard to the case of Japan, then it is necessary for there to be an alternation of power in the near future. Only then can we argue that a genuine two-party system has emerged.

The immediate post-war period of party politics is normally characterized as one of left-right contestation. Japan's defeat in World War II resulted in seven years of occupation by the Allied Powers. The key issue during this period was the alliance with the United States, and how it might be reconciled with the pacifist Constitution. The LDP placed emphasis on the significance of the alliance with the US, whereas the left-wing parties focused on the Constitution. Japan experienced rapid demographic, industrial and sociological transformation in a short span of time. Left-right confrontation at all levels was a symptom of these various developments.

The Japan – United States Security Treaty was revised in 1960 and left-right contestation reduced in intensity. The LDP dominated but did not have a two-thirds majority, as a result of which it was unable to revise the Constitution. The left-wing parties did not have a simple majority, as a result of which they were unable to remove the LDP from power. During this period the Yoshida doctrine was implemented. National security was delegated to the United States, and the Constitutional ban on the use of force in the settlement of international disputes was implemented. Energy and resources were focused on wealth accumulation. The period during which the Yoshida doctrine was pursued coincided with the period of high economic growth. The electorate became increasingly wealthy, but also discontented with what they saw as a redistribution mechanism which did not reward them appropriately. Support for the LDP decreased steadily as its power base (farmers and small business holders and manufacturers) was fundamentally undermined by unprecedented economic and social change.

The oil crisis took place at the height of the period of high growth, causing an economic slowdown. To the surprise of many observers, the steady decline in support for the LDP seemed to cease for a while during this period. There was no credible alternative to the one party dominance of the LDP. Nakasone presided over the core of this period, during which the developmental state partially transformed itself into a service delivery institution, focusing on pensions, health, welfare, medical insurance, and education. The bureaucratization of the LDP deepened, and the politicization of central bureaucracy intensified. The period ended with several scandals which hit the LDP hard and debilitated it for some time thereafter. The bubble economy, built in the latter half of the 1980s, collapsed in 1991, an event which coincided with the end of the Cold War.

The scandal-ridden and stagnating LDP experienced a large-scale exodus of members. The New Japan Party, which responded to popular demand for a fresh, clean, grass-roots based and pro-active party, took power in 1993. The LDP's postwar period of one party dominance ended in 1993. However, the New Japan Party and its successor held power for only one year. Thereafter the LDP resumed power in conjunction with the Socialists. After two years of coalition with the Socialists, the LDP regained a much more solid grip on power, but only in conjunction with shifting coalition partners.

In 2001, in response to popular distaste for the Nagatachō-Kasumigaseki establishment Koizumi gambled, and won, by slogan-eering that he would 'destroy the LDP, and rescue Japan with reform'. At this time, the LDP was extremely unpopular. The opposition was unanimously calling for economic recovery and reform of the whole system, especially with regard to social and defense policy. Koizumi outmaneuvered the opposition by championing himself as the leader of reform. In victory his coalition partners, as with his predecessor, were the new Kōmei Party and the Conservative Party.

When Koizumi scored a resounding victory in the LDP Presidential election in October 2003, he called a snap general election. But the electorate had become disaffected. The two largest opposition parties, the Democrats and the Liberals, united on the eve of the general election. The new Democratic Party posed a formidable challenge, and strongly advocated regime change. Civil society has also been maturing in Japan. As a result of all of these factors, the LDP ended up short of a simple majority, and the DPJ made a 40-seat advance. After the election, the Conservatives were absorbed into the LDP, which also collected some independent winners into its fold, and thereby regained a comfortable numerical majority in the National Diet.

This election campaign marked the first occasion when parties produced election manifestos. One legacy of the Koiziumi reform project was the fact that during the general election campaign there was transparent debate about which policies each party would pursue if they gained power. There were substantial debates on economic, social and defence policy. The new election manifestos played an important role in making these policy debates more familiar and intelligible to voters. The use of manifestos provided the DPJ with an opportunity to document and set out with clarity the long list of popular grievances voters had with regard to economic and social policy. The LDP repeated its reform slogan, but without being able to offer convincing evidence that it had lived up to its reformist pledges since the previous election. The LDP manifesto juxtaposed many diverse policy positions and pledges without a great deal of coherence. The manifesto also demonstrated that vested interests in various sectors were being protected.

The new Democratic Party of Japan repeated its demand for regime change, but without offering convincing, concrete and practical pledges to support their own economic, social and defense policies. Importantly, there was a general perception that Koizumi's reformist drive had faltered over issues such as the privatization of road construction and of postal services, and a reduction in the revenues made available to fund medical insurance, pension and social welfare. There was a feeling that despite his rhetoric Koizumi was more or less embraced by familiar vested interests. It was also becoming clear that the lack of order in postwar Iraq would make Japan's role in the reconstruction of its war-damaged economy and society dangerous and highly problematic. All these negative issues overlapped with and reinforced a sense that Koizumi's initially refreshing leadership powers were on the wane.

In terms of electoral mobilization, however, one could argue that the LDP did quite well, successfully activating its support bases in the districts, where the new DPJ did not have much time to cultivate support. What was most striking about the November elections, however, was the intensity of electoral mobilization by the new Kōmei Party. Its basic strategy was to offer electoral cooperation to parties whose candidate desperately needed substantial support from Kōmei voters. But this strategy was perhaps most successful in this last election. Kōmei now enjoys the status of a governing coalition partner. It has penetrated the LDP's support base by extending its electoral cooperation.

Kōmei is a comparatively small party and, as such, has enjoyed a disproportionate influence on public policy. Kōmei support for the LDP's policy of dispatching Self Defense Force troops to Iraq was decisive in determining the nature and timing of the dispatch. This new strength of the Kōmei Party has generated two responses. Some have suggested that Kōmei holds the electoral balance of power, and that the Kōmei Party can determine who will gain power by aligning or dealigning itself from particular parties as it pleases. Others have argued, however, that that the Kōmei Party's uneasy and opportunistic alliance with the LDP governing coalition visibly reduces popular support for the coalition government.

The Liberal Democratic Party lost power briefly in 1993, but has consistently been a key governing party since 1994. Four general explanations have been offered for the LDP's extraordinary electoral resilience during this period. These are: reform of the electoral system; the politicization of the bureaucracy; the limited effects of globalization; and the American promotion of polyarchy.

It has been suggested that the introduction of a mixed majoritarian voting system may be one of the major factors which has enabled the LDP to prolong its hold on power. This revised electoral system was introduced in 1993, with the aim of combining the best elements of two distinct voting systems, the majoritarian and proportional representation systems. Since this legislation was passed three general elections have taken place, in 1996, 2000 and 2003. There are signs that a genuine two-party system is emerging. The largest opposition party, the Democratic Party of Japan, has merged with the Liberal Party and successfully marginalized both the Social Democratic Party and the Communist Party. In doing so it has emerged as a party which is genuinely capable of assuming power, which is one of the criteria which need to be fulfilled in order that the Japanese system can be described as a genuine two-party system.

Japan's bureaucracy has been a key foundation of its politics. As a general rule of politics, it is clear that it is easier for a governing party to survive if it can successfully accommodate the modus operandi of the bureaucracy with which it has to deal. In its manifesto, the Democratic Party of Japan proposed that a substantial section of the senior bureaucracy should be politically appointable by a new governing party. This is one of the more original and distinctive policy proposals which the DPJ has come up with. But it is a worrying development for incumbent senior bureaucrats, because there is the possibility that they could lose their jobs if this manifesto pledge ever became policy. The existing bureaucracy, for this and other reasons, is therefore more supportive of the Liberal Democratic Party.

Substantial globalization would undermine the industrial and sociological power base of the Liberal Democratic Party. However the degree and rate of penetration of Japanese society by globalizing forces has been comparatively slow. This has allowed the Japanese economy, polity and society to adapt steadily to change without experiencing major disruption. Japan has a large population and a substantial economy, and this has allowed it to rely heavily on domestic markets. Within Japan, technological and economic adaptation to the pace of globalizing forces has been steady, and this is due to the way that Japanese handle industrial, financial and social adjustment.

Japan's increased economic competitiveness in the late 1980s and early 1990s gave rise to the suspicion in the United States and the rest of the world that Japan might be playing an unfair game, through its notorious industrial policy, its practices of administrative guidance and its keiretsu-style corporate organization. This suspicion led the United States government to make concerted attempts to unravel Japan's tightly knit business–bureaucracy nexus. At around this time there were a number of high profile LDP scandals, resulting in a pervasive distrust of the LDP amongst the Japanese electorate. The US found this environment helpful to its cause.

The LDP lost power in 1993. Hosokawa, head of the New Japan Party, became Prime Minister in 1993. The NJP and its successor, the New Frontier Party, believed that Japan should become an ordinary country, that is, it should embrace free trade, liberal market economics and liberal democracy, and should seek to become normal in the sense that it could use force in the settlement of international disputes. By 1994 the Socialist Party of Japan had left the NFP and formed a coalition with the LDP which was to prove sufficient for the LDP to return to power.

The economic goals of the United States government, namely market liberalization and the stimulation of international trade, were more or less achieved as the Japanese economy entered a prolonged period of stagnation, and thereby ceased to be a threat to US economic predominance. America's politico–military goal was to persuade Japan to use force to counter attacks on Japanese territory, and it was also successful in pursuing this objective. The 1997 Japan – United States Defense Guidelines recognize Japan as having primary responsibility for the repulsion of attacks on the Japanese mainland.

The terrorist attacks in the United States in 2001 prompted it to wage a global war on terrorism, in the course of which wars have been prosecuted in Afghanistan and Iraq. As a result of these developments Japan sent its Self Defense Force firstly to the Indian Ocean, and then to Iraq itself. These events have triggered a substantial debate within Japan as to whether troops should have been sent or not. This in turn has reignited older debates about the need for constitutional revision, with some arguing that the prohibition on the use of force for the settlement of international disputes, stipulated in the Constitution, should be removed.

In the early and mid-2000s, the United States government did not have to do much to promote polyarchy in Japan, because Koizumi Junichirö assumed power on the strength of his commitment to reform. This move towards polyarchy was a most welcome development for the US. The US government was also happy to see Prime Minister Koizumi steer Japan steadily in the direction of normal statehood, first by sending troops to the Indian Ocean and Iraq, and then paving the way for the revision of the Constitution.

The November 2003 general election has proved to be a watershed in a number of important ways. There has been a substantial move in the direction of a genuine two-party Japanese political system. The politicization of the bureaucracy has intensified. Japan's decade-long economic stagnation has led it to import a massive amount of foreign capital, and to shore up or purchase weak or bankrupt firms. Japan has invested massively in the overseas relocation of Japanese manufacturing. There has been much foreign direct investment, especially in China, and this has substantially facilitated the growth of globalization in both directions, and greatly diluted Japan's once-vaunted state-led developmentalism. The unipolar nature of the US's new foreign policy has led it to seek partners rather than allies, partners who are prepared to participate in contentious joint endeavors. Japan's transition may take a decade or more. But it is clear that the *ancien regime* characterized by one party politics, the ascendancy of the bureaucracy, state-led developmentalism and rigid alliance with the United States are gone.

Ordinary global power

Japan has chosen to define itself as an emerging global ordinary power, and it is in the process of consolidating this role for itself. Japan is becoming an ordinary power with Japanese characteristics. Although there have been substantial continuities in Japanese foreign policy since 1945, a closer look enables one to discern clear 15-year phases, and concomitant adjustments and shifts of emphasis to address emerging threats and conditions in world politics. These periods can be characterized as follows. The first entailed an internal battle between pro-alliance and anti-alliance sections of Japanese society (1945–1960). The second period was characterized by adherence to the Yoshida doctrine (1960–1975). The third period saw Japan tentatively emerge as a systemic supporter of the United States (1975–1990). The fourth period saw Japan attempt to pursue the role of global civilian power (1990–2005), and the fifth will see a gradual consolidation of Japan's emerging role as a global ordinary power (2005–2020).

The end of the Cold War set the stage for Japan and Germany, as 'global civilian powers', to play a more significant role in international relations. Both are populous, large and wealthy; both are pacifist; and both are good allies of the United States. However the legacy of the past and the ban on the use of force remains a burden for both countries. Despite these constraints, it was still possible for both countries to play a significant role in post-Cold War international relations. Using the emerging concept of human security as a guide for their actions, both countries engaged in peacekeeping operations and economic reconstruction projects in many parts of the Third World. During the early 1990s the United Nations, under the leadership of Secretary-General Boutros Boutros Ghali played a proactive role in the promotion of these activities. However, substantial problems began to emerge in the post-Cold War Third World. Global market integration deepened the predicament of poverty-stricken and strife-riddled countries. The end of U.S.–Soviet Cold War confrontation meant that both had a reduced stake in many Third World countries. This contributed to the creation of failed states and bankrupt economies. Addressing these tasks is beyond the self-proclaimed global civilian powers, the United Nations, other international organizations, and non-governmental organizations. Under such conditions the events of September 11 took place. These events have also paved the way for Japan to re-emerge as a global ordinary power.

Embracing defeat in 1945 resulted in two kinds of deficit which Japan must overcome as it attempts to become and behave like an ordinary power. Japan has a legitimacy deficit with regard to the use of force, and a capability deficit in using force as an instrument of defense, deterrence and diplomacy. Japan's legitimacy deficit manifests itself in a number of ways. First, Article Nine of the Japanese Constitution forbids Japan from using force to settle international disputes. The preamble of the Constitution also declares that Japan renounces war forever. The Constitution has played a strong role in shaping Japanese politics, and public sentiment has been tenaciously pacifist for more than a half a century. There are restrictions on the right of Japanese troops to use force. As Japan assumed a greater peacekeeping role, this created a new set of problems associated with the use of force in the execution of peacekeeping operations. Because Japan conceived of itself and promoted itself as a global civilian power, it was necessary to address such operational matters.

Japanese have invested a vast amount of time and effort, both inside and outside of the National Diet, to ensure that the participation of Self Defense Force troops in United Nations peace keeping operations has been Constitutionally appropriate. When this legislation was passed it was hailed as a major step towards Japan's re-assumption of the status of an ordinary power, although retrospectively this was only a comparatively minor step forward. This legislation stipulated that the overseas dispatch of troops for peacekeeping purposes could only be mandated by an appropriate United Nations Security Council resolution. It remained necessary for the overseas dispatch of troops to be legitimated by the United Nations.

There were further developments in the 2000s. Japan's participation in the Afghan war of 2002 was limited to the prosecution of tasks in the Indian Ocean. It was not necessary to legitimize these support activities with a UN Security Council Resolution, because the Indian Ocean was designated as a non-combat area. The stipulation of the Peace Keeping and Other Operations Law that Self Defense Force troops can only be sent to non-combat areas was not relevant for the same reason.

With regard to the Iraqi war, Prime Minister Koizumi indicated to the United States that Japan supported the war in Iraq shortly before the outbreak of hostilities in March 2003. The divisions between the members of the Security Council required Japan to perform a careful diplomatic balancing act. Japan justified its support for the coalition forces by referring to the fact that Iraq was in breach of numerous existing Security Council resolutions which had been passed since 1991. However, Japan did not make reference to the WMD issue in justifying its support for the intervention. By not invoking the WMD issue, Japan was simultaneously able both to sustain its argument that military action requires a United Nations resolution, and to remain a close and demonstrably reliable partner of the United States.

Japan's capacity deficit stems from the fact that the Self Defense Force was established on the assumption that it would operate for strictly defensive purposes. It is very important to underline the point that the SDF's role in the protection of national security was initially tertiary. The Constitution has effectively constrained and dictated the SDF's force structure up until the present time. Only in the mid-1990s has there been a general recognition that the most important function of the SDF is the protection of national security. Legal, institutional and public opinion have typically placed constraints on the kind of weapons and forces with which it has been felt appropriate for the SDF to be equipped. These constraints have contributed to the emergence of Japan's capacity deficit. The National Diet has stipulated all manner of constraints, specifying the nature and number of weapons that can be deployed. One problem for the Japanese government is that weapons technology is constantly evolving, and therefore even armed forces configured in an exclusively defensive manner are periodically forced to upgrade their weapons and revise their force structures to keep pace with new developments. Military configurations and threat perceptions have changed, and, as a result, so has Japan's alliance with the United States.

The events of the last decade, and in particular events since September 11, have highlighted the need for a re-appraisal of conventional national security strategy. Japan must decide precisely what role it intends to play in international relations, as it gradually comes to acquire the status of a global ordinary power. The Constitutional issue remains unresolved, but in the last three decades three other important elements of Japanese foreign policy have been addressed. There has been a gradual strengthening of the SDF, a consolidation of the alliance with the US, and a more substantial engagement in peacekeeping operations and disarmament.

An important outcome of the 2003 general election is that a two party system has emerged. However, neither of the two major parties, the Liberal Democrats and the Democrats, articulated their foreign and security policies with any particular clarity during the campaign. What is clear, however, is that both parties support the idea of Constitutional revision in the near future. The LDP supports a policy of *kaiken* (Constitutional revision) while the DPJ supports a policy of *sōken* (Constitution-creation). Prime Minister Koizumi's LDP found it impolitic to highlight the issue of Constitutional reform during the campaign. More importantly, the LDP was unable to articulate a clear foreign policy vision. It merely juxtaposed the three elements of foreign policy that I discussed above; self-strengthening, alliance consolidation and engagement in peacekeeping operations and disarmament initiatives. The DPJ was similarly unable to articulate a clear foreign policy vision. The merger of the two opposition parties, the Democrats (center left) and the Liberals (rightist) shortly before the campaign, meant that the new Democrats had insufficient time to forge a better-crafted manifesto on this particular issue. The DPJ's pro-UN and pro-alliance commitments were made clear, but it was less clear how these commitments might simultaneously be implemented within a coherent and practical framework.

The two minor leftwing parties lost many seats. The merger of the two largest opposition parties accentuated this trend. But the decline in support for these left wing parties is also due to the fact that their pacifist stances no longer appeal as strongly to the electorate. It is increasingly felt that the primarily pacifist stances of these two parties fail to address the pervasive sense of insecurity which Japanese voters feel as a result of aggressive American unilateralism, the North Korean threat and the postwar travails of Iraq. The new Kōmei Party's foreign policy manifesto is clearly pacifist, pro-UN and pro-alliance, as is that of the Democrats. But the major difference is that the Kōmei Party has made clear its (highly qualified) support for the decision to send SDF troops to Iraq, as well as stating its very strong pro-UN position.

Since the LDP and the DPJ have unmistakably moved in the direction of Constitutional revision, it is necessary to discuss what sorts of Constitutional revision they might promote. The LDP focuses on Article Nine, arguing that with respect to the use of force in the settlement of international disputes Japan should revert to the ordinary status enjoyed by all other sovereign states. The LDP has already announced that it will propose a draft of a revised Constitution in 2005. In justification of this position, the LDP argues that there has been a steady arms buildup in Japan's vicinity, and direct military threats have even been made. Furthermore, there is a new regional and global terrorist security threat and an ongoing need to consolidate the alliance with the United States. A number of specific incidents relating to

Japan's relations with the United States, North Korea, China and South Asia have persuaded the LDP to support Constitutional revision.

What will be the emerging nature of Japan's ordinary power from 2005 to 2020? Firstly, there is an emerging consensus on security policy based on the three key components; alliance, pacifism, and a pro-UN orientation. The two large parties, the LDP and the DPJ, agree on these matters, and these three issues will be the pillars of Japan's global ordinary power. Differences between the LDP and DPJ foreign policy stances are likely to be a question of emphasis with regard to each pillar, rather than disputes over fundamental issues. The LDP is likely to give greater weight to the pro-alliance orientation than the DPJ, and attach less significance to the pro-UN and pacifist orientations. The LDP is more likely to endorse the overseas deployment of troops than the DPJ, and less concerned than the DPJ about whether such a dispatch is authorized by a UN Security Council Resolution or not. The LDP would countenance the dispatch of Japanese forces to join a coalition not authorized by the UN, whereas the DPJ would not. The DPJ has been trying to differentiate itself from the LDP by giving greater weight to the pro-UN and pacifist orientations. The DPJ is more likely to come up with the line of giving a go-ahead to sending troops abroad to join UN forces, but not to join multinational forces, even with a UN resolution. It is also important to stress here that the new Kōmei Party, a coalition partner of the LDP, takes its strong pacifist and pro-UN orientations very seriously. In light of its growing influence within the current LDP–Kōmei coalition, the Kōmei factor remains an imponderable with regard to the issue of the overseas dispatch of troops.

Secondly, Constitutional revisions are more likely to take place during the 2005–2020 period if the LDP continues to hold power in one way or another. In that case, Constitutional revisions are likely to take the form of: endorsement of the ordinary use of force in the settlement of international disputes; greater empowerment of the Prime Minister in the direction of the 'Presidential Prime Minister' model, and an associated reduction in bureaucratic power; greater restraints on the scope, nature, and expense of social policy; and a greater inculcation of nationalism and patriotism. It is important to note here that the new Kōmei Party is unlikely to be comfortable with the first, second, and third of the four possible revisions that I have identified. The same is true of the DPJ, which would be especially unhappy about developments with regard to social policy and patriotism.

Third, in terms of external environments in Japan's vicinity, it is crucial that the following issues are handled deftly and cooperatively: the Korean peninsula; the Taiwan Straits issue; China's democratization and transition to market economy; and North Korea's democratization, re-unification and transition to a market economy. As these are enormously significant issues, it is expected that Japan will reorient itself and respond to new contingencies as it is required to do so. Needless to say, Japan's ongoing metamorphosis into a global ordinary power is a measured response to the potential enormity of these problems.

References

Alletzhauser, Al, *The House of Nomura*, London, Bloomsbury,1990.

Almond, Gabriel and Sydney Verba, *The Civic Culture*, Princeton, Princeton University Press, 1963.

Amaya, Naohiro, *Nihonkeizai: Utage no ato-eikō nōsangyōshakai wa dokoe ikunoka*, Tokyo, PHP Kenkyūjo, 1984.

Amino, Yoshihiko, *Nihonchūsei no hi nōgyomin to tennō*, Tokyo, Iwanami Shoten, 1984.

Amino, Yoshihiko, *Ikeino ōken*, Tokyo, Heibonsha, 1986.

Amino, Yoshihiko, *Nihonshakai to tennōsei*, Tokyo, Iwanami Shoten, 1988.

Amino, Yoshihiko, *Nihonron no shi za – Rettōshakai to kokka*, Tokyo, Shōgakukan, 1990.

Angel, Robert, *Explaining Economic Policy Failure: Japan in the 1969–1971 International Monetary Crisis*, New York, Columbia University Press, 1991.

Aoki, Masahiko, *Information, Incentives and Bargaining in the Japanese Firm*, Cambridge, Cambridge University Press, 1988.

Armitage, Richard et al. *The United States and Japan: Advancing Toward a Mature Partnership*, INSS Special Report, October 11, 2000.

Asahi Shinbun, 8–9 July 1992.

Asahi Shinbun, evening edition, 18 August 1992.

Asahi Shinbun, 'Seikatsu jūshi tsuranukeruka, Kōkyōjigyō, Nandai wa haibun danryokuka,' 11 December 1992.

Asahi Shinbunsha Yokohamashikyoku, ed., *Rikurūto giwaku o otte*, Asahi Shinbunsha, 1988.

Anderson, Benedict, *Imagined Communities: Reflections on the Origins and Spread of Nationalism*, London, Verso, 1983.

Anderson, Perry, *Lineages of the Absolutist State*. London, New Left Books, 1974.

Austin, Lewis, *Samurais and Saints*, New Haven, Yale University Press, 1972.

Banno, Junji, *Meiji kenpōtaisei no kakuritsu*, Tokyo, Tokyo Daigaku Shuppankai, 1971.

de Bary, Theodore, *East Asian Civilizations: A Dialogue in Five Stages*, Cambridge, Harvard University Press, 1988.

Bergsten, C. Fred, *The Dilemmas of the Dollar: The Economics and Politics of United States International Economic Policy*, New York, New York University Press, 1975.

Brodie, Bernard, *Strategy in the Missile Age*, Princeton, Princeton University Press, 1959.

Berkowitz, Edward and Kim McQuaid, *Creating the Welfare State: The Political Economy of Twentieth Century Reform*, New York, Praeger, 1980.

Bitō, Masahide, *Edo jidai towa nanika*, Tokyo, Iwanami Shoten, 1992.

Blaker, Michael, *Patterns in Japan's International Negotiating Behaviour before World War II*, NewYork, Columbia University Press, 1977.

Borg, Dorothy and Shumpei Okamoto, eds., *Pearl Harbour as History*, New York, Columbia University Press, 1973.

Broad, Robin, *Unequal Alliance: The World Bank, the International Monetary Fund, and the Philippines*, Berkeley, University of California Press, 1988.

Brown, Philip, *Central Authority and Local Autonomy in Early Modern Japan*. Stanford, Stanford University Press, 1993.

Buckley, Roger, *Occupation Diplomacy: Britain, the United States and Japan, 1945–1952*, Cambridge, Cambridge University Press, 1982.

Buckley, Roger, *US–Japan Alliance Diplomacy, 1945–1990*, Cambridge, Cambridge University Press, 1992.

Burns, John, *Political Participation in China*, Berkeley, University of California Press, 1988.

Calder, Kent E., *Crisis and Compensation*, Princeton, Princeton University Press, 1989.

Capling, M.A. and B. Galligan, *Beyond the Protective State: The Political Economy of Australia's Manufacturing Industry Policy*, Cambridge, Cambridge University Press, 1993.

Cheng, Tunjen and Stephan Hagaard, eds., *Political Change in Taiwan,* Boulder, Lynn Rienner, 1992.

Cipolla, Carlo, ed., *The Fontana Economic History of Europe*, 9 vols., Glasgow, Collins, 1972–1976.

Cooper, Richard, *The Economics of Interdependence*, New York, McGraw-Hill, 1968.

Cumings, Bruce, *The Origins of the Korean War*, 2 Vols., Princeton, Princeton University Press, 1981 and 1990.

Daikakai Naimushōshi Hensen Iinkai, ed. *Naimushōshi*, Vol. 2, p. 10, 1971.

Davis, Mike, *Prisoners of the American Dream*, London, Verso, 1986.

Davis, Winston, 'Religion and Development: Weber and East Asian Experience,' in Myron Weiner and Samuel Huntington, eds., *Understanding Political Development*, Boston, Little, Brown, 1987, pp. 221–80.

Dokyumento Nihon no kōgai, 8 Vols., Tokyo, Ryokufū Shuppan, 1986–92.

Destler, I. M., *American Trade Politics*, 2nd edition, Washington, D.C., The Twentieth Century Fund for Institute for International Economics, 1992.

Doi, Takeo, *Amae no kōzō*, Tokyo, Kōbundō, 1971.

Dore, Ronald, *Flexible Rigidities: Industrial Policy and Structural Adjustment in the Japanese Economy, 1970–1980*, London, Athlone Press, 1985.

Dore, Ronald, *Taking Japan Seriously: A Confucian Perspective on Leading Economic Issues*, London, Athlone Press, 1987.

Dore, Ronald, *British Factory – Japanese Factory: The Origins of National Diversity in Industrial Relations*, Berkeley, University of California Press, 1973.

Dower, John, 'The Useful War,' *Daedalus*, Vol. 119, No. 3, Summer 1990, pp. 49–70.

Dower, John, *Embracing Defeat: Japan in the Wake of World War II*, New York; London, W.W. Norton, New Press, 1999.

Downs, Anthony, *An Economic Theory of Democracy*, New York, Harper & Row, 1957.

Duverger, Maurice, *Les partis politiques*, Paris, Armand Colin, 1951.

Duus, Peter, Ramon Myers and Clark Peattie, eds., *The Japanese Informal Empire*, Princeton, Princeton University Press, 1989.

The Economist, 'The Endless Road: A Survey of the Car Industry,' 17–23 October 1992, pp. S1–S20.

Eberwein, Wolf-Dieter and Karl Kaiser eds., *Germany's New Foreign Policy: Decision-Making in an Interdependent World*, New York, Palgrave, 2001.

Emmott, Bill, *Japan's Global Reach: The Influence, Strategies and Weakness of Japan's Multinational Companies*, London, Century, 1991.

Evans, Peter, *Dependent Development: The Alliance of Multinational State and Local Capital in Brazil*, Princeton, Princeton University Press, 1979.

Fei, John C.H., Kazushi Ohkawa and Gustav Ranis, 'Economic Development in Historical Perspective: Japan, Korea and Taiwan,' in Kazushi Ohkawa and Gustav Ranis, eds., *Japan and the Developing Countries*, Oxford, Blackwell, 1985, pp. 37–64.

Ferguson, Thomas, 'Party Realignment and American Industrial Structure: The Investment Theory of Political Parties in Historical Perspective,' in *Research in Political Economy*, Vol. 6, edited by Paul Zarembka, Westport, JAI Press, 1983, pp. 1–82.

Ferguson, Thomas, and Joel Rogers, *Right Turn: The Decline of the Democrats and the Future of American Politics*, New York, Hill and Wang, 1983.

Finn, Richard, *Winners in Peace: MacArthur, Yoshida, and Postwar Japan*, Berkeley, University of California Press, 1992.

Flanagan, Scott, Shunsaku Kohei, Ichiro Miyake, Bradley M. Richardson and Joji Watunaki, *The Japanese Voter*, New Haven, Yale University Press, 1992.

Flynn, Dennis D., 'Comparing the Tokugawa Shogunate with Hapsburg Spain: Two Silver-Based Empires in a Global Setting,' in James Tracy, ed., *The*

Political Economy of Merchant Empires: State Power and World Trade, 1350–1750, Cambridge, Cambridge University Press, 1991, pp. 332–59.

Foucault, Michel, *Discipline and Punish: The Birth of the Prison*, New York, Vintage Books, 1995.

Friedman, David, *The Misunderstood Miracle: Industrial Development and Political Change in Japan*, Ithaca, Cornell University Press, 1988.

Fukushima, Akiko, *Japan's Foreign Policy*, London, Palgrave, 1999.

Fukuyama, Francis, *The End of History and the Last Man*. New York, Basic Books, 1991.

Fukuyama, Francis, *Trust: Social Virtues and the Creation of Prosperity*, New York, Simon and Schuster, 1995.

Funabashi, Yoichi. 'Japan and the New World Order.' *Foreign Affairs*, pp.58–74, 1991.

Gaddis, John, *Strategies of Containment: A Critical Assessment of Postwar American National Security Policy*, New York, Oxford University Press, 1982.

Gaddis, John, *The Long Peace: An Inquiry into the History of the Cold War*, New York, Oxford University Press, 1987.

Garon, Sheldon, *The State and Labor in Modern Japan*, Berkeley, University of California Press, 1987.

Gates, Hill, *Chinese Working Class Lives: Getting By in Taiwan*, Ithaca, Cornell University Press, 1987.

Gereffi, Gary and Donald Wyman, *Manufacturing Miracles: Paths of Industrialization in Latin America and East Asia*, Princeton, Princeton University Press, 1990.

Gerschenkron, Alexander, *Economic Backwardness in Historical Perspective*, Cambridge, Harvard University Press, 1962.

Gerschenkron, Alexander, *Bread and Democracy in Germany*, Ithaca, Cornell University Press, 1989 (with a new Foreword).

Giddens, Anthony, *The Constitution of Society*, Oxford, Polity Press, 1984.

Giddens, Anthony, *The Nation-State and Violence*, Oxford, Polity Press, 1985.

Gilpin, Robert, *War and Change in World Politics*, New York, Cambridge University Press, 1981.

Hagaard, Stephan. *The Political Economy of the Asian Financial Crisis*, Washington, DC, Institute of International Economics, 1999.

Hakuhōdō Sōgō Kenkyūjo, *Nihonjin no jishin*, Tokyo, Hakuhōdō, 1992.

Hanley, Susan, and Kozo Yamamura, *Economic and Demographic Change in Preindustrial Japan*, Princeton, Princeton University Press, 1977.

Harding, Harry, *The Second Revolution: Reform After Mao*, Washington, D.C., Brookings Institution, 1987.

Hatch, Walter and Kozo Yamamura, *Asia in Japan's Embrace: Building a Regional Production Alliance*, Cambridge, Cambridge University Press, 1996.

Hattori, Tamio, *Kankoku – nettowāku to seiji bunka*, Tokyo, Tokyo Daigaku Shuppankai, 1992.

Hawes, Gary, *The Philippine State and the Marcos Regime: The Politics of Export*, Ithaca, Cornell University Press, 1987.

Hayami, Tōru, *Nihon ni okeru keizaishakai no seiritsu*, Tokyo, Keiō Tsūshin, 1973.

Hayami, Tōru, *Kinsei nōson no rekishi jinkōgaku kenkyū*, Tokyo, Tōyō Keizai Shinpōsha, 1977.

Hayami, Tōru, *Edo no nōmin seikatsushi*, Tokyo, Nihon Hōsō Shuppan Kyōkai, 1988.

Hayami, Yūjirō, *Nōgyō keizairon*, Tokyo, Iwanami Shoten, 1986.

Hayami, Yūjirō, *Japanese Agriculture under Siege*, London, Macmillan, 1990.

Hayashi, Fusao, *Daitōa sensō kōteiron*, Tokyo, Banmachi Shobō, 1964.

Held, David, *Models of Democracy*, Oxford, Polity Press, 1987.

Henderson, Gregory, *The Politics of Vortex*, Cambridge, Harvard University Press, 1969.

Hirschman, Albert, *Exit, Voice and Loyalty: Responses to Decline in Firms, Organizations and States*, Cambridge, Harvard University Press, 1970.

Hirschman, Albert, 'Exit, Voice, and the Fate of the German Democratic Republic, An Essay in Conceptual Analysis,' *World Politics*, Vol. 45, No. 2, January 1993, pp. 173 202.

Huntington, Samuel, *American Politics: Promises of Disharmony*, Cambridge, Belknap Press, 1981.

Hosono, Akio, *Raten Amerika no keizai*, Tokyo, Tokyo Daigaku Shuppankai, 1983.

Hosono, Akio and Tsunekawa Keiichi, *Raten Amerika kiki no kōzu*, Tokyo, Yūhikaku, 1986.

Igarashi, Takeshi, *Tainichikōwa to reisen-sengo nichibeikankei no keisei*, Tokyo, Tokyo Daigaku Shuppankai, 1986.

Iida, Tsuneo, *Nihonteki chikarazuyosa no saihakken*, Tokyo, Nihon Keizai Shinbunsha, 1979.

Iida, Tsuneo, 'Ginkō ni motomerareru kiritsu, Tokyoku mo keizaiunei machigau,' *Asahi Shinbun*, evening edition, 21 December 1992.

Ikegami, Eiko, The *Taming of the Samurai: Honorific Individualism and the Making of Modern Japan*, Harvard, Harvard University Press, 1995.

Ikenberry, G. John and Takashi Inoguchi, *Reinventing the alliance: U.S.–Japan security partnership in an era of change*, New York, Palgrave Macmillan, 2003.

Inada, Kenichi, Sueo Sekiguchi and Yasutoyo Shōda, eds., *The Mechanism of Economic Development: Growth in the Japanese and East Asian Economies,* Oxford, Clarendon Press, 1993.

Inoguchi, Kuniko, *Posuto haken shisutemu to Nihon no sentaku,* Tokyo, Chikuma Shobō, 1987.

Inoguchi, Kuniko, *Sensō to heiwa,* Tokyo, Tokyo Daigaku Shuppankai, 1989.

Inoguchi, Takashi, *Gendai Nihon seiji keizai kōtō,* Tōyō Keizai Shinpōsha, 1983.

Inoguchi, Takashi, 'The Sources of Japanese Political Stability,' in Ronald A. Morse and Shigenobu Yoshida, eds., *Blind Partners: American and Japanese Responses to an Unknown Future,* Lanham, University Press of America, 1985, pp. 43–50.

Inoguchi, Takashi, 'Japan's Images and Options: A Supporter, Not a Challenger,' *Journal of Japanese Studies,* Vol.2, No.1, 1986, pp.95–119.

Inoguchi, Takashi, 'The Japanese Double Election of 6 July 1986,' *Electoral Studies,* Vol. 6, No. 1, April, 1987a, pp. 63–9.

Inoguchi, Takashi, 'The Legacy of a Weathercock Prime Minister,' *Japan Quarterly,* Vol. XXXIV, No. 4, October–December 1987b, pp. 363–70.

Inoguchi, Takashi, 'Gendai Chūgoku seiji taiseiron,' *Higashi Ajia hikaku kenkyū nyūzu retaa,* No. 1, 5 November 1987c.

Inoguchi, Takashi, *Kokka to shakai,* Tokyo, Tokyo Daigaku Shuppankai, 1988.

Inoguchi, Takashi, 'Nichibei kankei norinen to kōzō,' *Rebaiasan,* No. 5, Autumn 1989a, pp. 7–33.

Inoguchi, Takashi, 'Children of Tradition,' *Far Eastern Economic Review,* 26 December 1989b, p. 15.

Inoguchi, Takashi, 'The Political Economy of Conservative Resurgence under Recession: Public Policies and Political Support in Japan, 1977–1983,' in T. J. Pempel, ed., *Uncommon Democracies: The One-Party Dominant Regimes,* Ithaca, Cornell University Press, 1990a, pp. 189–225.

Inoguchi, Takashi, 'Japan's Politics of Interdependence,' *Government and Opposition,* Vol. 25, No. 4, Autumn 1990b, pp. 419–37.

Inoguchi, Takashi, 'Japan's Response to the Gulf Crisis: An Analytic Overview,' *Journal of Japanese Studies,* Vol. 17, No. 2, 1991a, pp. 257–73.

Inoguchi, Takashi, 'Asia-Pacific since 1945: A Japanese Perspective,' in Robert Taylor, ed., *Handbooks to the World: Asia and the Pacific,* Vol. 2, New York, FactsOnFile, 1991b, pp. 903–20.

Inoguchi, Takashi, 'Japan's Response to the Gulf Crisis: An Analytic Overview,' *Journal of Japanese Studies,* Vol. 26, No.2, Spring 1991c, pp. 257–273.

Inoguchi, Takashi, 'Awed, Inspired and Disillusioned: Japanese Scholarship on American Politics,' in Richard Samuels and Myron Weiner, eds., *The*

Political Culture of Foreign Area and International Studies, Washington D.C., Brassey's, 1992a, pp. 57–74.

Inoguchi, Takashi, 'Japan's Role in International Affairs', *Survival*, Vol. 34, No. 2, Summer 1992b, pp. 71–87.

Inoguchi, Takashi, 'Seiji kaikaku toiu genei to rejiimu no henkō,' *Ekonomisuto*, 18–25 August 1992c, pp. 104–6.

Inoguchi, Takashi, 'Japan's Foreign Policy in East Asia,' *Current History*, Vol. 91, December 1992d, pp. 407–12.

Inoguchi Takashi, 'In Search of Japan's Normal Role in the Wake of the End of the Cold War,' *Adelphi Papers*, No. 274, 1993a.

Inoguchi, Takashi, *Keizai Taikoku no Seiji Unei*, Tokyo, Tokyo Daigaku Shuppankai, 1993b.

Inoguchi, Takashi, 'Factional Dynamics of Japan's Ruling Party, the LDP,' *Asian Journal of Political Science*, Vol. 1, No. 1, 1993c.

Inoguchi, Takashi, 'Dialectics of World Order: A View from Pacific Asia,' in Hans-Henrik Holm and Georg Sorensen, ed., *Whose World Order? Uneven Globalization and the End of the Cold War*, Boulder, Westview Press, 1994a.

Inoguchi, Takashi, 'Democracy and the Development of Political Science in Japan,' in David Easton, John Gunnell and Michael Stein, eds., *Regime and Discipline: Democracy and the Development of Political Science*, Ann Arbor, University of Michigan Press, 1994b.

Inoguchi, Takashi, 'Distant Neighbors? Japan and Asia,' *Current History*, Vol. 94, no. 595, pp. 392–6, 1995a.

Inoguchi, Takashi, 'Japan's United Nations Peacekeeping and Other Operations,' *International Journal*, Vol. 50, no. 2, pp. 325–42, 1995b.

Inoguchi, Takashi, 'Three Frameworks in Search of a Policy: US Democracy Promotion in Asia-Pacific,' Michael Cox, G. John Ikenberry and Takashi Inoguchi eds, *American Democracy Promotion: Impulses, Strategies and Impacts*, Oxford, Oxford University Press, 2000, pp. 267–86.

Inoguchi, Takashi, *Global Change: A Japanese Perspective*, London, Palgrave, 2001.

Inoguchi, Takashi, 'A Northeast Asian Perspective,' *Australian Journal of International Affairs*, vol. 55 no. 2, 2002a, pp. 199–212.

Inoguchi, Takashi, 'Festina Lente or Hurry Up Slowly: Why Japan is Fast and Slow,' *Journal of Japanese Trade and Industry*, Jan/Feb, No. 6, 2002b, pp. 16–20.

Inoguchi, Takashi, ed., *Japan's Asian Policy: Its Revival and Response*, New York, Palgrave, 2002b.

Inoguchi, Takashi, 'Governance Across Borders in Northeast Asia: Shaping and Sharing Identities, Ideas, Interests and Institutions', paper prepared for presentation at the conference 'Governance Across Borders: National, Regional, and Global' organized by the delegation of the European Commission in Japan and the United Nations University, January 24–25, 2002c Tokyo.

Inoguchi, Takashi, 'The Japanese decision,' *openDemocracy*, 7 August 2003a, www.openDemocracy.net.

Inoguchi, Takashi, 'An ordinary power, Japanese-style,' *openDemocracy*, 26 February 2004b, www.openDemocracy.net.

Inoguchi, Takashi, 'America and Japan: the political is personal,' *openDemocracy*, 17 June 2004c, www.openDemocracy.net.

Inoguchi, Takashi and Iwai Tomoaki, *Zoku giin no kenkyū*, Tokyo, Nihon Keizai Shinbunsha, 1987.

Inoue, Hisashi, *Kome no hanashi*, Shinchōsha, Tokyo, 1992.

Inoue, Kiyoshi, *Nihon teikokushugi no keisei*, Tokyo, Iwanami Shoten, 1988.

Iokibe, Makoto, *Beikoku no Nihon senryōseisaku-sengo Nihon no sekkeizu*, 2 vols., Tokyo, Chūō Kōronsha, 1985.

Irie, Takanori, *Haisha no sengo*, Tokyo, Chūō Kōronsha, 1989.

Iriye, Akira, *After Imperialism*, Cambridge, Harvard University Press, 1965.

Ishida, Takeshi, *Nihon no seiji bunka – Dōchō to kyōsō*, Tokyo, Tokyo Daigaku Shuppankai, 1970.

Ishigami, Eiichi, et al., eds., *Zen kindai no tennō*, Vol. 1–6, Tokyo, Aoki Shoten, 1993.

Ishihara, Shintarō and Morita Akio, *No toieru Nippon*, Tokyo, Bungeishunshō, 1989.

Ishii, Takashi, *Meiji ishin no kokusaiteki kankyo*, revised edition, Tokyo, Yoshikawa Kōbunkan, 1966

Ishii, Takashi, *Nihon kaikokushi*, Tokyo, Yoshikawa Kōbunkan, 1972.

Ishii, Takashi, *Meiji shoki no kokusaikankei*, Tokyo, Yoshikawa Kōbunkan, 1977

Itagaki, Yūzō, ed., *Chutō: Wangansensō to Nihon*, Tokyo, Daisanshokan, 1991.

Iwai, Tomoaki, *Seiji shikin no kenkyū*, Tokyo, Nihon Keizai Shinbunsha, 1990.

Jaenicke, Martin, *The Failure of Politics: The Importance of Politics in Industrial Society,* Oxford, Polity Press, 1990.

Johnson, Chalmers, *MITI and the Japanese Economic Miracle*, Stanford, Stanford University Press, 1981.

Johnson, Chalmers, 'Political Institutions and Economic Performance: Government–Business Relations in Japan, South Korea and Taiwan,' in Frederic Deyo, ed., *The Political Economy of the New Asian Industrialism*, Ithaca, Cornell University Press, 1986, pp. 136–64.

Johnson, Chalmers, *Blowback: The Costs and Consequences of American Empire*, New York, Metropolitan Books, Henry Holt, 2000.

Kabashima, Ikuo, 'Supportive Participation and Economic Growth: The Case of Japan,' *World Politics*, Vol. 36, No. 3, April 1984, pp. 309–38.

Kabashima, Ikuo and Taku Sugawara, 'Sōsenkyo Kekka wo Bunseki suru, Kōmei ga dotsira wo Ebrabuka de Seiken ha Kawaru,' Tokyo, Chūō Kōron. Jan 2004, pp. 90–9.

Kaldor, Mary, *The Imaginary War: The East-West Conflict*, Oxford, Blackwell, 1990.

Kamata, Satoshi, *Jidōsha zetsubō kōjō*, Tokyo, Gendaishi Shuppankai, 1981.

Kamata, Satoshi, *Kyoiku kōjō no kodomotachi*, Tokyo, Iwanami Shoten, 1984.

Kanō, Yoshikazu, *Nihon yo, Nōgyōkokkatare*, Tokyo, Tōyō Keizai Shinpōsha, 1984.

Karatsu, Hajime, *Gijutsu taikoku ni koritsu nashi*, Tokyo, PHS Kenkyūjo, 1990.

Kasaya, Kazuhiko, *Shukun oshikome no kōzū*. Tokyo, Yoshikawa Kōbunkan, 1989.

Katada, Saori, Hanns Maull, Takashi Inoguchi, *Global Governance: Germany and Japan in the International System*, London, Ashgate, 2004.

Kataoka, Tetsuya, *Saraba Yoshidashigeru-Kyokōnaki sengo seijishi*, Tokyo, Bungei Shunjū, 1992.

Katō, Kunihiko, *Hekichi no jimintō den*, Tokyo, Jōhō Sentaa Shuppankyoku, 1985.

Kawaguchi, Kaiji, *Chinmoku no kantai*, Vol. 1–16, Kōdansha, 1988.

Kawato, Sadafuni, *Nihon no seitō seiji, 1890–1937 nen-gikaibunseki to senkyo no sūryōbunseki*, Tokyo, Tokyo Daigaku Shuppankai, 1992.

Keeler, John, and Martin Schain, Eds., *Chirac's Challenge: Liberalization, Europeanization, and Malaise in France*, New York, Palgrave, 1996.

Kennedy, Paul, *The Rise and Fall of the Great Powers*, London, Unwin Hyman, 1988.

Kihl, Young Whan, *Politics and Policies in Divided Korea: Regimes in Contest*, Boulder, Westview Press, 1984.

Kim, Young-ho, *Higashi Ajia no kōgyōka to sekai shihonshugi*, Tokyo, Tōyō Keizai Shinpōsha, 1988.

Kissinger, Henry A, *Does America Need a Foreign Policy?: Toward a Diplomacy for the 21st Century*, New York, Simon & Schuster, 2001.

Kitaoka, Shinichi, 'Nichibei Anpo o kijiku nishita [Kokuren Jūshi] e, Nihon ga Kokuren chūshin shugi datta koto wa katsute itshidomo naishi, watashi wa sore ni hantai demoaru,' Tokyo, *Chuō Kōron*. May 2003, pp. 56–61.

Klingemann, Hans-Dieter, Richard I. Hofferbert, Ian Budge, with Hans Keman., eds., *Parties, Policies, and Democracy (Theoretical Lenses on Public Policy)* Boulder, Westview Press, 1994.

Koh, B. C., *Japan's Administrative Elite*, Berkeley, University of California Press, 1989.

Kolko, Gabriel, *Railroads and Regulation, 1877–1916*, Princeton, Princeton University Press, 1965.

Kolko, Gabriel, *Anatomy of a War: Vietnam, the United States, and Modern Historical Experience*, New York, Pantheon, 1985.

Kolko, Joyce, and Gabriel Kolko, *The Limits of Power: The World and United States Foreign Policy 1945–1954*, New York, Harper and Row, 1969.

Kojima, Keizō, *Nō ni kaeru jidai*, Tokyo, Daiyamondosha, 1992.

Kōsai, Yutaka, 'The Politics of Economic Management,' in Kozo Yamamura and Yasukichi Yasuba, eds., *The Political Economy of Japan, Vol. 1: The Domestic Foundation*, Stanford, Stanford University Press, 1987, pp. 555–62.

Kōsaka Masataka, *Saishō Yoshida Shigeru* (Prime Minister Yoshida Shigeru), Tokyo, Chuōkōronsha, 1968.

Kōsaka, Masataka, *Prime Minister Yoshida Shigeru*, Tokyo, Chüö Köron, 1994.

Kumon, Shumpei and Henry Rosovsky, eds., *The Political Economy of Japan, Vol. 3: Social and Cultural Dynamics*, Stanford, Stanford University Press, 1992.

Kurihara, Akira, 'Netto wākingu eno shōtai,' *Asahi jaanaru*, 29 January 1985.

Kurihara, Akira, Yoshimi Shunya and Sugiyama Mitsunobu, eds., *Kiroku: Tennō no shi*, Tokyo, Chikuma Shobō, 1992.

Kurosawa, Aiko, *Nihon senryōka no jawa nōson no henyō*, Tokyo, Sōshisha, 1992.

Kusano, Atsushi, *Daitenhō. Keizaikisei no kōzō*, Tokyo, Nihon Keizai Shinbunsha, 1992.

Kyōgoku, Junichi, *The Dynamics of Japanese Politics*, Tokyo, University of Tokyo Press, 1983.

Kyōgoku, Junichi, *Nihon no seiji*, Tokyo, Tokyo Daigaku Shuppankai, 1983.

Lee, Manwoo, *The Odyssey of Korean Democracy: Korean Politics, 1987–1990*, New York, Praeger, 1990.

Leiserson, Michael, 'Factions and Coalitions in One-Party Japan: An Interpretation Based on the Theory of Games,' *American Political Science Review,* Vol. LVII, No. 3, 1968, pp. 770–87.

The Liberal Democratic Party, ed., *Jiyū minshutō toushi*, Vol. I–III, Tokyo, The Liberal Democratic Party, 1978.

Lukacs, John, *The End of the Twentieth Century and the End of the Modern Age,* Boston, Houghton Mifflin, 1993.

Maddison, Angus, *The World Economy in the Twentieth Century* Paris, OECD, 1989.

Maddison, Angus, *Dynamic Forces in Capitalist Development*, New York, Oxford University Press, 1991.

Maier, Charles, *The Unmasterable Past: History, Holocaust, and National Identity*, Cambridge, Harvard University Press, 1988.

Mainichi Shinbun, 'Kokkai Giin Chose,' 28 September 2003.

Maruyama, Masao, *Gendai seiji no shisō to kōdō*, Revised edition, Tokyo, Miraisha, 1964.

Masumi, Junnosuke, *Nihon seitō shiron*, 7 vols., Tokyo, Tokyo Daigaku Shuppankai, 1965–1980

Masumi, Junnosuke, *Nihon-seiji shi*, Vols. 1–4, Tokyo, Tokyo Daigaku Shuppankai, 1988.

Maull, Hanns, 'Germany and Japan: a New Civilian Power?' *Foreign Affairs* vol 69, no.5, pp. 91–106, 1990.

Miller, Benjamin, *The Political Economy of Japan's Tariff Policy: A Quantitative Analysis*, Canberra, unpublished Ph.D. dissertation, 1987.

Minami, Ryōshin, *Nihon no keizai hadden*, 2nd edition, Tokyo, Tōyō Keizai Shinpōsha, 1992.

Mitani, Hiroshi, *Perry Raikō* (Perry's Arrival), Tokyo, Yoshikawa Kōbunkan, 2003.

Mitchell, Margaret, *Gone with the Wind*, London, Pan Books in association with Macmillan, 1974.

Miyamoto, Matao and Hayami Tōru, eds., *Keizaishakai no seiritsu*, 17–18 seiki, (Nihonkeizaishi, Vol. 1), Tokyo, Iwanami Shoten, 1988.

Miyata, Noboru, Amino Yoshihiko, Tanigawa Kenichi, Mori Kōichi, and Ōbayashi Tara, eds., *Umi to rettōbunka*, Tokyo, Shōgakukan, 1990–93.

Miyazaki, Yoshikazu, *Faking fluky*, <publisher, year?>

Mizutani, Mitsuaki, *Edowa yumeka*, Tokyo, Chikuma Shobō, 1972.

Morishima, Michio, *Why Has Japan 'Succeeded'?: Western Technology and the Japanese Ethos*, Cambridge, Cambridge University Press, 1982.

Morita, Akira, *Kyoninka gyōsei to kanryōsei*, Tokyo, Iwanami Shoten, 1988.

Morita, Akio and Shintarō Ishihara, *No toieru Nippon* (Japan that can say no), Tokyo, Bungeishunsho, 1989.

Morris, Dick, *Power Plays: Win or Lose, How History's Great Political Leaders Play the Game*, New York, Regan Books, 2002.

Morris-Suzuki, Tessa, *Beyond Computopia: Information, Automation and Democracy in Japan*, London, KPI, 1988.

Mueller, John E., *Retreat from Doomsday: The Obsolescence of Major War*, New York, Basic Books, 1989.

Murakami, Yasusuke, *Han koten no seijikeizaigaku*, Vols. 1–2, Tokyo, Chuo Kōronsha, 1992.

Murakami, Yasusuke, *An Anticlassical Political-economic Analysis: A Vision for the Next Century*, Stanford, Stanford University Press, 1997.

Murakami, Yasusuke, Kumon Shunpei and Satō Seizaburō, *Bunmeito shiteno ieshakai*, Tokyo, Chūō Kōronsha, 1979.

Muramatsu, Michifumi and Itō Mitsutoshi, *Chihō giin no kenkyū*, Tokyo, Nihon Keizai Shinbunsha, 1986.

Myers, Ramon, and Clark Peattie, eds., *The Japanese Colonial Empire, 1895–1945*, Princeton, Princeton University Press, 1986.

Nakamura, Takafusa, *Senzenki Nihon keizaiseichō no bunseki*, Tokyo, Iwanami Shoten, 1971.

Nakamura, Takafusa, *Nihon keizai no kensetsusha*, Tokyo, Nihon Keizai Shinbunsha, 1973.

Nakamura, Takafusa, *Nihon keizai-sono seichō tokōzō*, Tokyo, Tokyo Daigaku Shuppankai, 1978.

Nakamura, Takafusa, ed., *Senryōkinihon no keizai to seiji*, Tokyo, Tokyo Daigaku Shuppankai, 1979.

Nakamura, Takafusa, ed., *Senkanki no Nihon keizai bunseki*, Tokyo, Yamakawa Shuppansha, 1981.

Nakamura, Takafusa, *Meiji taishōkino keizai*, Tokyo, Tokyo Daigaku Shuppankai, 1985.

Nakamura, Takafusa, *Shōwa-shi*, Tokyo, Tōyō Keizai Shinpōsha, 1993.

Nakane, Chie, *Tate shakai no ningen kankei*, Tokyo, Kōdansha,1968.

Nakane, Chie, *Tate shakai no ningen kankei: Tekiō nojoken*, Tokyo, Kōdansha, 1976.

Nakane, Chie, *Tate shakai no rikigaku*, Tokyo,Kōdansha, 1978.

Nakanishi, Hiroaki, *Nihon kindaika no kiso katei-Nagasaki zōsenjoto sono rōshi kankei*. 1855–1900, 2 Vols., Tokyo, Tokyo Daigaku Shuppankai, 1982–83.

Nakasone, Yasuhiro, *Dotō o koete*, Tokyo, Seisaku kagaku kenkyūjo, 1986.

Nakasone, Yasuhiro, *Seiji to jinsei*, Tokyo, Kōdansha, 1992.

Nakasone, Yasuhiro, Murakami Yasusuke, Satō Seizaburō, and Nishibe Susumu, *Kyōdō kenkyū: Reisen igo*, Tokyo, Bungei shunshū, 1992.

Nathan, Andrew, *Chinese Democracy*, Berkeley, University of California Press, 1987.

Nau, Henry et al., At Home Abroad: *Identity and Power in American Foreign Policy*, Ithaca, Cornell University Press, 2002.

Nihon Keizai Shinbun, 1 January 1993.

Nihon Keizai Shinbunsha,*Isetsu. Nihonkeizai*, Tokyo, Nihon Keizai Shinbunsha, 1991, pp. 188–9.

Nihon Kokusai Seijigakukai, ed., *Taiheiyō sensō eno michi*, Vols. 1–8, Tokyo, Asahi Shinbunsha, 1987–88.

Nippon Research Center, 2003, *Asia Barometer*, November, Tokyo, NRC (in Japanese)

Nishikawa, Shūsaku, *Nihon keizai no seichōshi*, Tokyo, Tōyō Keizai Shinpōsha, 1985.

Noble, Gregory W. and John Ravenhill eds., *Asian Financial Crisis and the Architecture of Global Finance*, Cambridge, Cambridge University Press, 2000.

Noguchi, Yukio, *Baburu no keizaigaku*, Tokyo, Nihon Keizai Shinbunsha, 1992.

Nōrin chūkin sōgō kenkyūjo, ed., *Shokuryō o motanai Nihonkeizai*, Tokyo, Tōyō Keizai Shinposha, 1993.

Nye, Joseph, *Bound to Lead*, New York, Basic Books, 1990.

Nye, Joseph, 'Coping with Japan,' *Foreign Policy*, No. 89, Winter 1992–93, pp. 96–115.

Nye, Joseph, *The Paradox of American Power: Why the World's Only Superpower Can't Go It Alone*, Oxford, Oxford University Press, 2002.

Nye, Joseph, ed., *The Making of America's Soviet Policy*, New Haven, Yale University Press, 1984.

O'Brien, Richard, *Financial Integration: The End of Geography*, London, Pinter Publishers, 1991.

OECD, *The Newly Industrializing Countries*, Paris, OECD, 1979.

Offe, Claus, *Contradictions of the Welfare State*, London, Hutchison, 1984.

Offe, Claus, *Disorganised Capitalism: Contemporary Transformation of Work and Politics*, Cambridge, Polity Press, 1985.

Ohmae, Kenichi, *Heisei ishin*, Tokyo, Kōdansha, 1989.

Ohmae, Kenichi, *The Borderless Economy*, New York, Harper Business, 1990.

Ooms, Herman, *Tokugawa Ideology*. Princeton, Princeton University Press, 1985.

Orren, Karen, *Belated Feudalism: Labor, the Law and the United States*, New York, Cambridge University Press, 1991.

Ōtake, Hideo, *Adenauer to Yoshida Shigeru*, Tokyo, Chūō Kōronsha, 1987.

Ōtake, Hideo, *How Electoral Reform Boomeranged*, Tokyo, Japan Center for International Exchange, 1998.

Ozawa, Ichirō, *Nihon Kaizō Keikaku*, Tokyo, Kōdansha, 1993.

Packard, George, *Protest in Tokyo: The Security Treaty Crisis of 1960*, Princeton, Princeton University Press, 1966.

Palais, James, *Politics and Policy in Traditional Korea*, Cambridge, Harvard University Press, 1975.

Pempel, T. J., ed., *Uncommon Democracies: One-Party Dominant Regimes*, Ithaca, Cornell University Press, 1990.

Pempel, T. J. ed., *The Politics of the Asian Economic Crisis*, Ithaca, Cornell University Press, 1999.

Perkins, Dwight, 'Managing Development in Follower Countries: The Case of China and Korea,' paper prepared for a symposium on 'Technological Competition in the 21st Century,' Duisburg, Germany, 3–7 August 1987.

Perry, Commodore M. C., *Narratives of the Expedition of an American Squadron to the China Seas and Japan,* Washington D.C., Beverly Tucker, 1856.

Pharr, Susan and Robert Putnam, eds., *Disaffected Democracies*, Princeton, Princeton University Press, 1997.

Phillips, Kevin, *The Politics of Rich and Poor: Wealth and the American Electorate in the Reagan Aftermath*, New York, Narper Perennial, 1991.

Putnam, Robert, *Making Democracy Work: Civic Traditions in Modern Italy*, Princeton, Princeton University Press, 1993.

Pye, Lucian W., *The Spirit of Chinese Politics*, Cambridge, MIT Press, 1966.

Pye, Lucian W., *Power and Politics in Asia*, Cambridge, Harvard University Press, 1989.

Reed, Steven, 'Japanese Elections in 2003: The LDP Strikes Back?', *Japanese Journal of Political Science*, Volume 4 Part 2, 2003.

Reed, Steven and Michael Thies, 2001, 'The Causes of Political Reform in Japan' in Shugart, Mattew Soverg and Martin P. Wallenberg, eds., *Mixed-member Electoral Systems*, Oxford, Oxford University Press, 2001, pp. 152–72

Ricci, David M., *The Tragedy of Political Science: Politics, Scholarship and Democracy,* New Haven, Yale University Press, 1987.

Richardson, Bradley, *The Political Culture of Japan*, Berkeley, University of California Press, 1974.

Rohlen, Thomas, *For Harmony and Strength: Japanese Whitecollar Organizations in Anthropological Perspective*, Berkeley, University of California Press, 1974.

Rohlen, Thomas, *Japan's High Schools*, Berkeley, University of California Press, 1983.

Rosen, Howard, 'Education: The Search for Excellence,' *International Economic Insights*, Vol. IV, No. 1, January–February 1993, pp. 28–30.

Rozman, Gilbert, 'The Rise of the State in China and in Japan,' in Michael Mann, ed., *The Rise and Decline of the Nation State*, Oxford, Basil Blackwell, 1990, pp. 172–89.

Russett, Bruce, *No Clear and Present Danger: A Skeptical View of the United States Entry into World War II,* New York, Harper and Row, 1972.

Russett, Bruce, and Arthur Stein, 'Evaluating War: Origins and Consequences,' in Ted Robert Gurr, ed., *Handbook of Political Conflict, Theory and Research*, New York, Free Press, 1980, pp. 399–422.

Sachs, Jeffrey, *Macroeconomics in the Global Economy*, New York, Harvester Wheatsheaf, 1993.

Sadaka, Makoto, ed., *Nihon kaisha hakusho*, Tokyo, Shakai Shisōsha, 1992.

Saeki, Naomi, *Gatto to Nihon nōgyō*, Tokyo, Tokyo Daigaku Shuppankai, 1990.

Sakaiya, Taichi, *Nihon towa nanika*, Tokyo, Kōdansha, 1991.

Sakakibara, Eisuke, *Shihonshugi o koeta Nihon*, Tokyo, Tōyō Keizai Shinpōsha, 1990.

Sakamoto, Hideo and Yamamoto Kōzō, eds., *Monbushō no kenkyū*, Tokyo, Sanichi Shobō, 1992.

Sakamoto, Masahiro, *Zusetsu, niju seiki no sekai*, Tokyo, Nihon Keizai Shinbunsha, 1992.

Samuels, Richard, *The Business of the Japanese State: Energy Markets in Comparative and Historical Perspective*, Ithaca, Cornell University Press, 1987.

Sandholtz, Wayne and Michael Borrus, *The Highest Stakes*, New York, Oxford University Press, 1992.

Sano, Shinichi, 'Igyō no Hisyokan Iijima Isao no Takawarai,' Tokyo, *Bungei Shunjū*, November 2003 pp. 110–23.

Sasaya, Toshihiko, *Shukun oshikome no kōzō*, Tokyo, Heibonsha, 1988.

Satō, Seizaburō, 'Response to the West: The Korean and Japanese Patterns,' in Albert Craig, ed., *Japan: A Comparative View*, Cambridge, Harvard University Press, 1978. pp. 105–29.

Satō, Seizaburō and Matsuzaki Tetsuhisa, *Jimintō seiken*, Chuō Kōronsha, 1985.

Scalapino, Robert., *The Last Leninists: The Uncertain Future of Asia's Communist States,* Washington, D. C., Centre for Strategic and International Studics, 1992.

Schwartz, Adam, *Advice and Consent*, Cambridge, Cambridge University Press, 1998.

Schwartz, Adam and Susan Pharr, eds., *The State of Civil Society in Japan*, Cambridge, Cambridge University Press, 2003.

Schwartz, Hans-Peter, *Die Gezaehmten Deutschen: Von der Machtbesessenheit zur Machtvergessenheit*, Stuttgart, DVA, 1985.

Senzenki Kanryōsei Kenkyūkai [Hata Ikuhiko, ed.], *Senzenkinihon kanryōsei no seido, oshiki, jinji*, Tokyo, Tokyo Daigaku Shuppankai, 1981.

Shindō Eiichi, *Posuto. peresutoroika no sekaizō*, Tokyo, Chikuma Shobō, 1992.

Shinobu, Seizaburō, *Taiheiyō sensō*, Tokyo, Keisō Shobō, 1988.

Shugart, Matthew Soverg and Martin P. Wattenberg, eds., *Mixed Member Electoral Systems*, Oxford, Oxford University Press, 2003.

Shue, Vivienne, *The Reach of the State*, Stanford, Stanford University Press, 1988.

Singer, J. David, and Melvin Small, *The Wages of War, 1816–1965: A Statistical Handbook*, New York, Wiley, 1972.

Skowronek, Stephen, *Building a New Administrative State: The Emergence of National Administrative Capabilities, 1877–1920*, Cambridge, Cambridge University Press, 1982.

Solinger, Dorothy, *Business under Chinese Socialism*, Berkeley, University of California Press, 1983.

Solinger, Dorothy, ed., *Three Visions of Chinese Socialism*, Boulder, Westview Press, 1985.

Solomon, Richard, *Mao's Revolution and the Chinese Political Culture*, Berkeley, University of California Press, 1971.

Steinbrunner, John, ed., *Restructuring American Foreign Policy*, Washington, D.C., Brookings Institution, 1988.

Suleiman, Ezra, *Dismantling Democratic States*, Princeton, Princeton University Press, 2003.

Suzuki, Yuriko, 'Murayakunin no yakuwari,' *Nihon nokinsei 3: Shihai no shikumi*, Tokyo, p. 269.

Takabatake, Michitoshi, *Chihō no ōkoku*, Tokyo, Ushio Shuppansha, 1986.

Takahashi, Kō, *Tsugaru senkyo-chihō seiji ni okeru kenryoku no kōzō*, Tokyo, Kita no Machisha, 1987.

Tanabe, Akira, 'Sengo Nihon no sutoraiki,' *Tokyo, Tōhoku hōgaku*, Vol. 52, No. 6, 1988, pp. 1–36; Vol. 53, No. 3, 1989, pp. 1–48.

Tanaka, Kakuei, *Daijin nikki*, Tokyo, Niigata Nippō Jimusho,1972.

Tang, Tsôu, *America's Failure in China, 1941–1945*, Chicago, University of Chicago Press, 1963.

Taylor, A. J. P., *The Origins of the Second World War*, London, Hamilton, 1961.

Thorne, Christopher, *The Issue of War: States, Societies and the Far Eastern Conflict of 1941–1945*, London, Hamilton, 1985.

Thorne, Christopher, *Allies of a Kind: The United States, Britain, and the War against Japan, 1941–1945*, Oxford, Oxford University Press, 1978.

Toby, Ronald, *State and Diplomacy in Early Modern Japan: Asia in the Development of the Tokugawa Bakufu*, Princeton, Princeton University Press, 1984.

Tokio, Teruhiko and Sekyuritarianzu, 'Chinmoku no kantai kaitaihakusho,' *Sekyuritarian*, March 1993, pp. 32–9.

Tsokas, Kosmas, *Beyond Dependence: Companies, Labor Process and Australian Mining*, Melbourne, Oxford University Press, 1986.

Tsuji, Kiyoaki, *Shinban Nihonkanryōsei no kenkyū*, Tokyo, Tokyo Daigaku Shuppankai, 1969.

Tsuji, Tōru, *Ritsuryōkokka shihaikōzō no kenkyū*, Tokyo, Iwanami Shoten, 1993.

Tsurumi, Kazuko and Kawata Tadashi, eds., *Naihatsuteki hattenron*, Tokyo, Tokyo Daigaku Shuppankai, 1989.

Tsūshō Sangyō Kōzō Shingikai, *Keizai anzen no hoshō no kakuritsu o mezashite*, Tokyo, Tsūshō Sangyō Chōsakai, 1982.

Tyson, Laura, *Who's Bashing Whom: Trade Conflict in High Technology Industry*, Washington, D.C., Institute for International Economics, 1992.

Ueda, Kazuo, *Kokusai shūshifukinkōka no kinyu seisaku*, Tokyo, Töyö Keizai Shinpösha, 1992.

Uekusa, Kazuhide, *Kinri. Kawase.Kabuka no seijikeizaigaku*, Tokyo, Iwanami Shoten, 1992.

Umehara, Takeshi, *Nihonjin no anoyo kan*, Tokyo, Chūō Kōronsha, 1991.

Umemura, Matatsugi and Nakamura Takafusa, eds., *Matsukata zaisei to shokusan kōgyō seisaku*, Tokyo, Tokyo Daigaku Shuppankai, 1983.

Umemura, Matatsugu, and Yamamoto Yūzō, eds., *Nihon keizaishi*, 8 Vols., Tokyo, Iwanami Shoten, 1988–90.

Umesao, Tadao, *Nihon towa nanika-Kindai nihonbunmei no keisei to hatten*, Tokyo, Nihon Hōsō Shuppan Kyōkai, 1986.

Unger, Jonathan, *Education under Mao: Class and Competition in Canton Schools, 1960–1980*, New York, Columbia University Press, 1982.

Vogel, Ezra, *One Step Ahead in China,* Cambridge, Harvard University Press, 1989.

Vogel, Steven, ed., *U.S.–Japan Relations in a Changing World*, Washington D.C., The Brookings Institution, 2002.Wade, Robert, *Governing the Market: Economic Theory and the Role of Government in East Asian Industrialization*, Princeton, Princeton University Press, 1990.

Wagner, Edward, *The Literati Purges: Political Conflict in Early Yi Korea*, Cambridge, East Asian Research Center, Harvard University, 1974.

Wakabayashi, Masatake, *Taiwan-Bunretsu kokka to minshuka*, Tokyo, Tokyo Daigaku Shuppankai, 1992.

Wallerstein, Immanuel, *The Modern World-System*, New York, Academic Press, 1974.

Watanuki, Jōji, 'Patterns of Politics in Present Japan,' in Seymour Martin Lipset and Stein Rokkan, eds., *Party Systems and Voter Alignments: Cross-National Perspective*, New York, Free Press, 1967, pp. 447–66.

Weber, Max, *Politics as a Profession,* Japanese edition, *Shokugyō to shiteno seiji*, translated by Waki Kahei, Tokyo, Iwanami Shoten, 1980.

Weber, Steve, *Cooperation and Conflict in US-Soviet Arms Control*, Princeton, Princeton University Press, 1991.

White, Merry, *The Japanese Educational Challenge: A Commitment to Children*, New York, Free Press, 1987.

Williams, William Appleton, *Empire as a Way of Life: An Essay on the Causes and Character of America's Present Predicament, along with a Few Thoughts about an Alternative*, New York, Oxford University Press, 1980.

Wilson, Richard, *Learning to Be Chinese: The Political Socialization of Children in Taiwan*, Cambridge, MIT Press, 1970.

Wittfogel, Karl, *Oriental Despotism*, New Haven, Yale University Press, 1957.

Wolf, Arthur P., and Susan B. Hanley, 'Introduction,' in Susan B. Hanley and Arthur P. Wolf, eds., *Family and Population in East Asian History*, Stanford, Stanford University Press, 1985, pp. 1–12.

van Wolferen, Karel, *The Enigma of Japanese Power: People and Politics in a Stateless Nation*, New York, Basic Books, 1989.

Woo-Cumings, Meredith, eds, *The Developmental State*, Princeton, Princeton University Press, 1999.

Woodside, Alexander, *Vietnam and the Chinese Model: A Comparative Study of Nguyen and Ch'ing Civil Government in the First Half of the Nineteenth Century*, Cambridge, Harvard University Press, 1971.

Yamagishi, Toshio, *Shinrai no kōzō*. Tokyo, Tokyo Daigaku Shuppankai, 1998.

Yamaguchi, Jirō, 'Jimin-teki 'shinsetsu seiji' no owari', *Mainichi Shinbun*, 27 July 1998.

Yamamoto, Taketoshi, *Shinbunkisha no tanjo*, Tokyo, Shinyōsha, 1995.

Yamazaki, Hiroaki, 'Nihon kigyōshi josetsu,' in Tōkyō Daigaku Shakai Kagaku Kenkyūsho, ed., *Gendai nihonshakai 5: Kōzō*, Tokyo, Tokyo Daigaku Shuppankai, 1991, pp. 29–80.

Yergin, Daniel, *Shattered Peace: The Origins of the Cold War and the National Security State*, Boston, Houghton Mifflin, 1977.

Yoshimura, Tōru, Saitama University, interview, 11th January 1993.

Zysman, John, *Governments, Markets, and Growth: Financial Sectors and the Politics of Industry*, Berkeley, University of California Press, 1983.

Zysman, John, and Laura Tyson, *American Industry in International Competition: Government Policy and Corporate Strength*, Ithaca, Cornell University Press, 1983.

Index